Endorsement for *Stagi*

What a riveting, energising rea
research and extensive interviev ___ _ ...u s wno of
Australian cultural life from the 1960s and '70s recreates
so vividly the heady, hopeful, and often fraught times
of Melbourne's Pram Factory and the APG. Front row,
backstage, on stage – we discover how much we didn't
know about the fight for women's rights, the politics of
revolutionary theatre and the ongoing significance of
all the seemingly age-old battles for autonomy and self-
representation. *Staging a Revolution* is a stunning and
stunningly important book.

BERNADETTE BRENNAN

Women's liberation, consciousness raising and collective
processes. From the front line of feminism in Australian
theatre, a reminder of how much we owe these remarkable women.

WENDY HARMER

Staging
a Revolution

Kath Kenny

Kath Kenny is an essayist, arts reviewer and researcher.
Her writing on theatre, film, television and books has
appeared in publications such as the *Sydney Morning Herald*,
Meanjin, *The Monthly* and *The Saturday Paper*. She recently
contributed the lead chapters to the anthologies *#MeToo:
Stories from the Australian Movement and Fashion: New
Feminist Essays*. This book draws on her award-winning
PhD about the film and theatre groups that were part of
the Australian women's liberation movement. She lives in
Sydney's inner west on unceded Gadigal country.

Kath Kenny

Staging a Revolution

When Betty Rocked the Pram

First published in Australia in 2022
by Upswell Publishing
Perth, Western Australia
upswellpublishing.com

ISBN: 978-0-6452480-5-0

 A catalogue record for this book is available from the National Library of Australia

Cover design by Chil3, Fremantle
Typeset in Foundry Origin by Lasertype
Printed by McPherson's Printing Group

For everyone who has ever acted up

Contents

Author's note

The women in the following pages dreamt *Betty Can Jump* into being in the early 1970s. While they were busy making history, they also recorded their lives, their thoughts, and their feelings – in production diaries, in unpublished interviews, and in published articles and stories. I am grateful they had the foresight to project themselves into the future to consider a writer who might one day encounter the archives they created. I'm also grateful for their generosity in the present, when I asked them to project themselves back to the events of five and more decades ago, to remember what happened to whom, and when and how and why. I also benefited enormously from previous accounts of the Pram Factory world, particularly those published by Australian Performing Group members Graeme Blundell and Tim Robertson, and by the scholar Gabrielle Wolf. Sue Ingleton's online history of the Pram Factory was another rich source of stories and reflections from dozens of Australian Performing Group members. While this story is based on oral histories and archival records, in places I have recreated scenes and dialogue based on what I imagine someone might have done or said. Those scenes are signposted in the text, and in chapter notes at the end of the book, and I take responsibility for both any of the flights and any failures of my imagination. While the past can never be really known, what is clear is that something significant happened in the early 1970s in Carlton. And the world changed.

Abbreviations

ABC	Australian Broadcasting Commission (later Corporation)
ACT	Australian Capital Territory
AFL	Australian Football League, the top competition in Australian Rules football
ANU	The Australian National University
APG	Australian Performing Group
BBC	British Broadcasting Corporation
BCJ	*Betty Can Jump*
CR	consciousness-raising
GP	general practitioner
HLN	US cable news channel, formerly Headline News
MWTG	Melbourne Women's Theatre Group
NIDA	National Institute of Dramatic Art, Sydney
SP bookie	starting price bookmaker; unlicensed bookmaker at horse races
STC	Sydney Theatre Company
SUDS	Sydney University Dramatic Society
WA	Western Australia
WEL	Women's Electoral Lobby

Introduction

On the upstairs floor of the brick warehouse the curtains are drawn against Melbourne's midsummer twilight. The scent of old timber from the recently stripped and sanded floor mingles with the aroma of Harris coffee and the fumes of cars heading down Drummond Street, Carlton, to Melbourne's northern suburbs. No matter how many times the men's toilets behind the theatre are cleaned, the acrid base note remains undefeated and it drifts into the theatre space. Helen Garner, a 29-year-old schoolteacher, is feeling nervous as she prepares with four other women for the first run-through of their women's show. Yvonne Marini, her brown waist-length hair pulled back in a ponytail, has left her Greek family's home in Melbourne's northern suburbs to devote herself to the theatre collective that has taken over the empty factory in inner-city Carlton. The observant Claire Dobbin, a young lecturer at the nearby Secondary Teachers' College, wears her auburn hair in a short, shaggy style. Evelyn Krape has arrived at the Pram Factory via the college too, where she honed her stage presence – part clown, part chanteuse – in musical theatre. Tall Jude Kuring towers over the other women. She stands back, a wry look creeping across her long, handsome face.

The cast warm up with yoga and breathing exercises. They stretch and bend limbs, transforming into animals: a cat, a cow, a fish. As their play is about to begin, Helen watches the men from the Australian Performing Group file in. A year and a half earlier, in 1970, the group ('the APG', they call themselves) moved into the building to hold workshops, rehearse street theatre for moratorium marches, and stage new Australian plays. The group's writers include Jack Hibberd, a doctor who writes plays and poetry in the evenings; and John Romeril, a politics and literature graduate from Monash University. Other key members of the APG are Max Gillies, a drama lecturer at the Teachers' College, and a group of actors who all met each other when they were students at the University of Melbourne: Bill Garner; Graeme Blundell; and Kerry Dwyer, the woman who has directed tonight's play.

It was Kerry and Graeme who first found the warehouse for the group. A Paramount Prams logo from the building's previous tenant is still stencilled across the tower on the building's north side. A white plaster horse's head, a leftover from the building's days as a livery stable, looks out above a second-floor window to the police station and lockup opposite. The building's top floor has been converted into a theatre with movable scaffolded seating. The set-up for the women's show is plain. Seats are arranged along the room's two long sides; the audience will face each other across the room's floor. At one end of the stage is a ramp and multilevel platform.

Women from the Carlton Women's Liberation Group and the APG have spent the past five months devising the play. Just one man has been included in the cast: the Perth actor Vic Marsh. In the opening scene, Vic whips the women, who play convicts emerging from a ship's hold. The cast re-enact riots in early female factories, and tell stories about Louisa Lawson, Vida Goldstein and other women that have been ignored by an Anglo, male history. They also deliver intimate monologues they wrote during rehearsal exercises, where each cast member had to complete the phrase 'As a woman I feel like ...' Helen feels like a sharp glittering knife. Evelyn feels like a cushion plumped up and sat in. Yvonne feels like a mouth filled with laughing gas. The lights go out and the cast talk about their bodies and blood and sex and rape. In another scene, the cast don jockstraps and fake penises and mock ocker men drinking at a pub.

Standing on the platform, Evelyn helps dress Yvonne in a surrealist costume. A giant wedding ring hangs around her neck. She wears a stole made of rubber gloves and a bra with baby bottles hanging from it. Yvonne stands on top of the ramp, as if she is about to slide into a grotesque hell below. Helen notices the men in the audience staring stony-faced at the performers. She wonders what the point was of their months of wrestling with their feelings and experiences, trying to mould them into a show using methods none of them had tried before. To Claire, the men look not hostile, but rather bewildered and perplexed. She feels her heart sinking: 'Shit, we're right out of gear ... Where's the dramatic action?'

The play's director, Kerry Dwyer, heavily pregnant and sitting in a cloud scented with Johnson's baby oil, watches from the audience. Six months earlier she was on the same stage playing Susan, the bimbo role in *Don's Party*, David Williamson's play about a boozy, sleazy night when a group of friends gather for the 1969 federal election results. The play was a critical and financial success – and it kept the APG's accounts afloat – but it wasn't the kind of work Kerry had imagined doing four years earlier when she had travelled to France to study performance, and returned home with plans to form her own theatre company. Kerry recalls the day she stormed out of rehearsals for their first Pram Factory show, *Marvellous Melbourne*, a play about the city during the economic boom of the 1880s. It was meant to be a group-created show, but she accused the APG men, including her husband Graeme Blundell and his co-director Max Gillies, of dominating the production.

La Trobe University student Laurel Frank, who travelled to Sydney to research stories about women's history for the play, is in the audience too. So is Vic's partner, Carmen Lawrence, a 23-year-old psychology tutor whose observations from the bleachers helped Kerry and the cast during rehearsals. Operating the slide show that forms a backdrop to the performers is Micky Allan, a painter and Kerry and Helen's friend from university. As the cast perform, Micky shuffles through dozens of slides she has selected. A moustachioed weightlifter,

Playboy bunnies, and a mannequin dressed in fetish gear holding up a glass tabletop.

When the show ends, the men file into the back office and pour themselves drinks without saying a word. Helen frets. 'Have the currents that had run beneath those scenes when we first improvised them trickled away somewhere between the workshops and the run-through, leaving a rickety, empty, shell of form?'

Helen's worries are unfounded. In the weeks that follow, *Betty Can Jump* will play to packed houses. Women who come to see the show will rush up to the cast afterwards to talk excitedly about what they have just seen, the season will be extended for two more weeks, and critics will write glowing reviews. *Betty*, as it becomes known, will be the first of many women's shows to be staged at the Pram Factory over the next decade. The play will change the APG irrevocably (and prompt at least one spectacular resignation), it will shape the lives of *Betty* cast and crew, and it will help transform Australian performance culture.

* * *

When *Betty Can Jump* was performed at the Pram Factory, there were separate columns in the paper advertising jobs for 'women and girls' and 'men and boys', public bars still banned women, not one of the 125 electorates across the country was represented in Canberra by a woman, and access to safe abortions was only just beginning to see an end to women routinely dying in illegal backyard operations. The newly coined slogan of women's liberation, that 'the personal is political', was a revelation that became an incantation in lounge rooms and around kitchen tables across Australia, as women were starting to talk to each other about the most intimate and unexamined parts of their lives. They read Germaine Greer's 1970 feminist blockbuster *The Female Eunuch*, Kate Millett's *Sexual Politics*, and the Boston Women's Health Collective's *Our Bodies, Ourselves*, a pamphlet urging women to understand their bodies, explore their sexual desires and control their reproductive lives.

When *Betty Can Jump* was staged, the Australian women's movement was gathering force. As well as dropping into rehearsals and the occasional show at the Pram Factory, Carmen Lawrence (later to become premier of Western Australia) was working with another group of women to found the Women's Electoral Lobby. WEL helped to usher Gough Whitlam's Labor Party, which was promising a new inclusive vision for women, migrants and Indigenous Australians, to power at the December 1972 election. One of Whitlam's earliest acts was to appoint Elizabeth Reid, a philosophy tutor and women's liberation activist, as the world's first government adviser on women's affairs. Reid soon embarked on a tour around the country, listening to women talk about their need for childcare, and their desire for equality at work and better educational opportunities for their daughters.

As women's voices were beginning to ring out loudly in Canberra, they also started being broadcast on the nation's airwaves. In 1971, Australia's mainstream music charts had been dominated by men. Songs such as George Harrison's paean to a (male) higher being, 'My Sweet Lord', and the Mixtures' 'Pushbike Song', an ode to a bike-riding woman ('*You looked so pretty, as you were riding along*'). One of the few women in the top ten in 1971 was Helen Reddy, with her cover of 'I Don't Know How to Love Him' from the rock opera *Jesus Christ Superstar*. But in 1972 women's voices began to chart. Melanie was singing about her brand-new rollerskates in 'Brand New Key'. And Helen Reddy released her feminist anthem 'I Am Woman'; the song's roar grew slowly, until it reached number two in Australia the following year.

In 1973, women broke all sorts of song-writing taboos. Carly Simon sang about a man who was so vain he thought the world revolved around him and that her song was about him. Suzi Quatro, all black leather and playing a shiny new Fender, celebrated a dominant (if not very sisterly) woman in 'Can the Can'. Meanwhile, Roberta Flack's effortlessly luscious vocals curled like clouds of cigarette smoke around 'Killing Me Softly', a song I remember my mother playing repeatedly in the 1970s. The album cover's brown and yellow colourings, with Flack sitting in the dark behind a golden grand piano, was made for an era of Parker furniture and earth-coloured pottery. As she sang about a man who saw into her soul but still *looked right through me/as if I wasn't there*, she seemed to be speaking for all women who were demanding to be heard.

The sounds of women's voices playing from radios in cities and towns across Australia was accompanied by an outpouring of women's creativity in bedrooms, garages and empty warehouses. Groups with names such as Clitoris Band and Shameless Hussies formed and played at women's dances and women's festivals. Writers, photographers and cartoonists began publishing women's newspapers, including *MeJane* in Sydney, *Vashti's Voice* in Melbourne, and *Hecate* in Brisbane. Kate Jennings solicited poems from dozens of women for the 1975 anthology *Mother, I'm Rooted*. In Sydney, a group calling themselves the Sydney Women's Film Group produced and distributed hundreds of feminist films throughout the 1970s, helping to train a generation of women film- and television-makers.

Second-wave activists and movement historians Ann Curthoys and Susan Magarey have described this explosion of women's creativity in the 1970s as a 'cultural renaissance' (and Ann was at the centre of it: she appears barefooted and wearing blue jeans swinging from a tree on the cover of the first issue of *MeJane*). The scholar Margaret Henderson, picking up on their idea, argued these women should be recognised as the true inheritors of the avant-garde tradition that began in the early twentieth century with the Dadaists, Surrealists and Futurists: in making art collectively, they challenged the notion of the individual creative genius; and, in using the raw materials of their everyday lives to make art, they blurred divisions between the personal, the political and the creative, and divisions between audiences and performers. With its DIY sensibility, the creative outpouring of the women's liberation movement was also, in many ways, an early punk movement. Women taught themselves how to play guitar, shoot films and stage plays. They squatted in vacant

Anglican church houses and established a women's refuge in Glebe, Sydney; they graffitied slogans ('Lesbians are lovely') and threw bras on statues at Canberra's Parliament House; and, to avoid prosecution at protests, they gave their name as Vera Figner (a Russian revolutionary) when they were thrown into paddy wagons.

The women behind *Betty Can Jump* were at the forefront of this cultural renaissance. They had run through moratorium marches dressed as Viet Cong and American soldiers, so they were already familiar with the idea of political performance. But while the ostensibly collective APG styled itself as a radical collective that rejected not only Australia's unthinking deference to a British theatre tradition, but also the country's slavish support for the US in Vietnam, at the outset, it was itself dominated by men. Second-wave feminism helped the women in the group articulate the frustration they were feeling, both in their personal lives and in their lives at the Pram.

The *Betty Can Jump* women understood that theatre could be used to make people think about their lives. And they would have noticed that performance and spectacle were an important part of the new women's movement too. In the US, women protesting the 1968 Miss America pageant had marched a live sheep on the boardwalk outside the venue and crowned it Miss America. Taking their cue from the US, Australian women used carnivalesque theatre sketches to spread women's liberation ideas. Women at the University of Adelaide, led by Anna Yeatman, Anne Summers and Julie Ellis, protested the 1970 Miss Fresher competition. Students at the Australian National University entered a cow wearing a 'charming black and white coat' in the Miss University competition. Women stormed public bars that banned women; they protested equal pay when Zelda D'Aprano chained herself to Melbourne's Commonwealth Building in 1969; and they boarded Melbourne trams and insisted on paying seventy-five per cent of the fare – the proportion of men's wages that women earned. Elizabeth Reid knew that the social reforms women wanted, such as childcare and equal opportunities for work and education, would be vulnerable unless the entire culture – the stories we told about men and women – was transformed. When she set aside funding during the 1975 International Year of Women for women to make film and theatre and hold women's festivals, she was aiming to change the culture by altering the stories that were told.

Women's liberation spurred women to demand new kinds of relationships and new ways of living. Many women rebelled against the heterosexual nuclear family, and some set up households with children cared for collectively. Helen Garner later chronicled her experiences living in these improvised households (and her still compromised relationships with men) during these years, in the novel *Monkey Grip*. When I interviewed her about that time, she described the sensation of discovering women's liberation as like being hit by an epiphany. 'I felt as if I'd been underwater for my whole life. And now for the first time, I'd stuck my head out of the water and taken a breath ... looking around and thinking: "Now I get it. Now I get why my life is such a mess and why I've been so unhappy and wrecked everything."' It was also, she tells me, a time of anguish and upheaval – as all revolutions are. 'I can hardly think about those years without a sort of angst,' she wrote to me after we spoke.

I don't have many of my own memories of this period. As the *Betty Can Jump* women were learning their lines, I was learning to walk and talk. But I belong to a generation of girls born into a time marked by revolution. It is only in recent years that I've come to better understand just how profoundly our world was changed by women's liberation. The movement's success is, ironically, one reason for my own generation's amnesia about battles fought by earlier feminists in our name. We were generally aware of the broad outlines of earlier feminist struggles – the vote, equal pay, abortion rights and an end to sex stereotyping. We were brought up by our mothers to believe the mantra that we could be whatever we wanted to be, and many of us also took our freedoms for granted. When I started university, the work of Elizabeth Reid and women like the second-wave feminist Susan Ryan, education minister in Bob Hawke's Labor government, saw girls outnumber boys on campus for the first time.

I read feminist philosophy at university – it was a time when French theory was in vogue, and after Simone de Beauvoir we were encouraged to read the dense philosophical and psychoanalytical works of Hélène Cixous and Julia Kristeva. The second-wave feminist movement in Australia, if it was covered at all, was squeezed into the end of one week's lecture in an Australian politics course. I was so busy looking forward that it would take more than two decades before I would look back. And as I opened archive boxes in reading rooms in the state libraries of Victoria and New South Wales, and talked to women in lounge rooms, kitchens and studios in Sydney, Melbourne and country Victoria (and later by phone to Perth and a locked-down Victoria during COVID times), I listened as the women behind *Betty Can Jump* told me an extraordinary story.

As I was researching the story of *Betty Can Jump*, the #MeToo movement emerged almost overnight, starting a worldwide conversation about sexual harassment and abuse. While there are many differences between the feminist movement of the 1970s and the feminist movement of almost half a century later, I couldn't help but notice the many parallels between the two periods. Like the current moment, the late 1960s and early 1970s are remembered as a period of renewed feminist consciousness-raising, of women telling their personal stories. In Australia, during both moments, women from the performance worlds of theatre and film played key roles, albeit in different ways. And like the #MeToo movement, which came to Australia from elsewhere, the *Betty* women were profoundly influenced by ideas, people, texts and consciousness-raising practices that were circulating internationally. While the #MeToo movement was founded by the civil rights activist Tarana Burke and later taken up by women in film and theatre, 1970s women's liberationists were inspired by their activism in the civil rights and anti-war movements.

The connections between feminist generations are often lost in a media environment that thrives on conflict and feminist catfights. Feminist debates are reduced to clashes between celebrity personalities – between Germaine Greer and younger trans-inclusive feminists; between Miley Cyrus and Sinéad O'Connor, who warned the former she was prostituting herself in her revealing videos – or to a headline about Katie Way, the 22-year-old babe.net writer who broke the sexual harassment allegations against Aziz Ansari, and then accused the HLN anchor Ashleigh Banfield, who criticised her story, of being a 'second-wave feminist has-been' with 'burgundy lipstick [and] bad highlights'. Years ago, I found myself in the middle of another conflict between feminist generations when Helen Garner published *The First Stone*, her book about two women who accused the master of their university college of sexual harassment. Garner's book seemed to accuse my generation of feminists of losing our way, of going *too far*. In the middle of the media storm that followed the book's publication, we met over a cup of tea and looked hopelessly at each other across the generational chasm. I revisit this story, and the new ways I've come to think about it, in Chapter 8.

The history of feminism is often cast as a mother–daughter battle. In Freudian terms, you could say that each new generation of feminist daughters at some point rejects their political mothers and forges their own identity. Young feminist writers and activists deride the older generation's supposed lack of sophistication. Older generations, meanwhile, will often express feelings of betrayal and disappointment that their radicalism and example is being discarded and their achievements trivialised. In 2017, at a symposium in Canberra on the origins of second-wave feminism, I looked around and noticed how few young feminists were there to hear about the history of their movement. But the lack of comprehension works both ways: a veteran feminist rose to her feet after one panel to decry how her daughter's generation – who she said would schedule caesareans and return to their executive jobs as soon as their wounds healed – had turned their back on her generation's work fighting for the rights of mothers and babies. Her comment seemed to ignore that it was a second-waver, Shulamith Firestone, who championed the idea of test-tube babies to free women from what she saw as a barbaric connection between their bodies, pregnancy and women's oppression. And her comment ignored the modern movement of women who now champion natural births and intensive mothering and call themselves feminists.

There is an irony, as the Australian feminist scholar Margaret Henderson has written, 'that a movement which challenged conventional' institutions like the nuclear family, and traditional notions of the 'maternal', finds itself repeatedly locked in its own oedipal drama. I think Henderson is referring here to a particular tendency in white or Western feminism, but it's important to remember that second-wave feminism was not monolithic. Another feminist scholar, Avtar Brah, speaking on a recent panel about feminist generations, criticised the wave metaphor for not only setting up false divisions between feminist generations, but for unhelpfully homogenising feminists within each wave. Understanding our history better is one way to move past these fruitless conversations about feminism – conversations that replace understanding and empathy with stereotypes and generalisations, and that bring us no closer to solving the problems that each new feminist generation faces.

Why is *Betty Can Jump* – like so many of the women's films and plays and music of the 1970s – so little known? We've come to think of Germaine Greer and *The Female Eunuch*, or Anne Summers and her 1975 text *Damned Whores and God's Police*, as synonymous with the Australian women's liberation movement. The collectively authored nature of so many of the women's plays and films of the 1970s is one reason these works aren't well remembered – there is no star author to help sustain their afterlife in our historical memory. And, unlike written texts, which can be studied and circulated indefinitely, theatre is an ephemeral art form, its performance tied to a particular time and place, seen only by audience members who were there. If *Betty Can Jump* was filmed (the stories are a little hazy), no one seems to know what happened to the stock. The script was never written down in a complete form. It is not surprising then that the story of *Betty Can Jump* has rated barely a mention in official feminist history books. But it was a transformative consciousness-raising event for the thousands of women who saw the show. *Betty* anticipated Anne Summers' thesis in *Damned Whores and God's Police* that under white-settler occupation, Australian women were consigned to the categories of either saint or sinner; and it led to a slew of women's shows at the Pram Factory over the following years.

Perhaps more surprising is that the story of *Betty Can Jump* has also been squeezed into the margins of theatre history. For many, the Pram Factory and the APG are synonymous with the playwrights David Williamson, Jack Hibberd and John Romeril; the director–actors Max Gillies and Graeme Blundell; and the great Indigenous actor Jack Charles. But the director, cast and crew of *Betty Can Jump* were, in many ways, even more avant-garde and experimental than the men at the APG. Their influences were as diverse as the Polish theatre director Jerzy Grotowski, the surrealism of the US Bread and Puppet Theater, and the consciousness-raising practices and collective structures of women's liberation. And at a time when the APG and the new Australia Council were championing a national culture that told Australian stories, they insisted that women's stories be included.

Helen Garner is the best known of the *Betty Can Jump* collective, but she is celebrated for her later novels and non-fiction books rather than for her theatre work. Garner's first novel, *Monkey Grip*, is set against the backdrop of the Pram Factory and its Tower, where members of the APG lived. The story's main character Nora, Garner's fictional surrogate, attends plays at the Pram and goes to dinner with her lover after he's finished rehearsing a show in the back theatre. While Helen tells me now that she never formally joined the Pram Factory, the Australianisms that pepper her conversation – 'pash', 'boofhead' and 'knocked around' – remind me that, perhaps more than anyone, she was the most successful in following through with the APG's conviction that art could be created in the Australian vernacular.

The APG and the building it occupied for a decade on Drummond Street between Elgin and Faraday streets are long gone. The Pram was bulldozed to make way for a suburban shopping plaza, with an art-house cinema; the Brunetti cake shop, with its acres of sweet displays;

and a basement supermarket that stays open until midnight. As I write, the cinema is screening a new documentary, Catherine Dwyer's *Brazen Hussies*, about the Australian women's liberation movement. The filmmakers Margot Nash and Robin Laurie – themselves performers who were members of the Pram Factory – are interviewed in the film about their own 1975 short film, *We Aim to Please*, in which they stood stark naked throwing tomatoes at the camera lens and smashing watermelons. But like most of the official histories of second-wave feminism, *Brazen Hussies* doesn't mention the dozens of theatre productions and the women who created a feminist theatre movement in the 1970s. Fifty years after *Betty Can Jump* was first performed, this book tells the story of the women who rocked the Pram Factory, and the aftershocks that can still be felt today.

Chapter 1
A leap of faith

In 1961, eighteen-year-old Kerry Dwyer walks into the University of Melbourne to start her first year of university. With her straight back and dancer's posture, she appears confident and even taller than she is; but although she loves to perform on stage, she feels so shy and ill at ease at university that simply walking into a café on campus takes enormous effort. Kerry matriculated from Canterbury Girls High School in Melbourne's eastern suburbs the previous year, but at university female students are outnumbered three to one by male students. She has studied ballet for five years, but her parents don't think dancing or working in the entertainment industry are suitable careers for a girl. She is enrolled in an arts degree: along with French and English, she will study biology. With a bonded teaching scholarship, she will have to spend her first three years after graduating working for the Victorian Education Department. That pleases her father, a primary school headmaster, and her mother, who has recently managed to persuade her husband to let her work at the *Herald*'s phone booth on Saturdays, where she types while journalists dictate their stories.

Kerry is one of thousands of students who have enrolled in universities since 1951, when Prime Minister Robert Menzies introduced the Commonwealth Scholarship Scheme. The scheme waives university fees and provides a means-tested living allowance to top students. The University of Melbourne campus has been expanding to accommodate growing numbers of staff and students. The Old Quadrangle, with its neo-gothic arched colonnade, is still at the heart of the campus when Kerry arrives, but a few hundred metres west, at the bottom of a gentle hill, a row of two-storey terraces for professors and their families has been knocked down to make way for a new building to house the growing stacks of books that were threatening to spill into the hallways of the Old Quad. In 1959, Menzies stood outside the modern glass-curtained front wall of John Scarborough's Baillieu Library to officially declare it open.

While universities are changing, government in Australia in 1961 is remarkably stable. Federally, the Liberal–Country Party Coalition is in the middle of a 23-year rule. The coalition is also in power in Victoria, where Premier Henry Bolte is in the sixth year of what will become a seventeen-year term. Australia's involvement in the Korean War ended eight years earlier, and the country is yet to join the Vietnam War. Another kind of war, however, one over culture, is brewing.

Modern libraries such as the Baillieu and the University of Sydney's Fisher Library are being built just as authorities are banning a raft of books. *Lady Chatterley's Lover* has long been forbidden, and more recently, J.D. Salinger's *The Catcher in the Rye* and Grace Metalious's *Peyton Place* have been added to the list. (Publisher and writer Hilary McPhee would later recall that behind their semi-transparent glass facades, some of these libraries held books for 'legitimate study only' in special collections that required letters of authority before they could be read.) The Literature Censorship Board had assented to Penguin Books' 1960 request to lift the ban on D.H. Lawrence's *Lady Chatterley's Lover*, but in a cabinet meeting in February 1961 Denham Henty, the Minister for Customs and Excise, overruled the board's recommendation. Students arriving on campus at the beginning of the academic year will read about the case in the University of Melbourne's student newspaper *Farrago*, where a J. Metcalfe favours restricting the sale of *Lady Chatterley's Lover* on the grounds that the book's promotion of 'promiscuity and sex without love' and its 'pernicious moral standards could do a great deal of harm to people not intelligent and mature enough to make an evaluation for themselves'.

Elsewhere, there are signs that a newer, more open culture is emerging. Elvis Presley's 'Are You Lonesome Tonight?' has been charting over the summer. For the first time, women can buy the newly available contraceptive pill Anovlar, and enthusiastically respond to Presley's plaintive plea, knowing that sex can be liberated from the possibility of either a hazardous backyard abortion or a potentially life-altering pregnancy. The pill is technically only available to married women (and to women who have been given the name of a friendly doctor who will prescribe it for 'medical' reasons), but the question of sex and love (and whether the two can be separated) is occupying the student population in 1961. *Farrago* is full of articles debating the pros and cons of sex outside marriage. Much of the conversation is still cautiously conservative. One writer, Peter Mayne, argues for a modern take on marriage, where students live together like married couples, which he prefers to drunken student parties leading to 'lax student sex morals' and unwanted pregnancies. An opinion piece by Wendy Neilson argues for abortion to be legalised, then other writers pen articles and letters in furious disagreement for the following edition. Talk of university students having sex greatly disturbs one correspondent, a Christian and a science student who compares the idea to the decadence of Sodom and Gomorrah. Rather than living in de facto relationships, however, many university students are moving into residential colleges that ring the campus to the north, where new buildings are being added to the original halls.

In an address to mark the beginning of the academic year, the university's Vice-Chancellor, Sir George Paton, implores parents of girls to let go of the Victorian-era view that educating girls is a 'waste of money'. Above the coverage of the speech on the front page of *Farrago* is a picture of actress and French beauty Agnès Laurent in full make-up and dressed in academic gown. Laurent is starring in the film *A French Mistress*, playing a teacher at an English public school who drives male students to such distraction they burn down the gym. 'We have a good idea why,' the *Farrago* editors archly write. The story, titled 'So girls look better without gowns?', compares the actress's picture with a second image, on page three, of Laurent in a bikini.

In April and May, the Miss University quest provides a diversion for the student body before the exam period at the end of first term. Colleges and faculties across the campus have elected representatives to enter the competition. On the day of the contest, 3000 students crowd into the exam and graduation building Wilson Hall, a modern glass and decorative-brick building completed in 1956 after a fire destroyed the neo-gothic original four years earlier. The contestants, with neat upswept bouffant hairstyles and skirt suits, are met with whistles and catcalls; audience members are crushed against the stage, and a tussle between medical and engineering students ends in an ABC cameraman being injured. Students climb on the backs of chairs and, as they leave, windows are damaged and food and cigarette butts litter the empty floor.

Kerry notices all of this, and although she is poised and striking, she has no desire to parade in beauty contests; she's more interested in watching other people. She's drawn to the energy that seems to spark off the actors and directors and hangers-on in the student theatre world. They debate art and literature and politics in the Student Union café, or at one of the pubs adjoining the university. The students in the Architecture faculty, renowned for their satirical Architecture Revue, with its ingenious sets and inspired costumes, are among the most charismatic and interesting on campus. They wear blue jeans to classes when other students are wearing suits and ties, and drive Citroën 2CVs, with their bug-eyed headlights and convertible open roofs.

Kerry also gravitates to the musical theatre productions at the Secondary Teachers' College next door, joining the cast of Gilbert and Sullivan operas in her first and second years at university. At the beginning of her second year, Kerry is entranced by a performance by Max Gillies in a production of the eighteenth-century play *The School for Scandal*. The 20-year-old has a large rectangular face that would be leading-man handsome were his features not quite so oversized and mobile: he seems to have the ability to rotate each one independently, turning his mouth up like a villain or down like a clown, shrinking and expanding his eyes and cheeks at will.

In her fourth year, Kerry finds the courage to audition for a role in Ray Lawler's 1955 Australian play *The Summer of the Seventeenth Doll*. She is cast as Pearl, a young widow, when the actress originally cast in the role falls ill. Max Gillies plays Barney, a canecutter who romances Pearl during one summer-long house party that has become a tradition during the layoff season. A year later, when Kerry auditions to play opposite Graeme Blundell in the Harold Pinter play *The Birthday Party*, she is again cast when another actress falls ill: 'It's almost like I got into theatre by default,' she tells me now, adding of this period, 'I started to feel that I'd arrived. I'd grown up a little bit.' Kerry hadn't had any acting training, but when I ask him about that time, Graeme remembers her as 'an instinctual actor: she had stage skills that were innate, which a lot of people in university theatre didn't have'.

Micky Allan, one of Kerry's university friends, is also gravitating to the world of student theatre. She had wanted to enrol in art school, but her parents were worried she might meet a mad artist and run away to live in a garret. Micky studies philosophy, fine arts and English but feels uncomfortable at university ('Underneath I was wanting to go to art school and didn't realise how firmly I wanted that,' she says now.) Looking for somewhere to express her creativity, she falls in with student theatre director Patrick McCaughey; and Peter Corrigan, an architecture student who dresses like an English dandy and builds strange fantastical sets out of scavenged material.

Micky drinks with Kerry and their friend, Helen Ford, an English and French major, at the pub on Friday nights. Helen lives at the women's college Janet Clarke Hall (where prospective residents had to sit an exam in homecraft) but she also gravitates towards the architecture students, with whom she can discuss aesthetics and American literature and films. 'My boyfriend at the time was an architecture student, and everyone I knew was an architecture student,' she tells me.

A student theatre crowd gathers at Carlton's Mayfair Hotel, where they invent characters and voices and argue about art and sport. By 1964, Kerry is feeling at home on campus. To Graeme Blundell, Kerry and Helen come across as a formidable pair: Kerry is 'a strong woman, frank, funny and direct', while Helen is 'petite and spiky', with the gift of 'being able to see the bones beneath the skin'. Kerry finds the student Labor Club staid, but she joins the Rationalist Society gatherings at the Mayfair, where they drink and argue with student Christian groups who try to convince them to take a 'leap of faith'.

While male and female students mix in the Mayfair lounge, only men are allowed to enter the public bar and order drinks. In 1964, on a Wednesday afternoon in the middle of July, Kerry's boyfriend, John Helmer, a political science student and *Farrago*'s editor, leads Kerry and another woman into the Mayfair's public bar to protest the banning of women. The barman loudly tells the group women are not allowed, and men drinking in the bar chime in, telling them to leave. They refuse to move, and the barman returns to warn them a second time. 'The Licensing Act allows women to come into the public bar,' John says. The barman yells: 'Get the licensing squad if you like! In this hotel the law is "no women".' He grabs Kerry and pushes the group out of the bar.

A couple of days later, *Farrago* prints a front-page photograph of the protest and urges a 'girlcott' of the Mayfair. 'It is against the law to refuse to serve women in the Public Bar and that hotels do not observe this seems indicative of the general Victorianism of this state,' John Helmer is quoted as saying. The article describes the protesting students as 'Rick [i.e. Ric] Birch and John Helmer with female company'. John is author of the article, perhaps explaining why Kerry and the second woman come across as little more than secondary characters (when I speak to them more than fifty years later, neither Kerry nor John can recall who the second woman was). Kerry readily acknowledges now that John was the 'mover and shaker' behind the action at the Mayfair. Nevertheless, it predates by nine months a more famous protest in March 1965 at Queensland's Regatta Hotel, when postgraduate student Merle Thornton and her friend Rosalie Bogner chain themselves to the bar rail and demand to be served. Their protest is filmed by ABC television and receives widespread media coverage. Images of the two women in office suits and heels, their pantihosed ankles chained to the bar's footrail, are printed in newspapers and replayed on television. They gain the nation's attention in large part because their action is also a performance, and in the years since, their protest has often been remembered as the first major action of the nascent Australian women's liberation movement.

* * *

By the mid-1960s the theatre scene at the University of Melbourne and the adjacent Secondary Teachers' College was thriving. There were more than a dozen theatre groups across the university and at residential colleges, staging productions ranging from Shakespeare and Shaw to Pinter. Every few weeks a new play opened. In 1963, Commonwealth Scholarship student Hilary McPhee, the head of the student theatre group the Marlowe Society, mounted a season of works at the University of Melbourne's Union Theatre by European absurdist playwrights such as Eugène Ionesco and Fernando Arrabal. Patrick McCaughey directed Max Gillies in Ionesco's strange play *The Chairs*, where a couple converse in what seems to be a post-Apocalyptic world. In a review of the season, *Farrago* writer Beatrice Faust praised Gillies' performance, as well as the 'bucolic bawdiness' of McPhee's murderess maid in the Jean Genet play *The Maids*. Graeme Blundell performed in the Alfred Jarry play *Ubu Roi*. As part of the program, the cast and crew of the Sydney University Dramatic Society brought its own show, *A Revue of the Absurd*, to Melbourne. SUDS member Germaine Greer played multiple roles, including Miss Piffs in a Harold Pinter sketch, a character who peppers a job applicant, a Mr Lamb, with personal and sexual questions while administering electric shocks.

There were no theatre history or drama literature courses at the University of Melbourne or Monash University at this time, so the drama on university campuses was all 'student-driven', Max tells me. 'There was excitement about different movements that we were aware of millions of miles away, but Theatre of the Absurd was one that caught everybody's attention.' Plays and festivals were accompanied

33

by film screenings and programs of lectures and discussion with visiting experts and writers from Europe, Max explains. 'In the early 60s, theatre becomes a thing that engages a whole lot of people on campus doing other courses.' Hilary McPhee's 1963 season was a watershed moment for student theatre; the revue's absurdist and experimental works represented a rejection of the traditional canon of English and European plays.

Four years later, an Australian play by Jack Hibberd that broke with naturalism and conventional forms of theatre was another turning point. Hibberd was a moustachioed doctor at Melbourne's St Vincent's Hospital who dressed in colourful shirts and three-piece suits paired with pocket squares, and worked on poetry and plays in the evening. In 1967, his production at the University of Melbourne's Prince Philip Theatre, *White With Wire Wheels*, opened with one of the three car-obsessed central male characters announcing 'Root my boot ... what a night.' The cast also featured Sue Ingleton, a star of the Architecture Revue, as one of the women who orbit the three ocker male friends. The play's naturalistic beginning devolves into fantasy sequences and scenes that break the fourth wall. Hibberd told interviewer Catherine Berry he was influenced by Pinter, Ionesco and Harpo Marx, but he 'has assimilated the European theatre movements into an Australian matrix'. After a glowing review by Patrick McCaughey (by now working for *The Age*) the season was sold out. 'We had to put on extra shows and there were queues from the Prince Philip Theatre up to Swanston Street to get in,' the director David Kendall later recalled. The play's ocker stereotypes and vulgar Australian slang, meanwhile, became, according to the scholar Gabrielle Wolf, a defining feature of Australia's new-wave theatre movement.

* * *

Kerry misses out on seeing *White With Wire Wheels*. Thanks to her roles in *The Birthday Party* and other university theatre shows, she wins one of thirty French government scholarships for international students to study performance for a year at the University of Nancy,

France. The program includes a month-long workshop in 1967 with the Polish theatre director Jerzy Grotowski, who has been developing a theory of performance called 'poor theatre'. According to Grotowski, the unmediated relationship between the actor and audience sets theatre apart from other forms of spectacle, such as film. His actor training involves a radical stripping away of ego and self-consciousness; his workshops are designed to integrate 'all the actor's psychic and bodily powers which emerge from the most intimate layers of his [sic] being and his instinct'. In the performance, Grotowski writes, 'the body vanishes, burns, and the spectator sees only a series of visible impulses'.

For Kerry, the workshop experience, away from her home and familiar reference points, is life-changing. While the writers, directors and performers in the Melbourne University theatre world are beginning to explore Australian identity, Kerry's experience with Grotowski challenges her to search for her own identity. Grotowski introduces the students to his 'sacred' theatre in classes that begin with rigorous physical exercises, breathing techniques and extreme yoga. Kerry writes later about Grotowski's critique of her final acting exercise, an experience that leaves her in turmoil:

'Yes. Next! Ah, oui. Mademoiselle.'

He shuffles through his notes.

'You want to be an actor?'

'Yes, ... I think so.'

'You were hiding in your piece. I could not see you. Who are you?'

I did not know what to answer. At the age of twenty-four, I realised I had no idea who I was.

'Well, I will tell you that you will never be an actor as long as you keep hiding.'

I am struck dumb.

Somewhere deep within me, he has hit a dark secret place which was indeed hidden, but I didn't know how to release it. What did he see that I couldn't? What was I hiding?

I stumble out of the room, past [my friend] June, unable to speak to her before tears gush from my eyes. I barely make it back to my room before I collapse on to my bed, in paroxysms of grief and fear. And there I stay for three days, sobbing, unravelling until I feel I have lost layers and layers of old skin and can face the world of Nancy in the pale spring sunshine.

Working with Grotowski transforms Kerry's relationship to theatre. She learns a process of 'stripping back of all masks, the humiliation [of] destroy[ing] the ego, the training of voice and body to be perfectly lucid fluid channels for whatever the theatrical moment required'. At the same time, Grotowski awakens another, almost contradictory impulse, a desire to be 'seen': 'I yearned to explore what that might mean in my own town.' When she returns to Melbourne she is determined to set up her own theatre company:

My year in France gave me the confidence and the sense of direction necessary. I didn't know whether or not I was creative. I didn't know whether or not I could be an actress ... I only knew that I had discovered an enormous store of energy and if I did not use it, express it somehow, I would go mad.

* * *

In France, Kerry had also met a group of Marxist–Leninists, part of a movement of students and workers who would strike in their millions the following year, protesting capitalism, imperialism and the Vietnam War. This moment was when her political education about issues such as the Vietnam War 'really began', she tells me. While Australia had been involved in the war since it first sent thirty military advisers to

Vietnam in 1962, opposition to the war hadn't yet developed into a mass movement. Kerry's boyfriend in 1964, John Helmer, was one of the early voices questioning the war: 'He was politically aware, and even way back then in 1964, he was saying: "Why are we in Vietnam?"'

While Kerry was in France, Australian campuses were becoming sites of growing political discontent. In 1967, a referendum for Aboriginal citizenship was held, and Abschol, a student group raising funds for university scholarships for Aboriginal students, organised speakers on campus for the 'yes' campaign. *Farrago* ran reports from Harry Stein, a correspondent in South Vietnam, and stories about children being napalmed in the war. In July, the Vietnam Day Committee arranged a three-day festival against the Vietnam War. It began with a mock debate between a Thomas Jefferson in eighteenth-century period costume and a '10-gallon hatted President Johnson', and more than 1000 attended a 24-hour vigil outside the US Embassy. The American Left, and figures such as James Baldwin and Martin Luther King, influenced a growing New Left movement in Australia, and students were closely following the Black Power movement in the US.

The student scholarship scheme and the rapid of expansion of higher education institutions that Menzies had overseen had created a new grouping of educated and politically aware young people from the middle and lower middle classes. And many of them were increasingly opposed to his government's policies: Australia's involvement in Vietnam, the second-class treatment of Indigenous Australians, censorship and an imported British culture. Historian Michelle Arrow, in her book *The Seventies: The Personal, the Political and the Making of Modern Australia*, has written about this new group of young Australians who emerged in a period of postwar prosperity and were increasingly influenced by global political currents, conditions that created 'the rise of a new, more educated middle class, who articulated a liberal perspective'.

In the late 1960s, women's participation in the workforce was growing, thanks in part to the 1966 lifting of a ban on married women working for the Commonwealth public service. Women's liberation was not yet an organised movement in Australia, but even the beauty queens in the Miss University quest at the University of Melbourne were beginning to look different. *Farrago* still couldn't resist a double entendre – 'The 1967 Miss University Quest is now nearing a swinging climax' – read one feature introducing the year's candidates. But the prim skirt suits and carefully coiffed hairdos were no more. Miss Arts, Miss Science, Miss Law and Miss Ormond now wore casual polo neck sweaters, simple summer frocks and longer and looser hair.

It is easy to forget just how quickly the student life Kerry, Micky and Helen were leading in the mid-1960s was changing. The ban on Australian women drinking in many public bars carried on well into the 1970s, but by the time I enrolled at the University of Melbourne at the end of the 1980s, it never occurred to me that ordering drinks from one of the dozens of pubs in the suburbs next to the university (including those untouched by renovations since the 1960s) was anything other than our birthright. Instead of Miss University contests, we now had women's rooms where, we liked to say from mouths painted with bright lipstick, we were escaping the 'male gaze'. Student politicians organised at the Clyde, while an anti-war group I belonged to met at the further-flung Punters Club in Fitzroy to plan campaigns.

I didn't know, when I moved into a terrace house on Swanston Street in my second year of university, opposite the trimmed green lawns of the colleges that circled the campus, that Helen Garner (then known as Helen Ford) had lived in the terrace next door nearly a quarter of a century earlier after leaving Janet Clarke Hall. Helen's biographer Bernadette Brennan describes her lodging as more of a bedsit, but it was the beginning of an era when students and artists and activists could live in cheap and plentiful inner-city real estate. They moved into Victorian- and Edwardian-era terraces and cottages that had been little altered since families and many new migrants had moved out of Melbourne's inner city, as the population spread out to newer bayside and garden suburbs. For many in Helen's generation, going to university, making friends and creating new ways of living and thinking was also the beginning of a separation from their parents, one that could sometimes turn into a great rift that could never be completely repaired.

Helen was born in Geelong in 1942. Her father was a wool merchant, and her mother had been a physical education teacher before Helen, the first of six children, was born. Helen had been head prefect and dux of the Hermitage, an Anglican girls' school, but at university she dropped her studious persona, Brennan writes, skipping tutorials and ignoring prescribed readings from the literature course while discovering writers such as Hemingway. She threw herself into a social life filled with friends and lovers. Her crowd was a 'lefty' group, but not a 'highly organised one', Helen tells me. They were just people 'slightly more bolshie than their own parents'.

In a podcast with historians Clare Wright and Yves Rees, Helen spoke of the enormous shame and regret she feels about the 'smart-arse intellectual' she turned into around her mother.

> In my generation … a lot of us had mothers that had never studied, who'd never read, whose life was very bound by wifely-ness. And suddenly up sprouts some daughter who goes to uni and thinks she's the ant's pants and comes home full of scorn and contempt and god, I die of shame thinking about that.

Friends could become a new family. Brennan relates how at university Helen forged a close friendship with Axel Clark (son of historian Manning Clark). During the summer break when she was back at her childhood home she wrote to him: 'Gosh I'm sick of being so far away from all my people. I think I have stopped considering my family as "my people".'

In 1968, Helen attended an abortion rally with a friend. 'I shouted and jumped about and he freaked. It wasn't until afterwards that I worried about what he thought,' she later told Kerry. That year she had returned to Melbourne from travelling in Europe with Bill Garner, whom she had known from university. She was twenty-seven, and married Bill against her father's wishes. Bill was 'lovely', but 'we were both much too young to be married', she tells me now. Helen recalls the newly married couple attending a meeting with Bertram Wainer, an English-born doctor who lived in Melbourne and 'was trying to start the Abortion Law Reform Association'. She had two abortions during her student years, she explains: 'The first time I was pregnant, when I was in second year uni, I thought, "God, this is terrible." I didn't know what to do.' She can't recall all the details now, but someone sent her to a GP in Collins Street. 'He was quite an oldish sort of bloke, but very sympathetic and with a lot of feeling for women. And he said, "I don't do this kind of work myself, but I will send you to somebody who does."' He referred her to a specialist who conducted abortions safely, if not always legally. 'I never had to go through one of those abortion stories you hear about, where you go to an outer suburban house and everyone's lying on a bed with plastic under them.'

Helen remembers 'hundreds of people' attending the meeting with Dr Wainer, and organisers asking people to nominate themselves to be on a committee. 'Bill said to me, "Come on, Hel, you could do this." I said "No, I couldn't." He said, "Come on – it's important," so I volunteered to be on the committee.'

> Because I was quite timid and didn't think of myself as being political, I just volunteered to keep the minutes. And I'm an efficient sort of person, I can keep good minutes, and I went away and typed them up. So that was my involvement. I mean, I put myself at the service of this [movement]... I totally wanted the law to change.

It was both an exciting and a terrifying time, Helen recalls: 'The police were involved and there was a lot of bribery ... Some doctors paid off the police. It was a really corrupt scene.'

The movement for abortion law reform in many ways preceded the organised women's movement. 'Being active in the abortion movement [at that time] wasn't a feminist act so much as a libertarian one,'

Helen says. Over the following years, however, abortion rights work became a central campaign of the women's liberation movement. And Helen worked at the coalface:

> We had this set-up where the women came from New Zealand because they couldn't get an abortion there. And I remember once a Māori woman came, and it was my job to meet her and take her to the doctor, and take her home to my house afterwards, look after her, make sure she wasn't bleeding, and give her a cup of tea. She came back to my share house, and she was just this terrified, trembling woman who just got off a plane ...

Helen remembers this incident must have occurred in '1972 or 1973', after she had broken up with Bill and moved into a share house. The political and personal changes in her life over the previous four years – and in the lives of the women she knew – had been momentous. Years later, when Dr Wainer died, she was one of the thousands of women who attended his funeral at the Congregational Church in Collins Street, Melbourne. 'Just about everyone you knew was there. It was packed with women. It wasn't spoken, but you knew we were all there because he made it possible for us to get an abortion.'

Chapter 2
From La Mama to the Pram

When Kerry returns home from France in 1968, she puts her plans to form her own theatre company on hold: her friends from her student theatre days have already set up a regular performance workshop in a former underwear and shirt factory in Carlton. The two-storey brick building, at the bottom of a carpark on a small block on Faraday Street, is now called the La Mama theatre. A former schoolteacher, Betty Burstall, has leased the building for writers, performers and directors to perform poetry and music and stage experimental theatre. Betty had been a teacher at the high school in Eltham, where she and her husband, the aspiring film director Tim Burstall, bought land in the 1950s. They built a mud-brick house there and lived at the centre of a community of artists. In 1967, Betty and Tim had returned to Melbourne after a two-year stint in New York, where they visited small venues and coffee houses in Greenwich Village and the Lower East Side, including the La MaMa Experimental Theatre Club, which staged new works by avant-garde American playwrights and encouraged actor–audience interactions. In Melbourne, Betty settles on the La Mama name as a tribute to its New York forebear; it is also a nod to Carlton's Italian heritage, and a reference to her vision that her theatre would nurture new work.

When she opens La Mama on 30 July 1967, Betty charges fifty cents a performance, serves free coffee from a corner kitchen, and stokes a large fireplace built into one wall. She writes in the La Mama program notes that she is open to hearing all ideas for 'new Australian plays, sketches, inter-media experiments, improvisations [and] happenings'. Kerry can see why her friends have been drawn to the space. Betty, with her round face and cap of curly dark hair, often sits in the corner, quietly smiling. On Sundays, Kerry and Graeme Blundell lead performance workshops with Bill Garner and two filmmakers they know from the Melbourne University Film Society, Brian Davies and Alan Finney. They subscribe to the US journal the *Tulane Drama Review* to follow experimental theatre groups such as the New York–based Open Theatre, which is improvising works and involving audiences in interactive shows, and the political Bread and Puppet Theater, which is taking theatre to the streets with giant puppets that have become totems of the anti-war demonstrations in the US. Kerry describes Graeme as the group's 'intellectual and directorial driving force ... a theatrical magpie grabbing ideas from everywhere'. Kerry, meanwhile, introduces Grotowski's methods to the group, while Brian Davies brings experiences with psychotherapy, his training with encounter-group therapy methods popularised in the 1960s and, from his day job at a chemical company, with marketing focus groups.

The La Mama workshops are soon attracting a small crowd, including an art student from New Zealand called Bruce Spence, who looks down from his lanky six-foot-six height with startled blue eyes; and Meg Clancy, who had grown up in Carlton and now pulls beers for SP bookies and crooked cops at the University Hotel, where her parents are licensees. The group spends its early days experimenting with improvisation exercises drawn from a mix of theatre theory and counterculture influences. One day they take turns to face the wall and try to project their thoughts backwards. (Bill Garner, who had been president of the Rationalist Society at university, now says, 'I was totally sceptical about that exercise. I thought it was bullshit. But I did it ... we were teaching ourselves.') A popular activity is the group grope, where everyone falls in a heap together and limbs flail, as if the Hindu gods have become mortal and libidinous Melburnians. When someone hires a jukebox, the workshops end in dancing, followed by a drinking session at the Albion Hotel across the road. 'We danced ourselves silly,' Kerry remembers. 'We improvised until we were empty and then we danced ourselves silly again.' In the first few months the workshops attract so much interest, the group begins to run simultaneous sessions upstairs and downstairs.

The word went around that something 'seems to be happening at La Mama', Graeme Blundell would later write. People 'emerged from the cracks in the local footpaths ... drawn by the lure of something new'. John Romeril describes how they felt almost a sense of mission:

> Suddenly Australian reality seemed so real you had to record it, drag it on stage. With all stops out we simply sought to make meaning for ourselves because we felt so few around us were making sense. Hearing this great task was being tackled, a crowd gathered.

The group's international influences include Stanislavski's Moscow Art Theatre, but they are searching for an Australian style to set them apart from the drawing-room comedies favoured by the Melbourne Theatre Company.

There are no scripts to rehearse at the early workshops, but La Mama also attracts writers like Jack Hibberd. He had followed *White With Wire Wheels* with a series of short plays at the Prince Philip Theatre in 1968 under the umbrella title *Brainrot: An Evening of Pathology and Violence, Love and Friendship*. The period is the beginning of what has been called the New Wave of Australian theatre, an umbrella term that groups together a diverse group of writers with distinct styles, including David Williamson and John Romeril in Melbourne, and Sydney playwrights Alma De Groen and Alex Buzo. What unifies them is their interest in telling Australian stories with Australian characters.

Writing to Graeme Blundell from London, Jack Hibberd describes the theatre that is emerging at La Mama as 'indigenous and quasi-experimental, anti-downtown'. While First Nations Australians such as Jack Charles would later join the group at the Pram Factory and establish the Aboriginal theatre company Nindethana, the La Mama group uses the word 'indigenous' differently from the way we understand it now, to refer to theatre that told stories of Australian life. This emergence of a vernacular Australian theatre, despite its glaring omissions of fully fleshed-out characters that aren't white and male, is nevertheless a momentous event, as Kerry would later recall:

> In the late 60s and early 70s ... Even just to get up on stage and speak with an Australian accent and do a play that was written by an Australian was a radical event! ... It was part of a process of self-definition [that involved showing archetypal characters] back to you, as an audience.

The group that gravitates towards La Mama rejects theatre that slavishly follows London's West End and requires actors to 'put on pommy accents to get on the stage', Kerry writes. Her comments perhaps overstate just how new their project was: members of the APG were aware of Australian theatre traditions dating from as early as the late 1800s, thanks to research by Margaret Williams, a friend of John Romeril's from Monash University. But it was true for Kerry to say that Australian theatre in the 1970s was dominated by European, and particularly British, plays.

The La Mama theatre closes the gap between the audience and stage in other ways, too. John Romeril has described the theatre as 'a handkerchief-sized arena. You can touch the audience, and with no back stalls to reach, a big voice seemed ludicrous, while the fruity vowels of the BBC-inflected Anglophile always was, for an Australian actor, an obvious put-on.' The nature of the La Mama space means that 'vocally we operated in an easy, unforced, vernacular way'.

In 1969, the group's determination to bring Australian voices and language to the stage leads to a visit from the vice squad. The Alex Buzo play *Norm and Ahmed*, about a meeting one night between Norm, a battle-scarred Anglo veteran, and Ahmed, a Pakistani student, ends with a shocking act of violence. But the vice squad detectives are more concerned about Norm's last words – 'fuckin' boong' – and Graeme as director and Lindsay Smith, the actor playing Norm, are found guilty of obscenity and fined $10. Later that year the La Mama group perform a show in the La Mama carpark that satirises the experience. John Romeril's *Whatever Happened to Realism* features the comedic Ros Brown as Life, a character who keeps trying to escape a coffin but is thwarted by a group of 'Relevant Officials', dark figures dressed in raincoats, eyes covered with fedora hats, who repeatedly nail the lid of a coffin closed. On the sidelines, Bruce Spence plays GAP, the Great Australian Playwright, who intermittently appears to deliver a manifesto. Members of the La Mama group, meanwhile, hand out copies of the manifesto to the 1000-strong crowd, decrying censorship laws. The performance concludes with a band playing a song '*Shit, fuck, cunt, fart, bugger off, will ya?*' The show's run is cut short during an early performance, when ten plainclothes police officers leap from the audience and arrest nine actors, including their theatrical counterparts. The police walk the actors to the Carlton Police Station around the corner, and the crowd follows, chanting and singing – '*Shit, fuck, cunt, fart, bugger off, will ya?*' – as the band keeps playing.

The La Mama commitment to bringing Australian stories, and Australian voices, to the stage is matched by its conviction that the audience can become a part of the story. The group does away with elaborate props and staging; Graeme Blundell describes audiences at La Mama shows moving between upstairs and downstairs when scenes change, and plays spilling out onto the stairs and into La Mama's gravel courtyard. Writing in *Carlton News*, Jack Hibberd declares that La Mama's open space allows the actors to explore the freedom and 'intimacy of close contact' with an audience. John Romeril's early play *I Don't Know Who to Feel Sorry For* is directed by Graeme, and stars Kerry as one half of an Australian counterculture couple living in a bedsit, with a picture of Marlon Brando in *The Wild One* on the wall. The audience crams into the small set, watching as the couple's relationship falls apart. Actors deliberately make eye contact; those watching the show feel as if they are eavesdropping, Graeme recalls.

When audience members climb the La Mama stairs in 1969 to see the group perform *Dimboola*, Jack Hibberd's play about a country wedding, the father of the bride greets the audience at the door, shakes their hands and announces their arrival to the room as if they are members of the wedding party. Inside, in a room decked out in wedding decorations, they sit down at tables piled with drinks and wedding food. Cast members address (and sometimes insult) the audience during the show. Actor Peter Cummins recalls the La Mama actors drinking throughout a show: 'We used to say we'd never do a play without a six pack. We were always carrying a six pack on and drinking real beer. We deliberately set out to create a theatre that contrasted with the establishment drawing room theatre.'

Dimboola is now considered an Australian classic, and has been performed by professional groups and countless amateur theatres around the country. You can watch an adaption of the play in a 1979 movie of the same name. The film stars APG members Bruce Spence, Max Gillies, Kerry Dwyer, Evelyn Krape, Bill Garner and others. Watching the film you realise that it's not always clear if *Dimboola* is a celebration or a condemnation of the boozy ocker male. Kerry plays bridesmaid Shirl, a character who is the target of other characters' innuendos about her sexual relationships. In a still from a 1973 production of the show at the Pram Factory that seems full of loaded symbolism, Kerry as Shirl is pictured being hauled into the back of a Valiant ute by groom Morrie (Bruce Spence) and his best man Dangles (Bill Garner).

* * *

While the La Mama group was dragging the Australian character and vernacular onto the stage and conducting a war on cultural censorship, the collective also became increasingly drawn into the movement protesting Australia's involvement in the war in Vietnam. In 'Pramocracy', his history of the APG's early years, John Timlin, APG administrator and publicist, linked the group's growing politicisation to the involvement of John Romeril, Jon Hawkes and Lindsay Smith, new members from Monash University, home of a Marxist–Leninist faction in the student movement. The arrival of these three figures signalled the group's transition from a purely theatrical to a more overtly political outfit, Timlin wrote: 'The emphasis [in the beginning] was theatrical rather than political though this was later to change with the input of the energies of the Monash University denizens.' Writing in the APG newsletter, using the revolutionary phrasing of the era with an archly wry twist, Bill Garner similarly described the 'injection of three cadres from Monash – Smith, Hawkes and Romeril' as being responsible for the 'politicisation of the A.P.G.' He said these figures changed the group 'from an apolitical set of actors into a sentimentally radical propaganda organ committed spasmodically and ignorantly to some vague version of the revolution.' The new members influenced the La Mama company's move towards street theatre and agitprop sketches.

The La Mama group was also influenced by events that began in Paris on 13 May 1968, when thousands of students and workers initiated a general strike and occupied the Odéon-Théâtre de France, the national theatre. The strike began as a protest by university students against the ban on male and female students sleeping in each other's dorm rooms, but it soon enfolded opposition to the war in Vietnam, low workers' wages, and the entire political and cultural system. Actors and protestors raided costume boxes at the Odéon. Performers acted in the streets, and activists and leaders of the strikes took over the theatre to stage political performances.

The involvement of performers and avant-garde artists in the French strike and occupations was a significant event for the experimental and political theatre groups that were forming across the world. Australian theatre scholar Denise Varney has written about how the events in France both validated their rejection of realist theatrical traditions as instruments of the 'bourgeoisie', and put arts workers, cultural actions and politically engaged theatre at the centre of broader political actions. British playwright and critic Michelene Wandor has similarly written that the events of 1968 help take theatre in Britain 'out of its bourgeois citadels', where plays began to address 'the fabric of ordinary people's lives'.

From the beginning, the group that formed first at La Mama, and later at the Pram Factory, was spurred by a Marxist belief that the working class was a 'potential agent of social change'. The La Mama company began to work with protest groups, using acrobatics and commedia dell'arte techniques. 'We spent the summer of 1968–69 at La Mama making masks for street theatre,' Kerry remembers. 'I don't remember who suggested we do street theatre – maybe Lindsay Smith or Jon Hawkes ... Maybe Graeme, enamoured as he was of *commedia dell'arte* ... Maybe it was me – I was very inspired by the street theatre in Paris in May 1968.' Kerry recalls more than twenty people turning up to rehearse John Romeril's anti-war play *Mr Big, The Big Pig* for a May Day performance on the banks of the Yarra River in 1969. At first they rehearsed in a space lent rent-free by the New Theatre, and then in the Carlton Gardens opposite the house Kerry was by then living in with Graeme. Some of the La Mama actors resigned when they realised the black costumes and white papier-mâché face masks evoked the soldiers of South Vietnam's National Liberation Front. For those who stayed, though, the politics of the emerging counterculture was of a piece with the group's rejection of theatre of the proscenium arch and fourth wall.

The May Day play was in many ways a dress rehearsal for the group's performances at mass anti-war demonstrations. The actors dressed in black costumes, red bandanas and face paint. Kerry recalls sewing the costumes with Julie Ewington and Margot Lindsay in her front room, and practising cartwheels, chants and sketches on the grass. Bill Garner remembers one of the group's members, Martin Phelan, teaching the group tumbling: 'We'd haul mattresses out of [Kerry and Graeme's] house and practice.'

The Bulletin's Leonard Glickfeld described the group on 8 May 1970 'whirring down Bourke Street like American fighter pilots in the vanguard of the Moratorium march'. Kerry has written about the day, when the APG street theatre performers joined the movement organisers, Jim Cairns and Sam Goldbloom, 'tall and upright' men, at the front of the crowd, leading thousands of protestors in a march down Bourke Street. The street theatre group had assembled at dawn in Treasury Gardens behind Parliament House:

> The sun was barely up when we got there. I have an image of Doug Anders burned into my brain. A tall thin man, he is silhouetted against the crisp early morning sky. The sun is shining through the leaves of the trees and hits the top of the big bass drum strapped to his chest. Boom!! He strides through the milling crowd, gathering us up and signalling the beginning of a sketch. Boom! Boom! Boom!!
>
> We were not the first to arrive, but we were certainly the most visible – our faces painted white, black and red gashed across our cheeks, running down from eyes and mouth. Around our heads we wore a red band. The pyjamas gave us speed and ease of movement and white sneakers gave us stealth and a spring in our step ... In true guerrilla style, we had strategies for moving through the crowd, for speeding through the terrain, and creating performance spaces.

The group repeated five or six prepared sketches during the day, with any member being able to take any role. Kerry describes the group marching and then gradually forming a circle, singing as they went:

> *When Johnnie comes marching home again, Hurrah! Hurrah!*
>
> *When Johnnie comes marching home again Hurrah! Hurrah!*
>
> *He hasn't an arm; He hasn't a leg,*
>
> *He's an armless, legless formless egg*
>
> *And we'll all be gay (fall down?)*
>
> *When Johnnie comes marching home.*

The group would crouch down and then burst out of the huddle 'as if bombed or hit by a landmine, leaving maimed tortured bodies writhing on the ground', Kerry later writes. 'Silently, the bodies picked themselves up and snaked out of the space to move on to the next site.' Lindsay Smith and Graeme Blundell ran ahead with signs saying 'Flying wedge', 'Free Zarb', 'Light at the End of the Tunnel', and 'All the Way With LBJ'.' 'Zarb' was 21-year-old Pascoe Vale postman John Francis Zarb, a conscientious objector who was sentenced to two years in Melbourne's Pentridge Gaol for refusing the comply with his call-up notice.

The Vietnam War is often called the first television war, and the group's sketches and songs can still be seen on YouTube today: actors running through the crowd form the backdrop to a report from Bob Higson on the ABC's current-affairs program *This Day Tonight*. As the troupe sing and run in the background, the suited reporter, his eyes framed by Buddy Holly–style glasses, walks through the crowd describing the 'motley collection of people' at the march, including 'one or two fine examples of the shock troops of the New Left'. Bill Garner later writes about the 'heady' experience of performing 'in front of one hundred thousand people and dancing your way down the road, watching the police and the army thugs dissolve in front because of the seamen and wharfies who were this guard behind you ...'

Kerry describes the point of the 'one-minute sketches on street corners':

> It was about inserting yourself not outside the audience, but within the audience. We developed these techniques for working in big crowds where we'd ... file into the crowd and we'd turn in like a corkscrew and create a circular space and sit down and do these two-minute routines, ten groups of five people.'

Bread and Puppet founder Peter Schumann, in a 1968 interview in the *Tulane Drama Review*, said: 'You don't make your point unless a five-year-old girl can understand it. If she gets it, the grownups will too'. Schumann believed that watching something exaggerated and confronting, like a grotesque, inflated President Johnson, would prompt audiences to become alienated from their assumptions about society, and start to think about the ideas being presented. The Carlton group likewise believed – like many on the New Left – that 'if enough people changed their personal lives according to the principles of socialism or feminism ... then the whole structure of society would eventually change,' Kerry later writes.

Fifty years later, the influence of Schuman on the group is clear when Kerry repeats his theory almost verbatim: 'We believed that by educating people and showing them images you could actually change the government ... The theory [was] that if a five-year-old child can understand it then it can work.' In one action, the APG made a human cage, she says: 'People in the street would go, "That's bizarre. What's this?" The questions would start as a result of the images, that was the theory.' The sketches were designed to give people 'a seed of information and draw people into discussions afterwards'. Bill Garner would describe the May Day play as a 'watershed' event: 'once we began to perform in the streets it was impossible for us to continue on in a non-political way'. The political theatre of the APG 'shattered the barrier between theatre and the world', he wrote, finishing with an optimistic note of hubris: 'a theatrical act is a political act'.

The year of the big moratorium marches, 1970, was also the year the La Mama group moved into a new home. The group needed a larger space, and the Sunday workshop at La Mama was beginning to dominate the small theatre: 'For a couple of years we essentially moved everyone else out,' Kerry says. Kerry and Graeme's house on Carlton Street had become the group's unofficial meeting space. Months of searching for a suitable rehearsal and performance venue ended when Dot Thompson, from the Melbourne branch of the left-wing New Theatre movement, asked the La Mama group if they wanted to share the rent on a vacant factory building on Drummond Street in Carlton. Graeme remembers climbing the cyclone fencing of the business next door with Kerry to peer through the building's 'dirt-encrusted windows ... The downstairs space was long and crypt-like and, as far as we could tell, the upstairs was spacious, with higher ceilings and three large windows looking out into the street.'

The sprawling building dated from 1912, when it was a livery stables for residents who could not accommodate their horses in the small backyards of Carlton's terraces. In later years the building was used for other kinds of transport – in the 1920s Paramount Prams manufactured baby carriages there, and at some point a panel-beating business moved into the ground floor. The building was a microcosm of Carlton's changing social history; at one time or another it had reportedly been a dance hall, a brothel and a boxing ring, a coke den during the Depression years and, more recently, a storage space for overflow from the Baillieu Library. John Timlin recalls it had even been used as 'a place where the Melbourne Theatre Company stored old sets, and older ideas'.

With no way of paying the rent, Kerry and Graeme approached John Timlin, a local businessman who enjoyed hosting writers at Sunday drinking sessions, and who had a gift for spotting an opportunity and bringing people together. Naming the building the Pram Factory was a nod to the building's recent past, but it also reflected the group's allegiance (in theory if not by background) to the working class. Timlin says the name was deliberately derivative and unembellished: 'It had long been a pram factory and that's what we called it. No pretension, no style you see. That was the style.' By this time, the group had also settled on a name for the company. Suggestions such as Lindsay Smith's 'Spectaculo', or Hibberd's Brecht-inspired offering from London,. 'Gestus Ensemble', were discarded, Graeme recalls. In contrast to the Pram Factory's matter-of-fact nomenclature, the name they settled on – the 'Australian Performing Group' – matched their audaciously ambitious mission to reinvent Australian theatre culture.

* * *

Kerry, Graeme and the founding members of the APG begin cultivating a group of like-minded performers. A group of lecturers and former students from the Secondary Teachers' College drama course join them, including Max Gillies, along with Claire Dobbin and Tony Taylor. Claire and Max worked at the Open Stage theatre, established by the head of drama at the Secondary Teachers' College, Ron Danielson, and modelled on the experimental Open Space Theatre in London, which encouraged actors' improvisation and abandoned traditional theatre fixtures such as an elevated stage and elaborate props. Danielson was staging Brecht plays such as *Mother Courage* and *The Caucasian Chalk Circle*, and introducing students to Brecht's notion of 'epic theatre', which favoured strange, alienating action that discouraged audiences from passively identifying with characters on stage.

The Pram also attracts Evelyn Krape, who had dropped out of law studies and then music at the Conservatorium to study drama at the Teachers' College, where her comic persona and stage presence attracted Kerry and Graeme's attention. Evelyn had grown up with Yiddish music and theatre: her mother and maternal grandfather had performed at the Kadimah Yiddish Theatre in Carlton. The original Kadimah theatre group first operated from a building on Drummond Street two doors south of the Pram Factory, before moving in 1933 to a purpose-built hall on Lygon Street opposite the Melbourne General Cemetery. Evelyn recalls Kerry and Graeme seeing her in a show at the Teachers' College: 'They said to me, "The APG is about to move into new premises in Drummond Street. Would you be interested in coming and having a look?"'

Evelyn first visits the Pram Factory one Saturday afternoon. The first thing she sees when she walks through the door is Bill Garner standing on his head. Her initial shock – she has never seen anyone standing on their head for so long – turns to panic when she realises they might ask her to do the same thing. But Bill stands up and mimes going into the Exhibition Building and coming out onto the balcony around the dome. Another group of actors are rolling around on the floor. Yvonne

Marini, acting spaced-out and floaty, is rehearsing a scene set in an opium den in Little Lonsdale Street.

* * *

'I didn't know what an opium den was. I was clueless,' says Evelyn, who was raised in a close-knit Jewish community in Kew. 'I didn't understand what they were doing ... I went to non-Jewish schools and I did have non-Jewish friends ... but I had grown up pretty much in a Jewish shtetl.' Evelyn's maternal grandparents were from Polish Jewish families who came to Australia before the war. Her father, Saul, arrived Melbourne after time in two displaced-persons camps. 'He was the only one who survived in his family,' Evelyn says. She had gone to University High School in Parkville, but when she came home to Kew after school she was immersed in a Jewish community. With her background in musicals, the physical style of improvised theatre at the Pram Factory was at first foreign to her. 'But interestingly, the kind of actor that I am suited that very well – I'm a physical actor and comic,' she tells me. Although Evelyn knew nothing about the history of Melbourne's sex industry, she was cast as the madam of a brothel in the Pram Factory's first show, *Marvellous Melbourne*.

Max Gillies tells me the group of staff and students from the Teachers' College and the La Mama group were like 'parallel outfits of roughly equal cohorts'. Max's group was also reading the *Tulane Drama Review* – 'the Bible all the drama nerds were reading'. *Marvellous Melbourne* grew out of an early Australia Council grant the Pram group won to do a six-month workshop, he recalls. The project began with the group interviewing their parents about 'growing up in Melbourne, growing up through the Depression with a view to eventually ending in performance'. In the early stages of the workshop Helen Garner acted as the group's scribe, organising the material, Max recalls. At some point, however, the project was redefined as an examination of Melbourne at the end of the nineteenth century. 'We decided there were similarities in the politics of the time, the events of the time, and Melbourne now,' Max says. The group saw parallels between the corruption of politicians in the nineteenth century and the 1970s government of Victoria. They also made a connection between the young men who were being sent to fight in the Vietnam War and the Australian troops who fought alongside the British Army in the Boer War.

As the APG was rehearsing *Marvellous Melbourne* in 1970, its members were simultaneously transforming the Pram Factory into a theatre space. Covering their faces with handkerchiefs to protect themselves from dust, the group began pulling apart the wooden beams and shelving, removing wooden pillars and the false ceiling and mezzanine floor modifications of the building's previous tenants. The working bees over the first six months were, Max tells me, 'as much as anything a discovery of the space and what you could do in it'. Meg Clancy recalls the group hired industrial sanders and set up a 24-hour roster of two people working at a time: after a shift at the Pram, 'we'd go home with white eyelashes and black shit up our nostrils'. The building's days as a printery meant that 'we had to sand about half an inch off the floor to get below the deeply embedded ink stains', Kerry wrote. Tony Taylor remembers someone spotted a fire hose in the building: 'I watched three guys holding the hose spurting the detritus of the last tenants out into the night. And we detritus moved in.'

The group's DIY approach to renovating the building led to unscripted dramas, Meg Clancy recalls. Without the mandatory three-phase power required for a theatre, the health authorities would shut down productions. An early show was 'closed down for two weeks, then I don't know how, but Timlin did something, maybe some money passed hands, but we were finally allowed to open even though we hadn't had the three-phase power fixed up'. During a 1971 performance of Romeril's *Chicago*, Meg was offstage with Graeme Blundell when they smelt something burning. They raced across the road to the house of an electrician who lived opposite, Graeme Leith, and got him out of bed saying 'Quick! The theatre's on fire!' The audience moved out onto the street without protest as the cast and crew pretended 'nothing was happening', and Leith performed a 'wire and chewing gum' repair.

The Front Theatre was the only theatre in the Pram Factory in the group's early years, but from the beginning the building was open to the local community and events. Underneath the Front Theatre, in the crypt-like basement, a flea market operated on weekends that was an early resource for the group. 'We used to go down and get costumes,' Evelyn recalls. She still has a red velvet coat she wore when she played Melba in Jack's play *A Toast to Melba*. Bands would perform there – the earliest iteration of Melbourne band Skyhooks played a show in November 1973. The Tower on the building's north side, meanwhile, was a home to APG members. Robin Laurie, an early Tower resident with Jon Hawkes and Lindsay Smith, remembers enjoying the communal meals, but also that 'no one would do the washing up, that's probably why we ended up eating out all the time at Tamani's [now called Tiamo]'. At some point a hole was punched into the wall between the Tower and the theatre space, meaning residents could tumble out of bed and into a rehearsal, while some of the rooms in the Tower became admin offices. 'People who lived in the Tower, on the whole, were idealists who wanted to live at work and work at play and avoid the nuclear family,' Tim Robertson writes in his recollections of the Pram.

In the late 1960s and early 1970s, experimental art cooperatives like the APG were taking over disused factories and warehouses in Australia's inner-city suburbs. While the APG was establishing a space for new theatre in Melbourne, the Melbourne Filmmakers Co-operative was working out of offices in Spring Street; the Sydney Filmmakers Co-operative was creating films in a warehouse in Darlinghurst; and the Earthworks Poster Collective was moving into the Tin Sheds opposite the University of Sydney on City Road, screen-printing political posters for demonstrations, art happenings and events. These collectives took advantage of increasingly affordable and accessible technologies, such as offset printing and Super 8 and 16 mm cameras. John Hughes, a member of the Melbourne Filmmakers Co-operative, says these groups acted as 'hubs' that 'performed the zeitgeist' for the newly emerging 'identity' groups opposed to the war in Vietnam overseas, and a sexual and cultural conservatism at home.

While groups such as the APG were opposed to many of the conservative Holt and Gorton federal government's policies at the beginning of the 1970s, they also shared with them, somewhat inconveniently, the aim of creating a 'vernacular' Australian culture. As historian Michelle Arrow observes, American programs had dominated small screens since the introduction of television in 1956, raising 'the stakes in the debate about a national culture'. There had always been Australian plays and Australian playwrights – including many female playwrights, as Arrow notes in her 2002 book *Upstaged*. But in the 1960s, there was little that cohered into a living, thriving performance tradition – or so it seemed, at least in the eyes of those who formed the APG.

In 1963, the Vincent Report – named after its author, a senator for Western Australia, Victor Seddon Vincent – argued that Australia's performing arts industries were at the heart of the country's cultural life and should receive government assistance. Australian film and television would thrive if they were underpinned by a healthy live performance culture, the report argued. It recommended that live theatre be shown on television, that actors' pay and conditions be improved, and that young Australian actors be given scholarships to train overseas. The Vincent Report influenced the government to establish the Australia Council for the Arts in 1967, the Australian Film Development Corporation (AFDC) in 1969, and the Australian Film and Television School in 1972. The Australia Council administered grants and government subsidies for Australian artists and Australian arts companies, and groups like the APG found themselves in the paradoxical position of applying for funding from the very government they frequently criticised in their work.

In contrast to established theatre companies, which brought in new directors and performers for each new show, from the beginning the Pram Factory was run by its members. But it was the company's need to raise funds from outside bodies that prompted the APG to formalise its structure, with a constitution and an executive and regular meetings. In 'Pramocracy', John Timlin describes the APG as 'a democratic collective of actors, writers, designers etc'. An anarchic kind of socialism might be the best way to describe the group's ethos in the early years. The APG's philosophy was that there would be no stars or iconoclastic directors, and everyone was expected to take a turn running front of house. 'There was a sense that actors weren't more important than cleaners, and that directors were a bit of an aberration,' Max Gillies says.

Some of the members of the Pram, including Max and Claire Dobbin, were also involved in an 'economic union', a scheme where members pooled their income in an attempt to create a small socialist cooperative in Carlton. Claire says the economic union was formed 'because we believed that people should be paid according to their needs, regardless of their income, within the resources available. It was an attempt to separate earnings from financial needs.' The system was good for actors who didn't have a regular income, Max says. 'Or if you're a couple of young teachers ... and you had a couple of little kids, the pressure would be for the male to be the breadwinner and the partner to stay at home with the little kids, just because of the earning differential [between male and female teachers].' The group would do a collective shop and have a meal together once a week to decide which projects were a priority to support. 'You'd get all your groceries and meat and fish and vegetables from the market and distribute them at the meal. Somebody would do the books, keep the accounts going. The difficulty we had was there's nothing in the tax system that works for this. So we had to ... not fudge things, but it was a nuisance.'

A principal of communal egalitarianism operated at the Pram too. Before they were an actor or director or playwright, everyone was simply a 'member'. Pram member Robin Laurie remembers a kind of open-door democracy operating for the street theatre performances. 'We'd rehearse in the morning, perform in the afternoon, and everyone who turned up in the morning could be in the show in the afternoon.' Member John Smythe recalls: 'It seemed to be an unwritten rule that anyone succeeding at any one thing, like directing a play, should then do other things to prove they were no better than anyone else and preserve the egalitarian nature of things.' While decisions were voted on during collective meetings, as is invariably the nature of such groups, factions would develop (and then often dissolve). Not everyone had equal amounts time, or the skills to write, direct or act. And not everyone had the confidence to lobby in the pubs and cafés where decisions were often made. (Bill Garner has described the café Tamani's as place where 'lives turned … It was the stage on which bedmates were declared, feuds conducted, subtle degrees of status displayed.')

There were ongoing debates at the Pram about whether the APG was primarily a writers' or an actors' theatre, a theatre for political work, or a space for more esoteric and experimental work. There were tensions between directors who wanted to stage plays from overseas, and actors who favoured improvisation and experimentation. Laurel Frank remembers 'writers who wanted the purity of their work and their text to be at the forefront'. 'Hibberd wrote the most amazing stuff,' Vic Marsh recalls. 'There was this group of fabulous experimental writers, and they were a bit suspicious about improv and all that stuff … The written word was the key.' Collective meetings, Laurel Frank remembers, could turn into 'full-on' debates about where the group's energy should go:

> People would just say really blunt and astonishing things about other people who were in the room. Lindsay [Smith] had a lot of radical American plays that he wanted to produce as well as creating new work, whereas the writers' group tended to be pushing the Australian writers' voice.

Max recalls one meeting that went on to 1.30 am, discussing a piece Jack Hibberd had written about one of the high-rise housing estates in Carlton where he worked as a doctor:

> His piece was about a picnic with all the different ethnicities of the people who lived in the flats, it was a broad caricature, and comic in

intent ... There was a huge discussion about whether the piece was politically correct ... It was a proper and animated discussion about the content ... how it should be played, if it should be played at all.

Jack wasn't at the meeting, and 'tempers were getting frayed ... people were going berserk', Max remembers. 'In the early hours of the morning, Evelyn said: "Where's Jack? Where's the fucker? He's not here." So she went off and rang him up. In the middle of the night.'

From the group's earliest years, Jack Hibberd and John Romeril were its most prolific writers. La Mama's July 1969 program, a season that included the hit *Dimboola*, starkly demonstrates how directing roles at the APG's predecessor, the La Mama group, were also dominated by men. Just one woman, Judy Gemes, is named in a list of sixteen directors who produced plays at La Mama. Gemes is credited as directing one play, while the leading male directors, Graeme Blundell and Brian Davies, had directed eight and six plays respectively. In contrast, of the eighty actors listed in the program as appearing in La Mama plays, thirty-three seem to be women. This imbalance – a company approaching an equal number of male and female performers while men dominated writing and directing roles – became untenable for Kerry at the beginning of the 1970s, during rehearsals for *Marvellous Melbourne*.

Marvellous Melbourne has been described by theatre scholar Denise Varney as the APG's first genuinely group-devised show, but women in the APG, led by Kerry, rebelled when it became clear the show, written by men, would tell only men's stories. Kerry says that while *Marvellous Melbourne* was 'ostensibly' a group-created show, the production was dominated by four APG men: playwrights John Romeril and Jack Hibberd, 'who controlled the content of the show', with directors Graeme Blundell and Max Gillies 'making executive decisions about the form'. While the *Marvellous Melbourne* cast included equal numbers of women and men, scenes 'arrived in the rehearsal room with five parts for men, none for women [or] seven parts for men, one for a woman', Kerry says. The directors would come to 'rehearsals with the actors' moves already worked out'.

The show – with actors on stage speaking in Australian accents, and telling Australian stories, nevertheless 'struck a nerve' with a preview audience, Max tells me. 'On the strength of that we decided to mount it as a full production ... we dressed it up a bit and refined the dramatic presentation and it had the first season of what became the APG.' But for Kerry, the radical nature of the play was limited by the fact that the men behind *Marvellous Melbourne* assumed the audience was 'male and white and Anglo-Saxon' and focused on the stories of white men. Kerry described the show to me as 'a corny larrikin boys' own romp with virtually no roles for us [women]. We were half the company, but we were ignored, invisible. In fury I became a committed feminist.' Three of the women who would go on to perform in *Betty Can Jump* were members of the *Marvellous Melbourne* cast – Evelyn Krape, Claire Dobbin and Yvonne Marini – but 'no one else felt as strongly as I did', Kerry has recalled:

> I had not given up the comfort of a good job as a teacher to play male roles, and eventually I hit flash point. I stormed out of rehearsal feeling frustrated, betrayed and deeply hurt. And above all ENRAGED ... that in the theatre women were considered incapable of writing or directing ... Rage that female culture was not respected, and not nurtured ... That history ignored the lives of women as if men were born fully-fledged at the age of 21, already full of testosterone and braggadocio ... And above all, rage that at the Pram Factory ... women were being pushed into invisibility.

In her Pram Factory memories, Yvonne Marini writes that, in the beginning, *Marvellous Melbourne was* a truly group-developed piece. 'You brought in the idea, it got developed and researched, and you did it – I remember researching the history of the Exhibition Buildings at the end of the 1890s and that became the first scene of the show.' At some point though, the writers and directors took charge.

Claire Dobbin would later recall, in a 1975 interview with Kerry, feeling 'totally in the dark and inadequate to the task of acting out the prototype of people in public life (usually men)' during *Marvellous Melbourne*. In a 1984 interview in *Meanjin* about women's theatre at the Pram Factory, however, she placed some responsibility for the situation in the Pram's early years on women: 'The big drawback was always that the women couldn't write – or that they didn't write.' When I talked to her in 2020, Claire recalled the time with perhaps an even more generous hindsight. 'I would have played male roles [in *Marvellous Melbourne*], but I would have played male roles everywhere before this ... The issue wasn't that women had to play men – I've directed plays where I've got boys to play pregnant women,' she tells me. 'I think the issue is that ... it didn't cross [the men's] minds that the decision-making structure would only allow for a certain kind of theatre which did not give voice to women, because nobody thought like that, nobody talked like that then.' It wasn't that the women didn't have anything to say, she tells me, it was that in the beginning the men 'had a strong sense of what they were doing ... They were visionaries and they were committed to creating an authentic national theatre, but it didn't occur to them that women were also part of the national story.' There were few roles for women in a story 'of the domination of the land-booming class in Melbourne' she says. 'It became clear very quickly that if we're going to be part of this, we're going to have to take some space for ourselves.'

The absence of a language, or a space, for women's stories saw Kerry fall into a period of deep depression and overwhelming grief after the *Marvellous Melbourne* run. Tensions at the Pram Factory over the stereotypes of the ocker man and bimbo woman in the group's plays only grew during a July 1971 production of David Williamson's *Don's Party*. Kerry was cast as Susan, a character she considered insubstantial and vacuous. Writing in the APG newsletter in 1972, Helen described the feelings of women at the Pram Factory:

Many women working in new Australian theatre have been frustrated and disappointed by, firstly the dearth of women characters in recent plays, and secondly, by the presentation of what women characters there are as simply vicious, or scatter-brained or superficial, or pathetic, or (perhaps worst of all) enigmatic.

The male characters were not much of an improvement, in Kerry's view. Many of the APG members strongly identified with the working class – 'attendance at football matches is compulsory. We all had to support the right team and go to the bloody matches,' Vic Marsh recalls when I speak to him in Perth, where he is in the middle of watching the AFL finals. But Kerry believes there was a disconnection between the lives of the men in the APG and the ocker and larrikin characters they were writing about. 'I think it was all patronising because those guys who wrote those plays were not larrikins themselves.'

Kerry had hoped *Marvellous Melbourne* would give the company a chance to 'go beyond the superficial larrikin stereotypes, which frankly give nothing to the women in the company, other than the chance to be seen on stage'. For her, the group's move to the Pram Factory and transition to a legal entity triggered a 'dampening down of the raw ecstatic power of the early days', and it led to a period of male dominance: 'That glimpse of a spiritual dimension of the theatre began to fade. The voice of the women became more and more feeble. We lost the immediacy of creating on the floor in favour of moves worked out at home by the directors and then imposed on the performers.' Kerry describes this period as 'the beginning of many bitter arguments at the Pram Factory about bringing women's reality, women's culture more to the front'.

Yvonne Marini describes one night at the APG when Kerry and Evelyn's frustrations came to a head:

> Betty was born out of a big confrontation that had happened in the collective, about there not being enough roles for women. It happened one night whilst we were rehearsing some show ... and there was this big, explosive debate about the dissatisfaction in the

group. Kerry and Evelyn brought it up and the whole show came to a standstill. It was a huge issue and as a result of that the Women's Project came into being.

Women at the APG were developing a feminist consciousness in response to their personal and professional frustration with APG men. But it was their active involvement in the anti–Vietnam War movement and left-wing politics that gave them 'the strength and confidence to confront the war closer to home – male dominance', Kerry writes. As she told me, their political activism:

> gave us the confidence to say, 'We've done that and ... we can do anything.' I think in a lot of the left-wing movements in those days, men would say: 'We'll worry about feminism [later], let's get this class war happening.' We thought, 'Hang on. It's not going to work unless we address this issue as well first.'

10

11

12

13

Chapter 3
As a woman ...

In 1971, as Kerry Dwyer wraps herself in knitted layers as a shield against Melbourne's long winter, her anger at the way the Pram men had dominated the production of *Marvellous Melbourne* is turning into depression and grief. She and Graeme Blundell have moved into a terrace opposite the Carlton Gardens, and their house is the social heart and unofficial office for the Pram Factory crowd. Every night their lounge room is filled with people laughing, drinking, arguing and dancing into the early hours to the Beatles and the Rolling Stones, or sometimes Jose Feliciano singing 'Light My Fire'. Most nights Kerry leaves the parties early and goes upstairs so she can wake in time for her job teaching drama to students at Moreland High School. She is sick of banging on the bedroom floor to ask for quiet. The group that she and Graeme have cultivated at the Pram Factory has begun to take over the house in another way; to Kerry, the stack of papers and unread plays Graeme leaves lying around the house are just another sign of the vanishingly few spaces they can exist in as a couple.

When she discovers she is pregnant, Kerry's grief turns to rage. Why, she asks herself, are the boys in my family considered far more important than the girls? Why are women in the theatre considered incapable of writing? Or directing? Why does football dominate the television and radio for more than half the week? Why is female culture not respected and nurtured? Why have women been subjugated to men? And why has history ignored the lives of women? She has been collecting ideas for a women's play for two years, but the material has no structure, no shape. Now this. Graeme's life is barely affected by her pregnancy. Soon he will soon be leaving for a trip funded by the Australia Council to study alternative theatre groups in the UK and New York. Kerry, on the other hand, has started going to a group closer to home, in a lounge room in Fitzroy where women had begun to meet and talk about the things that were wrong with their lives.

The Carlton Women's Liberation Group's early meetings are held at Helen's house in Kerr Street, Fitzroy. Bill is banished from the gatherings to look after baby Alice. Kerry and Helen's friend Micky comes to her first meeting the night she separates from her husband, Rod. The couple had followed the hippie trail – Darwin, Bali, Timor, India, Turkey – to London, where she worked as a supply teacher in schools during the day, getting up in snowy weather to be at school at 8.30 am. Micky tells the group they had shared a small apartment where she and Rod both tried to paint.

I imagine Micky plonking herself down on an armchair as she begins to relate the story to the group, her face flickering between embarrassment and indignation.

'I had a little cupboard off the kitchen which was my studio, and he took over our living room as his. When I came home in the afternoon, I couldn't get in without him making a big fuss about having to move a giant painting blocking the door.'

Rod had asked her why she needed to paint: 'If you're painting too, who will bring in the cup of tea?'

Kerry groans in sympathy. Helen leans forward, her eyes bulging.

Micky explains she started taking up pottery at nights. 'But he smashed my favourite pot.'

Then Micky – never really wanting to give up painting in the first place – tells the group she smashed her second-favourite pot. And she tells them why, when Kerry and Graeme had offered her paid work at the Pram Factory, she had turned it down: 'It would have meant working at night, and not being home to get Rod's dinner.'

It hadn't helped that her father – an otherwise good man – had once told her, 'Women can do quite well if they work hard, but they can never have an original thought.'

When Kerry's university boyfriend John Helmer returns home in 1971 after years away at Harvard University, she invites his wife, the actress Maggie Helmer, to come to the women's meeting too. Maggie had taught drama at Harvard summer schools, and met John when she was in a production of Henry Purcell's *The Fairy-Queen* and he attended a cast party. Maggie belonged to the Caravan Theatre, a political theatre troupe, based in a church hall next to Harvard University, that developed antinuclear pieces and shows about the civil rights movement, then took them on the road in refurbished buses.

In 2019, Peter Kovner, an actor who had performed alongside Maggie in Caravan productions showed me around Harvard University and Cambridge, Boston. He explained, with a shake of his head, how some members of the group were on such a radical fringe that he passed up the chance to go to Woodstock: 'We thought it was too commercial.' The Caravan Theatre was formed by married couple Bobbi Ausubel, a Harvard biology student, and Stan Edelson; both Bobbi and Stan were activists, and Stan was involved in the Communist Party. In 1967 Bobbi, who had read Simone de Beauvoir's *The Second Sex* and was distressed at the way her equal partnership with Stan changed after they had children, approached the company with the idea of doing 'a play about a woman's life'. The first women's liberation play in the US, *How to Make a Woman* was a group-created production, inspired by Ausubel's feelings that motherhood and heterosexual marriage had 'suffocated her personal ambition and stifled artistic expression'.

It told the story of two women in a dress shop who must learn how to look and behave like acceptable women – until one of them rebels.

The Caravan first performed the play at a folk music club in a basement in Harvard Square. When Peter shows me the club, still operating today, the walls are filled with photos of performers who played there, including Joan Baez and Bob Dylan. Then, as the women's movement gathered momentum at the end of the 1960s, Caravan members, along with members of newly formed women's liberation groups like Redstockings, would lead men and women in the audience in discussions about the feelings that came up during the performance (at first together, and then, when the women wouldn't speak up around men, separately).

Kerry has invited Maggie to speak to the Carlton group's conscious-ness-raising meeting about *How to Make a Woman*, and a few dozen women from Carlton and the Pram Factory have come to hear her. Maggie runs the group through the exercises she had led after Caravan shows, and asks everyone to finish the phrase 'As a woman I feel like ...' Helen feels so uncomfortable she starts to get up to leave, but she wills herself to stay, and imagines herself as 'a piece of elastic that is stretched and stretched and stretched'. (Later, she would confess to Kerry how confronting she found Maggie's exercises: 'I was so freaked out at the thought of having to do anything like that.')

Kerry tells the workshop her fears about motherhood: 'I feel like I'm going to stick a nappy pin into the baby's belly.' She is worried that having a baby will push her to the margins at the Pram Factory, where she has seen that women with children are not well supported. When Kerry discovered she was pregnant she gave Graeme an ultimatum. She wanted him to commit to looking after the baby with her. 'If you want to get married, that's good, but if you don't, I'm going to have this child by myself,' she told him.

Maggie gives the Melbourne women another exercise, one where they act out their fears. The women start to workshop small scenes. Helen acts out bringing baby Alice home from hospital, one of the most traumatic days of her life, with Kerry playing her husband Bill. 'I was estranged from my parents at that point,' Helen tells me now. Her father hadn't approved of the marriage, and had tried to stop it going ahead and banned her mother from attending. 'I've got no ... family backing,' she recalls. It's as if she's back in that moment. 'They didn't even come to see me after I had the baby.' Bill, meanwhile, was spending more and more time at the La Mama group. 'The nature of [that sort of theatre group is] that it's hard to be in one if you're married ... They were having so much fun. And they were drinking a lot, and he sometimes wouldn't come home at all. I just didn't know what to do.'

During the day, Helen is working four days a week as a teacher at Fitzroy High School. At home with Alice at nights, she feels like a theatre widow, 'left out and lonely', Helen told her literary biographer, Bernadette Brennan. She tells me it is difficult – distressing – recalling the year leading up to the play: while there were 'times of laughter and enjoyment, of working in a group to try to get this play together', it was also 'a moment of my life that was cataclysmic. Not because of the play; it was a year of incredible smashing and breaking things in my personal life.'

When I speak to Helen now, she doesn't claim any credit for starting the Carlton group – 'There are a lot of people around who say they started the women's movement', she rolls her eyes and laughs. 'I don't remember starting anything!' While Helen now recalls the consciousness-raising group as a fairly 'ad hoc' affair, APG News stories written in the weeks before *Betty Can Jump* opens credit the group with playing a formative role in the play's genesis. 'I remember there were about eight of us or nine sitting in ... a room in the house that I lived in,' Helen says now. 'Everybody told their little grievance story, whatever their father had done, or whatever it was.'

Ad hoc or not, the group was one of Melbourne's first consciousness-raising collectives – small groups where women met regularly to talk about their lives, often picking a different topic each week, such as sexuality, friendships, work and love. Unlike meetings at the Pram Factory, where the most confident and articulate men held the floor, the consciousness-raising meetings gave women the opportunity to speak freely to each other about their lives and frustrations.

Some of the women at the Pram Factory, on the other hand, are already living what might be described as independent feminist lives. Yvonne Marini was born in Greece to parents who had been through guerrilla movements and two wars. By the age of fourteen she already felt politicised. She had left home when she was young and unmarried. She would later write this was 'unknown in my culture at the time. You just got married – that's how you left a Greek home, but both my sister and I were rebellious.' Yvonne had joined the La Mama group when she returned to Melbourne after failing NIDA, the acting school in Sydney – she would joke that failing NIDA made her acceptable to the Sunday workshop actors. When she first started working at the Pram Factory, she travelled from her family home in Maribyrnong, in Melbourne's north-west. 'There's no way I can get to the Pram every day from here,' Yvonne told her father. With fingers yellowing from the constant roll-your-own cigarettes she smoked, she packed her possessions in boxes and moved into the loft at the back of APG administrator John Timlin's Rathdowne Street home.

Yvonne's issues with the male playwrights and performers at the APG were about cultural difference as often as they were about gender difference. She felt no connection to – and often had no understanding of – the Australianisms in a Jack Hibberd play, like a reference to a Mechanics Institute. In the 1971 production of Don's Party in the Pram's Front Theatre she played Jody, 'the prim and proper one who let loose at the end'. She felt as if she was stumbling through it, struggling to do the Australian accent. 'I hadn't experienced a society like that, it was right out of my world view ... I had a Greek accent and I had great difficulty doing the Australian accent. Don's Party wasn't the kind of theatre I wanted to do, and I nearly left the Pram,' she later wrote. On the last night of the production, she stood backstage and, for one terrible moment, froze: 'I'm not going to be able to go on for the last scene,' she thought. 'No one thought about the cultural difference that I brought in except for Kerry Dwyer, who'd taught migrant kids at school, and perhaps Bill Garner, who seemed to realise I was from a different culture,' she would later reflect in her memories of the Pram years. 'I never felt really confident with the language, it took a long, long time to feel I was fluent or expressive enough.'

Student Laurel Frank, more reserved and younger than many of the women in the Carlton group, had also gravitated to the APG. She felt on the outer at the Pram at first, not only because she was a woman, but because of her working-class background. Her father was an electrician, and her family was peppered with unionists and Communist Party members; Laurel's aunt and grandmother had worked at the International Bookshop, and communist books and magazines, and Russian and Chinese novels, were scattered around family homes. She had followed an older cousin to La Trobe University, believing it would suit her more than the elite University of Melbourne. At university Laurel became involved in anti–Vietnam War actions and a demonstration against the Springbok rugby team tour in 1971. But university was still a culture shock. 'Over my three years at university I ditched my broad working-class Aussie accent in favour of proper pronunciation,' she says now.

When she arrives at the Pram Factory, where the APG is embracing Australian stories and Australian voices with flat vowels onstage, Laurel has to reverse her now modulated accent. Offstage, however, APG members are introducing her to a middle-class world. Kerry's visits to markets in France had introduced her to food such as artichokes in garlic butter, and Graeme cooks dishes from Elizabeth David's *French Provincial Cooking*. Visiting their home to talk about a job at the Pram, Laurel is struck by the elegant way Kerry presents a lunch of steamed beans and bratwurst sausages from the Victoria Market, two items she has never seen before. And she is amazed when she sees Bill Garner buying avocado and prosciutto.

Because Laurel is not married or living with a man, she doesn't experience the 'contradiction of working all day and being equal in a creative life, then going home and being expected to do the major share of the domestic work', she tells me: 'I did what I wanted, so I was very privileged in that way.' Working as a volunteer on the phone lines at a Rape Crisis Centre, however, played a key role in her developing feminist consciousness: 'It made me put myself in that position, and [think] about "How would I deal with someone with that attitude towards me, wanting to limit my life that way, or thinking they had the right to abuse me?"' Laurel remembers the phrase 'the personal is political' as something of a 'mantra' in early consciousness-raising meetings. 'I did start to automatically re-evaluate everything that happened, and every decision I had to make, and the way I was treated and the things that I was offered.' Micky Allan, too, says the women's group gave her a powerful 'sense of justification ... that you weren't the only one who felt that way'.

* * *

The consciousness-raising practices that women at the APG, and across Australia, began to use had their origins in the US. In her memoir, second-wave feminist Susan Brownmiller describes a 1967 meeting of the early women's liberation movement in a New York apartment where she says the term 'consciousness raising' was first used. The assembled women, mostly veterans of the old and New Left and civil rights movements, were influenced by the Marxist notion of 'false consciousness'. Activist Anne Forer spoke up, asking: 'Would everybody please give me an example from their own life on how they experienced oppression as a woman? I need to hear it to raise my own consciousness.' Brownmiller credits another woman at the meeting, the writer Kathie Sarachild, with coining the term 'consciousness raising' (the women's movement slogan 'Sisterhood is powerful' is also Sarachild's). Another early women's liberationist, the author of the influential pamphlet 'The Personal Is Political', Carol Hanisch, has said the women's liberation practice of consciousness raising was also influenced by the 'tell it like it is' practice of civil rights movements, and the Chinese Revolution's 'speak bitterness' practice. (With its

Maoist members, the notion of 'speaking bitterness' was a familiar one to women at the Pram too, later member Jane Clifton tells me.)

By the early 1970s, consciousness-raising groups were forming in capital cities across Australia. Marilyn Lake, a historian of the Australian women's movement, writes that 'groups sprang into existence all over the country, each a small unit in a grand movement'. The first public meeting of Sydney's women's liberation movement was held in a hall on Druitt Street in the CBD on 14 January 1970, while the Canberra Women's Liberation Movement's first meeting was held on 31 October 1970. The Carlton group was one of Melbourne's earliest, and by 1973 there were thirty-four groups listed in the Women's Liberation Newsletter. Women's groups were importing feminist books and pamphlets from overseas to discuss in consciousness-raising groups, and Australian women were soon printing their own material and starting women's liberationist newspapers and journals.

Not all of the early groups involved women sitting in a circle talking about their personal lives. Some groups were based around political campaigns, others, like the Carlton group, around common creative interests. A collective of women filmmakers formed in 1970 at the Sydney Filmmakers Co-operative in Darlinghurst, an avant-garde group that, like the APG, wanted to create a new Australian culture and tell Australian stories. (Jan Chapman, who was a member of the Sydney Women's Film Group at the Co-op, would go on to produce films written by Helen Garner.) Other groups organised around practical concerns. Libby Lloyd, a qualified osteopath, a diplomat's wife and a young mother of three in the 1970s, for example, remembers forming a childcare co-operative called Tuggeranong Family Action in Canberra with other working women.

It is hard to overstate just how transformative the experience of joining the movement was for many women. Feminist author Sara Dowse describes the intoxicating mood of a moment when anything seemed possible: 'For three months I didn't know a single person's name. Because people couldn't be bothered with names. We were just women on fire.' When I visit Julie Gibson, one of the founders of the Sydney women's film group, in her cottage in New South Wales's Capertee Valley, she describes a time when 'Everything sparkled – even if the world was dreadful out there, we were together in now tackling it. And I had huge faith in how wonderful the women I was with were.'

Some women left their husbands, some women came out, and countless others demanded wholesale changes to their private lives. Libby Lloyd's daughter, Justine, recalls a moment when she, her brothers and her father would not come out of their rooms to the dinner table. Her mother 'dumped the dinner on the floor and said to us: "There are five people in this family. You will all be cooking dinner one night every week."'

The women's movement and the sexual revolution were intimately entwined. In 1970 Germaine Greer was urging women to taste their menstrual blood and find liberation through orgasms, women were reading about open relationships and sexual identity in the Boston Women's Health Collective's handbooks *Our Bodies, Ourselves*, and in Australia, the first issue of *Dolly* magazine launched with a Dolly Doctor page answering questions about periods and women's anatomy. For many of those who converged around the APG at the beginning of the 1970s, it was the beginning of a period of experimenting with different kinds of relationships and new ways of living. Kerry says now that it was 'almost like we had to go through that process of trying out the traditional relationship before rejecting the nuclear model'.

At Pram Factory meetings, overt displays of affection were seen as crass, and couples would avoid sitting next to each other. 'Jealousy and possessiveness was frowned upon while open free relationships were encouraged,' writes Ponch Hawkes, a photographer who chronicled the Pram Factory and Carlton world. It was not always easy in practice (in *Monkey Grip*, as Nora visits the Tower and the share households of her inner-city community, she constantly steels herself for the possibility of seeing her lover Javo emerge from another woman's bedroom). People, Ponch writes, 'couldn't say they were very hurt, or act hurt [when they] had to see you the next day, or the same day, in the hall'; they had to 'wear it'.

For all its radicalism, the sexual revolution at the Pram was still a partial and fraught one. One night in 1971, the APG invited Dennis Altman, who had just published his first book, *Homosexual*, which championed gay liberation and a polymorphously perverse sexuality, to a meeting at the Pram Factory. 'My then partner Barry Prothero and I started to sketch out a play on gay themes, but it didn't eventuate,' he says now. Jude Kuring was an enthusiastic supporter of the project, but other Pram members were uncomfortable with the idea. 'The Pram factory didn't deal with homosexuality very well at all,' Kerry acknowledges now. Pram actor Tony Taylor, who had not yet come out, remembers 'being appalled at my performance of a camp flag designer in [*Marvellous Melbourne*]. I was so inwardly ashamed of all that stereotype poncing. The mob seemed to love it but I always felt like going home and having a good wash'. Vic Marsh, who joined the Pram when he was recruited for *Betty Can Jump*, recalls: 'There was a lot of critique of monogamy, but it was still a heterosexual sort of world.' It would be another couple of years before some of the Pram women – newly emboldened by the success of *Betty Can Jump* – would produce a show with lesbian themes.

The Pram Factory men, meanwhile, were worried about what the women were starting to talk to each other about. Pram member Bob Thorneycroft recalls a story circulated among the men that the 'women even got down to the nitty gritty ... the size of their men's penises'. Bill Garner recalls that 'second-wave feminism hit us like a tidal wave. The men were totally paranoid about consciousness-raising groups, suspecting that every detail of our private lives, sexual lives, married lives, our lives as fathers was being discussed.' Bill tells me now that 'some of the slightly older men' at the Pram were particularly wary of the emerging women's movement. But he, along with the 'revolutionary Monash crew', such as 'Johnno [Hawkes] and Lindsay [Smith] and [John] Romeril', were supportive. They were accused of a certain amount of opportunism (not unfairly, he says): 'If we didn't side with the women ... we would never get another fuck,' he happily admits. But throwing your lot in with the feminists was also 'a sine qua non moment' for the possibility of friendship, let alone sex, he adds.

A few fitful attempts were made to start men's groups, but they didn't last. When Vic Marsh arrived from Perth in the middle of the political and sexual revolution at the Pram, he noticed that while some of the APG men were happy that the cultural changes might have reduced the inhibitions of some women in the group, others 'grumble into their beer ... that the [women were discussing] intimate details of their private lives ... The men really needed to catch up because they hadn't had their unconscious male privilege questioned or interrogated.'

Evelyn recalls a friend inviting her to go along to her first consciousness-raising group in 1971 after she finished her university exams, but the personal exploration she was interested in wasn't on offer: 'We tried to engage the group in personal discussions, but the women in it would always rather objectify issues, and talk about them in a very general way.' Working with the women at the Pram was a chance to talk about the personal, but in the context of theatre. Evelyn tells me the Pram men weren't always accepting of the women's cells:

> the men had real problems when we said, 'We want to have meetings with just women.' There was a lot of discussion at the Pram Factory about women's meetings. The men were saying that 'the whole point of the Pram Factory is that it's open to everybody and nobody should be allowed to have closed meetings'.

The APG men regarded the women's complaints about their personal life as 'bourgeois individualism', Helen Garner told Bernadette Brennan. 'But we didn't think it was bourgeois at all to claim that the personal was political,' Kerry says now. 'Most of the men in our lives were anxious, angry, scornful or just plain scared, but we surged on anyway.'

Women did not have to be members of a consciousness-raising group to be part of the women's liberation actions. My mother was the same age as many of the women at the Pram Factory, but while they were studying at university, she was training to be a nurse and midwife. She had seen an aunt go through a backyard abortion, and as a trainee nurse she remembers the silence and shame around unmarried pregnancy. One day in theatre she worked on an operation where doctors removed a young woman's perfectly healthy appendix while doing a curettage. 'They took her appendix out so she had a reason for the surgery. We all went along with the illegal abortions.' When she moved to a small country town in Gippsland in the early 1970s, she saw women who were pregnant with babies they didn't want, and nowhere to turn. The sexual revolution had not necessarily been accompanied by more *information* about sex, or easy access to contraception. My mother took herself to Melbourne for a week-long family planning course. When she came home, she held sessions for women in the local hall. Thanks to the help of the local doctors, a young couple who advertised her work, women flocked to her talks. So did the local Catholic priests, who sat at the back of the hall, watching her, the wife of the local Anglican priest. She vividly remembers them now: 'Sitting together stiffly, real frowns on their faces, their hands clenched on their knees and glaring at me.'

Some of the APG men's reactions to women's liberation at first mirrored those of New Left men Carol Hanisch described in her pamphlet 'The Personal Is Political'. Hanisch, who had worked as an organiser with the civil rights group the Southern Conference Education Fund, was defending consciousness raising from accusations from within the New Left that women discussing their lives in small groups was merely a form of personal 'therapy', and a self-indulgent focus on spheres of life – women's bodies, abortion, housework and relationships – that should remain private. But Hanisch rejected the notion that personal issues were trivial and collective consciousness raising was unnecessary, writing: 'There are no personal solutions at this time. There is only collective action for a collective solution.' Many in the early Australian women's liberation movement agreed with the early US model of consciousness raising that said self-analysis and transformation, or even an analysis of power, were important but not ends in themselves. They needed to be matched, as Marilyn Lake writes, with 'action and outreach'.

In the early years of the women's liberation movement, women were organising and protesting about discrimination in every sphere of life. The Carlton Women's Liberation Group were discussing matters well beyond men's sexual abilities. They wanted to raise their own consciousnesses, but they also wanted to create a consciousness-raising event for other women. Maggie's visit had crystallised the idea for a women's play. Kerry, Micky and Helen were the driving forces at the start, Kerry says now. 'The three of us decided that we would do a show based on the ... images and the work that was coming out of doing those exercises with Maggie. We thought, "Theatre, why not? We can do anything." We knew nothing, so we could do anything.'

Their experience in the moratorium movement had given the women at the Pram Factory a new confidence. For Kerry, putting on a women's play would create the space she desperately wanted for women's stories. Micky remembers now that when the Carlton group came along, she felt a 'new-found freedom' and a chance 'to activate my own creativity'. Helen recalls being drawn to the idea of a women's show during a frightening period: 'It happened at a stage of my life when my marriage was breaking up, and I realise now how freaked out I was.' Over the following months, women from the Carlton group and the Pram Factory would take the lessons of Kerry's experience studying with Grotowski, and the APG's commitment to telling Australian stories, and combine them with the women's liberation process of consciousness raising and collective processes to create their women's show.

Chapter 4
Rehearsals for revolution

Micky Allan remembers how appealing the Pram's collective approach could be. She recalls 'huge discussions' over issues such as whether the group should have an administrator who would be paid: 'everyone decided everything. That was extremely attractive, the collective side of it and the camaraderie of being part of this whole with everybody doing their bit.' Meetings could devolve into interminable discussions about what colour to paint the toilet, Robin Laurie recalls: 'People got drunk, knitted, spun wool, fixed their bicycles, shouted, doodled, argued, performed, cried, stormed out and slept through them.' 'Quite a lot of knitting went on,' Max Gillies tells me. 'And when you're chairing a meeting you can become aware that there's some furious knitting going on in different places ... the knitting was an expressive part of the group.'

Not everyone was enamoured with the group's collective decision-making though. Graeme Blundell writes that he 'was never quite sure about the idea that we were all equal in the workforce and that we all possessed equal skills as performers if only we were given equal chances'. In practice, democracy at the Pram was often haphazard. Collective meetings would make decisions about which shows would go on, but it was often the loudest, the most articulate and those most adept at meeting processes – more often than not men – who held sway.

Pram members could bristle at efforts to distribute onstage and offstage roles equally. Meg Clancy supported Kerry's boycott of the second production of *Marvellous Melbourne* ('She felt that it was sexist, and she was right,' Meg later wrote). But she also recalls a time, just before the opening night of the show's first season, when she was welding rostra frames with Yvonne Marini – 'Neither Yvonne nor I had ever made a rivet or used a welding tool' – in the basement carpark. They were 'furious with Kerry':

> she had spent the whole afternoon swanning around doing the publicity and delivering press kits here and there while Yvonne and I had black faces and were still in these hot sweaty metal masks 15 minutes before the show started. I recall Kerry driving up in the Volkswagen with full makeup on as Yvonne and I were sawing up bits of wood.

Factions and divisions inevitably formed. According to Kerry, there were the 'Irish Catholic' drinkers, mostly men, who would spend the day at the pub. Another group who 'liked drugs and were radical in their politics and lifestyle' gravitated to the Tower. In the middle were a group who were more 'moderate in their vices' and liked 'light-hearted popular musical theatre'. Then there was the often unacknowledged power of romantic alliances: 'There were always new hierarchies springing up, and quite often the hierarchy would be based on who was in a new relationship, so the energy from that relationship would bring them to the top of the pile.'

Timlin, in 'Pramocracy', writes that the APG attempted to break down silos and factions by giving everyone a vote and introducing a policy of all members performing multiple tasks: 'All shared in programming; roles were multi-functional – writers could act, actors write, administrators build the set.' While these developments were radical shifts for Australian theatre at the time, it was only a partial revolution. Underneath the promise and pretence of democracy, many of the women felt it was 'more one <u>man</u>, one vote', Timlin notes. It was the very 'looseness' of the APG structure that allowed power to 'accrue to too few people'. But the APG women drew on the group's commitment to democracy and collectivism – however flawed in practice – when they invited women from across Melbourne to contribute ideas for a women's show at the Pram.

* * *

In September 1971, Kerry, suffering from pregnancy nausea, drags herself along to a feminist conference at the University of Melbourne's Guild Theatre to advocate for a women's liberation play to be staged. 'I just managed to utter some incoherent account of what we would like to do and asked for support,' Kerry would later write. Word about a group of women planning a women's play spreads, and Kerry and the Carlton group send invitations to a planning meeting to women they know in Carlton and Fitzroy and Parkville, and from as far afield as Lower Plenty, Elwood and Mt Buller.

On a rainy Monday at the end of September, nearly fifty women turn up to the first of two open meetings at the Pram Factory to talk about what the play should say, and how it should say it. There are young women and middle-aged women, South Yarra working girls and frustrated housewives, teachers and students. Winsome McCaughey (who would later become Lord Mayor of Melbourne) attends, as does the folk singer and anti-war activist Glen Tomasetti, already celebrated for the song she penned in support of the 1969 equal pay case, 'Don't Be Too Polite, Girls', sung to the tune of the Australian shearing ballad 'All Among the Wool, Boys'.

Taking over the Back Theatre, women break into small groups. One group discusses the communication gaps between older women and younger women, along with the conflict women feel between caring for children and having an intellectual life, and they wonder how the play might reach working-class women. A second group discusses religion and US feminist Kate Millett, binary stereotypes like 'mother earth v male technology', and whether the play should be serious or satirical. A third group talks about sexual hypocrisy and double standards when it comes to males and females. Another group talks about lesbianism, sex stereotyping and the oppressive notion in heterosexual relationships of women needing to 'keep the man'. And they wonder 'how can you possibly reverse sex-role conditioning when it begins so early and when schools are full of people who hate children?'.

One man also attends the first planning meeting with a couple of scripts he's written about men and women. The women ask him to join the large circle for general discussions, but instead he storms around the edge and shouts from the top of the rostra that they will get nowhere without men: 'Damnitall! I don't know how you are going to achieve anything at all if you won't accept help and advice from us.' Kerry later writes in her production diary that 'he kept trying to interpret women's lib for us, but wouldn't join'. The man gives Kerry all the justification she needs to close future meetings to men. They don't need more ideas, Kerry writes in her diary: the group is already 'brimming with ideas that we might explore in our feminist play'. The second planning meeting is strictly for women only.

The group insists on creating a space separate from men, where they can talk and share their ideas uninterrupted. Claire recalls the mood of the time: 'When we announced we were going to be doing a women's theatre project, no one was hostile to it, but we insisted on hiving off and doing it ourselves ... We needed the space to make mistakes and to work out what we were doing and ... to find our voice.' Kerry recalls the 'Pram men were like, "They'll never get a show together." They were really scathing ... We had to do it. Not to impress the men, but to say: "We can do it. You're not going to stomp on us."'

Over the following weeks, the planning meetings turn into a series of acting workshops to select performers (some of whom, Kerry realises, might need a 'crash course in elementary stage craft'). The group uses exercises from overseas women's liberation groups, including a list of topics for discussion from the New York Women's Liberation Movement. They use the list to act out their first experiences of sex, what it's like to be a girl in school and then a woman at work, to be married, and a mother.

As the workshops and the demands of time and commitment increase, Kerry notices that many 'talented and enthusiastic women drop away'. Those who stay begin acting workshops and improvisations using the 'As a woman I feel like ...' prompt. They discuss relationships with mothers, and they talk about how older women in their families would brush off their questions as they were growing up, saying: 'There are some things you don't need to know yet.' They also come up with images they might use in the play; someone suggests depicting women as marionettes, with someone else pulling the strings. In a word-association exercise, boys are horses stampeding in a paddock.

This smaller group also chooses a name for the show. *Betty Can Jump* is a reference to lines from *John and Betty*, a 1951 children's reader produced by the Education Department of Victoria. The story begins with a boy and girl doing the same thing ('John can jump, Betty can jump') and then separating. John plays with his truck and dog, and Betty plays with a toy pram and her cat. The book was still being read by children starting school well into the 1970s. The younger members of the group, like Evelyn and Claire, might have read it in their first years of school. It was one of the first books I picked up when I was learning how words sounded and stories were made.

The story of a girl playing games, jumping and then pushing a pram is a fitting inspiration for a show made by women rebelling against partners and husbands who expect them to have their dinner ready in the evening. Who can leave them – literally – holding the baby. That it will be performed in a space that once manufactured babies' prams seems nothing if not poetically subversive.

By mid-November a cast of five women is chosen: Helen Garner, Yvonne Marini, Jude Kuring, Evelyn Krape and Claire Dobbin. Micky Allan takes responsibility for design, Laurel Frank and Kay Hamilton are chosen to carry out historical research, and musicians Lorraine Milne and Sarah de Jong are responsible for the score, with Glen Tomasetti contributing additional music and lyrics. Kerry takes on the role of the director, a first for a woman at the APG. The group is a blend of theatre professionals and amateurs like Helen, who had no previous performing experience. Kerry would later write that the raw talent and resolve of *Betty* collective members was more important than theatre experience: 'Helen was not yet known as a writer, but her letters were brilliant ... Micky was a painter with an exceptional sense of colour and form. Their enthusiasm and commitment were sure signs we were on the right track.'

The closest Helen had come to performing was play acting with her siblings. She would later tell Kerry she was 'amazed' when she was chosen for the cast. 'I was pleased and flattered and terrified ... I was [also] incredibly tired and drained. I had never been so exhausted. What with splitting up with Bill, teaching 8/10 time, looking after Alice and doing the show at night.' Laurel has not worked in theatre before either. Her glasses, petite and neat frame and quiet, sharp mind suggest literary scholar rather than live performer. But when she hears about it though university friends she finds herself drawn to the energy of the project developing at Pram Factory. Micky now recalls the time as a period of great possibility: 'It was just this sense of enormous enthusiasm and exhilaration, of 'Why not? Why don't we just do it? We can do whatever we want.'

* * *

The collective received some funds for the production from the APG, thanks to a small grant from the Australian Council for the Arts. Rehearsals were scheduled every weeknight for three hours and all-day Sunday. In Micky Allan's poster design, the play is billed as jointly presented by 'APG, carlton women's lib'. Twenty-three women are credited for the show; Micky took their names, and turned them into a design of three nested circles. The largest circle is made from the names of the cast and key crew members, while two smaller circles inside spell out the names of other women in the collective who built sets, helped make props and costumes and managed front of house. Micky's design evokes both the consciousness-raising circle, and the way the work of the performers has grown out of the contributions of those named in the inner circles.

The tall and gangly Jude Kuring had played Evelyn's mother in *Dimboola*. She towered over the other women in the cast – on the comp cards the APG's Actors Agency produced for commercial work, Yvonne, Evelyn and Claire are all listed as just five feet tall. (Evelyn describes herself, along with Yvonne and Claire, as earthy, grounded performers, 'as if our centre of gravity was sort of in the hips and uterus'. Helen was just a couple of inches taller.) Jude had a reputation as a 'good bloody actor', Evelyn says now. Charismatic and unpredictable, she had been known to fall asleep on stage. One night, during a performance of *Dimboola*, Evelyn had to poke Jude in the ribs to wake her up. Jude was also famous for a prank she liked to play sitting on the floor of Jimmy Watson's courtyard on Saturday mornings. As the crowd grew, she would fill her mouth with claret and let it slowly trickle down to her trousers until someone called for help. Onlookers fell for the trick the first time, calling for medical help, but after the fifth time 'people were not impressed', her good friend Soosie Adshead would remember. She was a droll and almost mocking presence in the collective, Claire recalls: 'That was quite useful, because we were probably too earnest at times.' She adds that Jude's approach helped the group quell their anxious questions – 'What are we doing again? Why are we doing this?'

In photos of Yvonne from the period, she projects a kind of vulnerability, openness commingled with intense focus. Claire remembers Yvonne 'bringing a kind of Greek longing' to her performances, 'a sense of ache, a sense of loss'. Evelyn recalls that she and the 'warm and earthy' Yvonne were 'a bit Bobbsey twins ... We worked well off one another ... we were in similar territory in terms of our approach to things.' Evelyn and Claire already knew each other from the Secondary Teachers' College. Claire remembers Evelyn as 'a ball of energy and very brilliant and always completely out there in terms of what we can do ... A total risk-taker as a performer, and that encouraged the rest of us'. Evelyn's ability to connect with the audience, and to connect with her emotional core 'really inspired the rest of us'. Overseeing it all was Kerry. Vic Marsh, who was cast late in the process, remembers her as 'this tall, strong Amazonian woman making her voice heard'.

Kerry longed for a rehearsal process like the one she had experienced at La Mama in 1969, when she and two other women performed *Calm Down Mother*, a play by Megan Terry from the New York Open Theatre. Terry's play allowed for improvisations – actors' personal experiences and creative contributions were central. Kerry remembers she and the play's other two cast members, Lindy Davies and Kim O'Leary, had 'slipped into a stream of unlimited possibility; creating, discovering, exploring, with heightened awareness and exquisite sense of connectedness and wholeness'. Graeme Blundell directed by 'not directing ... [He] sat and watched, not judging, yet discerning all.'

> *Calm Down Mother* began with each of us improvising around an opening riff. Mine, significantly, was 'Hit! I want to hit! Hit! Hit! HIT! HIT!' accompanied by increasingly violent swipes at the air. What ecstasy! From the rage came a creative force on which the rest of the performance flowed effortlessly. In my everyday life I always tried to control the rage, but my gimlet eyes always gave it away.

The trust between the *Calm Down Mother* cast carried into the performance. One night, a drunken actor in the audience, drinking from a flagon of red wine, kept heckling, Kerry remembers: 'I assumed a character who went and sat on his knee, gave him total attention for a minute or two. He quietened down.' Lindy led him to the door, ushered him outside and re-joined the play without a pause. Another night, Lindy ended a dramatic speech by grinding her cigarette butt into the back of Kerry's hand: 'She was oblivious. I looked at her in amazement, but I felt no pain.' Kerry hope to create the same kind of trust and sense of connectedness and flow between cast members in the *Betty Can Jump* rehearsals.

* * *

In the middle of November, Kerry writes a plan for the ten weeks of rehearsals before the show is to open. Each session begins with warm-up exercises. Yvonne leads the group in a physical warm-up exercise. Helen, who has begun learning yoga in the studio recently opened by Mrs Mangiamele on Lygon Street, leads the cast in breathing and yoga exercises. Evelyn, the group's singer, runs them through vocal warm-ups. They try Grotowski-like exercises: they assume cat poses, work on head and shoulder stands, and do an exercise to help actors concentrate 'on how their bodies occupy, fill, displace & vacate the space'. Kerry directs the cast to concentrate on a sphere of air around them: 'Shape the air using all parts of your body to alter the contour of the mass of air. Enclose yourself in it. Touch the air and leave your imprint on it with different parts of your body.'

Yvonne would recall how these exercises helped the actors 'tune into each other before they get into the work'. Grotowski 'had a huge influence on me' during the production of *Betty Can Jump*, Kerry says now. The yoga and meditation exercises that begin rehearsals, and the relaxation exercise that end them, are unheard of at the Pram Factory. But her rehearsal process is aimed at 'going beyond the critical mind to a more intuitive freedom ... It's about finding that connection between the numinous and the physical which has to come through the body, it has to come through the intuition.' Grotowski's exercises were premised on stripping away the physical layers to uncover a 'core self', while women's liberation consciousness raising was commonly understood as throwing off women's layers of social conditioning to find a more authentic self beneath. Kerry described what she was trying to achieve in rehearsals in her production diary:

> The exercises are to help actors confront themselves – especially in relation to the way they've been influenced by society. Finding out about yourself in as many different ways (not just the safety of the images you try to present for your everyday public life) and learning to trust yourselves and the others around you.

Reading Kerry's explanation of Grotowski's exercises makes me think of my experience in yoga classes during the Savasana pose at the end, lying in repose, palms facing upwards on the mat. Savasana is the *point* of the class, not the exercises beforehand, one of my teachers would often say. (In Savasana, an instructor will often tell you to empty your mind, but in those five minutes I find my mind often makes the most creative associations for something I'm writing, or solves a puzzle I've been thinking about, as if my unconscious has been working as hard as my body in the previous hour.)

Rehearsals for *Betty* often leave the cast utterly exhausted. That, in one sense, is the point. Evelyn recalls many late-night sessions, and Kerry's 'belief that you should ... rehearse until everybody got so tired that ... you could break down people ... their acting habits and expose something really new and fresh'. The physical exercises, improvisations, and word-association games were a means to help cast members uncover memories, images and dialogue from their life. Kerry's aim was to create theatre that 'communicated not only through words and interactions between people, but [through] a non-verbal language'.

At a rehearsal on Sunday 12 December 1971, the group develops scenes using Maggie Helmer's 'As a woman I feel like ...' phrase, and variations such as 'Men make me feel ...' The 'As a woman ...' exercises gave them material right from the first session, Kerry writes:

> Evelyn Krape felt like a cushion plumped up and then sat on. Claire as a teenager was a 'spiky pineapple in a bowl of perfect pomegranates'. Yvonne was a 'huge laugh' that kept on going until it choked her. With super academic men Helen felt like a 'big pulsating heart just seething with intuition' and with stupid men, 'like a sharp glittering knife only a little bit out of its sheath'.

'I remember lying on the ground and imagining that I was being pumped up with a bicycle pump,' Evelyn tells me. '[I was] full of air, getting to standing, kind of almost floating and then being punctured.' She makes a sound with her lips like air escaping from a balloon.

For Kerry, the process is a clear break from the *Marvellous Melbourne* rehearsals of actors performing scripts already worked out. Claire, however, sees more continuity between *Betty* and earlier APG shows, where scripts built on actor improvisations: '[I think *Betty*] went further [than] *Marvellous Melbourne* ... but it was a kind of Pram Factory style.' It was not an unfamiliar way to work, Claire says, adding an important qualifier: '*Marvellous Melbourne* ... was an investigation into the corrupt roots of Melbourne, [*Betty*] was an investigation into crimes against women.'

While Claire describes creating the show as a 'very organic kind of process', she adds that Kerry was clearly the director. 'It was not collaborative to the extent where there was no director ... Kerry was ... the one who jumped off the high diving board and she had a much stronger sense of what she was trying to do than any of us did.' Claire recalls the pressure that Kerry – who was preparing for the double arrival of a show and a baby – was under: 'She was the one that had gone out on a limb and said, "I'm going to make it happen."' Kerry would 'come to rehearsal and she would have worked at what we were doing and what was working and what we might build on. And you needed it because we were inside the improvisation, and we couldn't tell what was working ... Somebody needed to be outside to be watching or else ... we'd still be rehearsing.' For Kerry, making *Betty* helped her answer the question Grotowski's workshops had posed: 'Through consciousness-raising, the rigour of our rehearsal process, and the powerful performances of the cast, I was beginning to see glimmers of light in response to Grotowski's probing question. I was beginning to find out who I was.'

* * *

While workshops were taking place in Melbourne, Laurel Frank and Kay Hamilton travelled to Sydney to research the history of women in settler Australia at the Mitchell Library. Some of the stories they found would later be explored by Anne Summers in *Damned Whores and God's Police*, as Laurel now recalls: 'Anne Summers ... landed on the same research that we had found in the Mitchell Library and elsewhere.' Being in Sydney and researching women's history was a revelation, Laurel says. 'That was a really amazing experience for us that none of the other women participated in ... We were in the library going "Look at this, look at that!", discovering and photocopying madly and trying to structure some sort of female history.' An APG News item notes that in Sydney, Laurel and Kay uncovered 'official records, diaries, journals, newspapers, magazines, letters, and plays, poetry, prose and songs from different periods of our history'. They discovered tales about convict women, the female factories where they were put to work, and how they were auctioned off as wives. They also uncovered archives about women such as Caroline Chisholm, Vida Goldstein and Louisa Lawson. Writing in the radical journal *Dissent* when the play was over, Helen Garner compared their discovery of women's history to demands from 'black militants for the rewriting of American history to include their experience'.

When Laurel and Kay returned to Melbourne, the collective combined the historical stories they had found with the scenes and images the cast was creating. According to the APG News, the documents Laurel and Kay discovered helped 'place the experience of the group – cast, director and "writers" – into some sort of context'. Their research, in other words, was an attempt to find the historical threads that led to their own experiences of patriarchy in the 1970s. And the material Laurel and Kay brought back to rehearsals 'proved to be a goldmine', Kerry has written.

The cast began to make connections between their own stories and the historical stories of women that had been ignored by the kind of male view of history epitomised by *Marvellous Melbourne*. In a rehearsal plan for 3 January 1972, Kerry writes in her diary that after a 'warm up' the cast are to 'Begin with the bush woman stuff [then] keep eye open to ways of opening out → contemporary life. Isolation, incessant work, desolation ... holding the fort, helping the man.' Evelyn recalls the 'nights we sat around passing documents' as a revelation: 'I found it terrific to see those documents in a time scale;

to piece things together and then go out and create something ... Even though we were working in the dark, I never lost confidence.'

The intense energy of rehearsals did not, however, always translate to the performance. Evelyn describes one four-hour rehearsal that went until midnight, where the cast played convicts being whipped. 'By the end I was totally drained ... We weren't *pretending* to laugh or cry, we actually were, and we were confronted by total emotional anarchy.' But the problem for the performance, she goes on to say, is that 'theatre is not about uncontrolled emotion, because ... you have to laugh or cry each night at a particular point in the text'. The intensity of rehearsal and improvisations, being open to your past experiences and emotions, posed a technical challenge: how do you find the truthfulness in a performance each night without 'spending four hours to get there'?

The historical stories Laurel and Kay uncovered were revelatory, but they also created a problem of narrative cohesion. 'When we came back, it was almost like we had two different plays that were possible,' Laurel recalls. 'There was this amazing historical material and there was the very intense material that came out of the consciousness raising and improvisations.' It was, Laurel says now, 'quite remarkable how Kerry pulled all that together. She just reconfigured the scope of the play.'

The collectively authored script – developed from the cast's personal experiences and Laurel and Kay's research, knitted together through Dwyer's directorial eye – challenged the idea of the individual artist as a lone creative visionary. But while their method was collective, Evelyn describes it as process in which 'each of us developed individually'. According to Evelyn, cast members took on different roles. Helen, for example, 'was like the mind and was allowed by the group to express ideas', while Jude, tall and loose-limbed, was 'like a solid, rather passive base'.

Evelyn's descriptions match Kerry's production diary notes: 'Helen is always the one to see a new opening ... Judy [i.e. Jude] always on the ground in the middle of it all.' Watching from the outside was Kerry. 'You seemed impenetrable,' Evelyn later told her. 'Sitting there with your legs apart and your hands on your knees, smelling of Johnson's baby oil and looking like a pregnant buddha.' Kerry notes in her production diary how Evelyn and Yvonne riff off each other during rehearsals with improvisations that 'are nearly all funny'. Evelyn now recalls Claire as a great team player and collaborator: 'Offstage [Claire] is hilarious. She's a great storyteller.' Helen, too, remembers Claire as 'really funny and clever'. Evelyn was not as close to Helen as she was to Yvonne and Claire, but she remembers Helen as 'brutally honest', with the gift of instant intimacy: 'She had a way of addressing you personally. I remember going to her place ... in Carlton and Helen calling out to me and saying, "Evelyn, I'm in the toilet, down in the backyard, come and talk to me."'

The consciousness-raising circle and the rehearsal room were both places where intimacies and vulnerabilities were regularly exchanged, and transformations of identity and character occurred. Bonding between members of the group was inevitable. When the *Betty* women combined consciousness raising with the daily discipline of the rehearsal room, the intensity of the experience was magnified.

Although the rehearsal process was bringing members of the group closer, for Kerry, it was a time when her relationship with Graeme, who had gone overseas on his three-month study tour of alternative theatre groups, was strained and distant. 'He had gone overseas six weeks into rehearsals. He wasn't there to influence me or undermine me, but he also wasn't there to comfort and cuddle me,' she wrote. Helen and Jude, in the meantime, embarked on an intense flirtation. 'We had this sort of mad crush on each other,' Helen says now. 'Everything in my life was blowing up ... and we used to go and lie in her bed and pash. That's all we ever did, but I'd never kissed a girl before and it was really nice.'

While the cast and researchers were in the rehearsal room, Micky Allan was planning costumes and an elaborate slide show for a screen that would be placed behind the actors. Micky's costumes consisted of cotton T-shirts and loose pants, dyed a different colour for each cast member. 'Their plainness went with the elementary nature of the set with its ramp and a screen,' she says. Micky's projections were a relatively new innovation for Melbourne theatre. She collected dozens of slides, including images of Salvador Dali paintings, bridal pictures, *Playboy*-style images of women, and a picture of Caroline Chisholm on the $5 note, and used two projectors to screen the images behind the actors. 'Sometimes the slides bonded the show together, sometimes they bridged parts and added another dimension ... And often they took the pressure off the actress so that they didn't have to act out unfortunate stereotypes, like the woman with silicon tits,' Laurel recalls. An image of a weightlifter, for example, was a reference to the schoolyard chant 'Boys are strong, like King Kong; girls are weak, chuck 'em in the creek.'

Although the collective's original plan was a show with an all-female cast, they made what Kerry describes as a 'difficult decision' to include Vic Marsh, an actor she had met at the 1970 Perth Arts Festival, to play the male roles. Kerry had been trying to entice him to Melbourne ever since the APG's Perth visit, and during *Betty* rehearsals, she realised that to 'examine the repressive historical male attitudes towards women it would be useful to have a man in the cast'. Vic was an actor and a theatre critic writing what he describes as 'fiery columns' in a weekly paper:

> Most of the conventional Perth theatre folk hated me because I was too outspoken. I was looking for some form of theatre that would change the world, and when the APG brought a couple of plays to perform at the Perth festival, I hung out with them and reviewed their work very positively ... I just found most theatre completely irrelevant to current Australian life, and here they were, a performance collective and a bunch of writers and political radicals.

Vic had trained in mime and, like Kerry, he was interested in Grotowski's method, one he describes to me as 'trying to find the real key to the text in your own psyche'. He looks back at the period with humour and a note of self-deprecation: 'I was just sort of an air head. The APG offered me a fare to get to Melbourne to join the collective. I guess because I said all the right things in my column. And they recognised a flailing, wannabe spirit.' When Kerry asked him to come to Melbourne, Vic was in Sydney facing charges after being arrested while tripping on five tabs of acid, wandering the streets lost for twenty-four hours before walking into a stranger's house. 'I suppose I was in a psychotic state, so when they said "Come to Melbourne and join us," I was desperate to go somewhere else other than Perth, and Carmen said, "Yes, let's do it."'

'Carmen', as we saw earlier, was 23-year-old psychology tutor Carmen Lawrence, Vic's then girlfriend. She had excelled as a student at the Perth Catholic boarding school Santa Maria College and matriculated with distinctions in 1964. At the University of Western Australia she threw herself into campus politics, lobbying for the campus beauty contest to be abolished and joining groups such as the Marijuana Law Reform Society. An activist in the anti-war movement in Perth, she had spoken at rallies urging young men to burn their draft card. Her activism introduced her to Vic and a group of 'people who were doing street theatre'. Carmen was also involved in an anti-censorship push in Perth:

> We called ourselves, rather bizarrely, the Libertarian Socialists ... Things like [Henry] Miller's *Sexus*, for instance, you couldn't buy in Australia. There was a constant tug of war between people in the arts and those people who were trying to keep us attached to a kind of moral compass that bore more resemblance to the fifties.

In 1971, she worked backstage on the first production of Dorothy Hewett's *Chapel Perilous* at Perth's New Fortune Theatre. The play told the story of Sally Banner and her rebellion and search for sexual liberation (Hewett has said she only finished the play after witnessing the 'bombshell' of the Pram Factory's Perth Festival plays. She invited the group to a reading of *Chapel*'s first act, and 'Jack Hibberd laughed madly all through it.') Vic played two of the main character's lovers in the New Fortune production of *Chapel Perilous*, which was marked by poetic and musical interludes.

When Kerry asked the couple to come to Melbourne, Carmen, newly pregnant and working as a researcher at the University of New South Wales, found a more attractive job at Melbourne University as a tutor, and they moved into a room in Kerry and Graeme's terrace. At first the cast was nervous and apprehensive. The group was hypersensitive to outsiders, particularly men, Helen recalled when Kerry interviewed her three years after the play ended. 'We had closed rehearsals, and I remember when a man just came to the door once I went and told him to "Piss off! Go Away!" We were really freaked out by men.' When Graeme Blundell attended a rehearsal, Vic remembers he was not well received. 'He came and watched a rehearsal, and it was just after improvising and he decided it didn't have any coherence at all ... There was a general feeling that really they needed a writer to come in and give shape to the play. And you can imagine how that went down among the women.'

The initially apprehensive cast welcomed Marsh's presence in rehearsals when they saw his willingness to take direction from women and bear the brunt of playing the unflattering male parts. 'Whichever male figures were required, I played them all. I just had to be the butt of everything,' Vic says now. 'I wasn't really very good,' he claims. 'I remember wandering around at one stage shouting at the audience: "Woman! Woe Man! Woman, the Woe of Man!" Throwing out these stupid fucking slogans. And they were coming up with really good, original little set pieces.' Vic recalls the play's opening scene, a convict transport ship coming to Australia from England. 'All the women were rolling around suffering and moaning. And I was this horrible male guard, lashing them.' One of the most memorable moments for Vic was devising an improvised scene, one that wasn't used in the end:

> All the women were giving birth to this baby, which was me, and I was trying to add my bit to it. I came out with 'Mmmmm mamamama

mee, like trying to sort of extricate myself from the mother's womb ... That was my only ideological contribution, and it never got used, but I remember after that, when we were discussing what we'd done. Helen said it was quite extraordinary ... the feeling of a man's leg (I was pretty athletic back then). Grasping my leg, she felt like, 'Oh, that's a real male leg!' That's the kind of energy I brought to it somehow. It was all totally accidental.

'Vic made me laugh, I liked him. I like men,' Helen later told Kerry when she asked her how she felt about Vic joining the cast. Vic's inclusion also replicated her own childhood sibling structure of five girls and a boy. (When I asked her if there was something familiar to her about the grouping, she replied, 'Gosh I hadn't thought of that! ... It's a nice idea,' she laughs. 'It does hold up!' Helen, after thinking about it, later writes.)

Kerry recalls Vic as 'a very generous performer ... Sometimes he seemed more female than some of the women.' In the opening convict ship scene, Vic remembers, 'I was so skinny and fit and wiry, that when I was doing the lash thing I was trying to embody a lash and torture these women on the ship because that opened the bloody play. And I was terribly embarrassed by it.' Rehearsing the scene one day he felt a sharp pain and thought he had a heart attack. Jack Hibberd, the resident doctor, was on hand. 'He assured me that I hadn't damaged my intercostal muscles. I hadn't even heard of intercostal muscles.'

Vic had to 'wear the sins of ... male Western civilisation,' Claire recalls. 'I'm sure it was quite hard for him, but he was very, very good about it ... I imagine Carmen was a huge support to him.' Vic and Carmen would separate later that year, as Vic began to confront his sexuality and seek answers in spirituality, leaving Carmen to raise her son alone, but she is magnanimous and philosophical looking back on the period now. Vic received a small weekly wage from the APG, but he acknowledges that it was her work that kept the couple afloat. 'Without income from me [Vic] wouldn't have survived,' Carmen says. Kerry remembers Carmen also contributing to the play's collective authorship: 'We had the double blessing of Carmen's brilliant mind occasionally clarifying some muddy patch.' Claire recollects Carmen would come and watch rehearsals:

> You need that outside eye as somebody making the connections … She was a very quiet, rational, watchful, observant person who helped create a kind of sense of confidence and calmness, and "We can do this" … It was clear then how smart she was, and to have that kind of endorsement was actually important.

Fifty years on, Carmen says she 'honestly' doesn't remember her contribution:

> I mean, I clearly was sitting in the bleachers while they were rehearsing … maybe waiting for something to happen, to go somewhere else or do something else … So maybe at those moments I made some comment or comments that were helpful. I had my own project, so I just popped in there occasionally. I was deeply immersed in the women's movement at that time though.

Carmen's 'project' was a plan to influence the upcoming election between Gough Whitlam's Labor Party and the incumbents, William McMahon's Liberal–Country Party Coalition. She was one of twelve women who met in Beatrice Faust's Carlton lounge room before the 1972 election to set up the Women's Electoral Lobby. WEL played a key role in the election when they surveyed candidates about their attitudes to issues such as abortion and childcare, campaigning with the memorable slogan 'Think WEL before you vote'. Iola Mathews, one of the women at WEL's founding meeting, remembers Carmen breastfeeding her newborn son at an early meeting and telling the group: 'We must feed our babies in the boardrooms of the nation.'

In creating *Betty Can Jump* collectively, the group emphasised the importance of the women's liberation principle of valuing each member's contribution over the end result. Yvonne Marini later commented: 'In a sense, the process of working was more important than the production itself.' Their approach was unprecedented for the APG, despite the company's ostensibly collective structure. *Betty's* production philosophy was that the 'group process is more important than the genius of any one individual', Kerry later wrote. The collective method *was* the political statement, an APG News editorial noted: 'BETTY CAN JUMP continues an APG tradition of political theatre, but its politics differs from the factories' [sic] tours, etc. Not a statement of dogma or ideology, the revolutionary statement becomes a process, as women's liberation is a process, not a blueprint.'

The *Betty* women's commitment to working collectively was not absolute, however. Cast and crew members' outside responsibilities meant the ideal of collective decision-making was not always possible. Those with jobs couldn't easily attend the daytime planning meetings to make their January opening date. *Betty Can Jump's* short run could not be changed because the APG had already programmed other shows to follow, and because, as Kerry remarks now, 'I was about to drop a baby.' The collective also wanted the show to coincide with Germaine Greer's arrival in Australia for a tour to promote *The Female Eunuch* (although there is no record of Greer attending the play). 'We had to work every day, every night. During the days, Helen and Vic and Micky and anyone else who was available would meet at my place and we'd go through and make decisions about what we were going to work on.' Kerry's memory is that the daytime meetings 'really pissed Evelyn off because she wanted to be part of all that, but she had to work in her parents' dress shop' (Evelyn's memory differs: 'I wouldn't have been working there during the day then,' she says now.)

Although Kerry had been furious about the way final scripts were presented at *Marvellous Melbourne* rehearsals, she acknowledges that the unilateral decisions made during the smaller group's daytime meetings also led to 'tensions and misunderstanding'. Helen reflected on the difficult process of creating the show in the journal *Dissent*:

> The lack of a writer began to make itself felt, and as we were drawn on in an exhausting way day after day, both by rehearsal demands and by our outside commitments to work, marriage, children and

so on, bad vibes sprang out of the necessity for fast decisions to be made in extra daytime script meetings.

While the decisions made in planning meetings were 'not intended as fait accompli, they could be taken that way when presented at rehearsals,' wrote Helen. A democratic process can be slow and exhausting, she reflected, and in a small group, 'personal tensions can be more urgent to solve than theatrical problems'. Members of the group felt involved in Kerry's pregnancy, Helen wrote, and when she experienced complications, sometimes 'dissension' from decisions she made as director were 'bottled up' for fear of causing anxiety. Helen also describes how, for the first time, 'I think ... we had all a very real experience of sisterhood'; on the other hand this sibling-like closeness meant that personality clashes and 'hard banter', if taken the wrong way, could wound more painfully than it might otherwise. 'If we'd known how time consuming these methods were going to be,' Helen suggests, 'I don't imagine we would have tackled the project so blithely.'

The *Betty Can Jump* collective attempted, as best they could, to take account of each other's lives and responsibilities. Kerry's diary contains a note at the beginning of the rehearsal period about a 'salary and babysitter allowance for Helen and Kristin [another mother in the group]'. Kerry later wrote, however, that mothers found it hard to commit to the demanding rehearsal schedule: 'Only one mother was able to find the time to cope with the demands, Helen Garner, and I think her greater experience, just in living, in being married and in having a child was invaluable in giving depth to the material.'

Claire doesn't remember it being a particularly 'difficult rehearsal time', but that doesn't mean there weren't arguments about the work. 'There's always arguments about the work and there need to be: if there aren't arguments about the work it's not going to be any good.' There were no precedents for *Betty*:

> The much-praised *Marvellous Melbourne* had set a kind of APG style and form which was firmly positioned in a historical and

male perspective. There were no personal stories of victims of landgrabbers or the experience of being homeless. It's no surprise we felt uneasy about whether this reimagining of how to dramatise female experience would work … It was tense from time to time, but I don't think it was because people were hostile to each other. It was a real sense of: 'What the fuck are we doing? Can we do this? … We open in two weeks and we still don't know what the fuck we're doing.'

Chapter 5
Betty's run

On the 26 January 1972, the North Vietnamese government rejects Richard Nixon's peace plan as an attempt to install a puppet government in Saigon. Germaine Greer is publicising *The Female Eunuch* in Melbourne, where book reviewer Thelma Forshaw recently compared it to something written by a 'deranged' patient in a 'mental asylum'. A car parts manufacturer in the northern Melbourne suburb of Broadmeadows, meanwhile, gives notice to seventy men amid some of the worst unemployment levels since World War II, and a photographer from *The Age* newspaper, looking for an image for the next day's page three, spots Sandy, an eighteen-year-old with long blond tresses and a silky slip, standing knee-deep in the river that runs through the property where the first Sunbury pop festival is about to begin. Later in the evening, a Wednesday night, a group of actors are laying out their costumes, testing stage lights and running through lines at the Pram Factory's upstairs theatre. Across the city, around 100 people are making their way to the APG's headquarters. Those coming from nearby streets and suburbs walk on paths lit up by Melbourne's long summer twilight. Others travelling from addresses further away ride bikes and catch trams. At the box office they pay an admission of $1.50, climb the concrete stairs to the Front Theatre, and take a seat in rows that rise towards the ceiling along the room's two long sides.

As the theatre fills, 660 kilometres to the north-east (give or take) four Indigenous men are driving towards the lawn opposite Parliament

House with a tiny tent, a beach umbrella and a hastily scrawled sign that says 'Aboriginal Embassy'. Earlier that day, the men had driven from Redfern when they heard Prime Minister McMahon announce that his government was rejecting land rights and offering Indigenous people leases instead. As the four men in Canberra – Michael Anderson, Billy Craigie, Tony Coorey and Bert Williams – are preparing a form of political theatre in the darkness of the nation's capital, in Carlton the opening night of the women's show begins. Vic, a British officer, descends the ladder of a ship that has just landed in the colonies. He grabs one of the convict women milling around in the ship's hold, fucks her on the stairs and seizes and whips her when she tries to defend herself. Evelyn's character laughs hysterically and Vic turns on her too. With little appetite to fight back, the convict women languish on the rostra and a series of platforms at the end of the stage. The audience's seats turn in towards the deck where the actors are performing; it's as if they are a part of the ship, looking at the action from seats that make up the vessel's hull. The space from one side to the other is not much wider than five metres. Vic's whip causes the air to swoosh past audience members. He rounds the women up like sheep dogs and directs them to leave the ship's hold. As the women move they cry out: 'I want to die; Let me die', 'Shut up, leave me alone', 'Don't touch me'.

Betty's opening night, on 26 January, is a quirk of the show's scheduling around other productions in the Pram's program. It was a 'total coincidence', Kerry says now, that the show's opening scene, of a convict ship's arrival in Australia, evoked the day exactly 184 years earlier when Captain Arthur Phillip's flag-raising ceremony Sydney Cove marked the beginning of Indigenous dispossession.

* * *

Helen wrote that the night the cast improvised the opening scene was one of the most exhausting and painful times of my life ... Each of us was to think of an image which would express for us the essence of our existence in that hold: a cow, crammed in and helpless; a wire stretched taut and yet not breaking; a huge aching expanding cunt with the ability to endure pain; a vicious ferrety animal; a fish, caught and gasping.

The images 'had to be painfully dragged out of ourselves'.

As I researched this story, I asked people if they could recall whether the 45-minute show was ever recorded, and no one could recollect anyone filming the performances. Then, in one of my final interviews, Bill Garner tells me he believes a recording of the show *was* made, and that it sat in the back room at the Pram along with other films, but at some stage someone took it. Or maybe it was lost when the building was sold and the props and paraphernalia of the past decade were cleaned out. No one seems to know. The photos in this book were taken hurriedly, Micky tells me, when someone realised on the show's final night that no one had taken any pictures. In an APG News story, Helen wrote that 'BETTY CAN JUMP was by its nature ephemeral ... It has never been, and probably never will be written down in any complete and communicable form, and so, in a sense, except to the people who took part in it and who saw it, it has been lost.'

Kerry describes the show as a 'pastiche'. 'It was a very complex show. There were slides, there were puppets. We just flung everything at it ... It was a very, very dense show.' 'We were afraid (until we read Virginia Woolf's *A Room of One's Own* of the necessity for women to create their own forms of expression) that the show would be too short,' Helen wrote. Although Kerry tells me 'not very much of [the script] was written down', when I comb through the APG archives at the State Library of Victoria, I find a stapled document that appears to be a near-complete script for the play. A cover note in thick red texta suggests Yvonne kept a copy of scenes and the notes they made as they rehearsed. 'Dear Laurel. Here is the BETTY CAN JUMP script. It's a complete one & probably the only one in existence. See you soon. Love. Yvonne.' In faded purple ink on roneoed pages are scenes of Beckett-like brevity. Characters speak in half sentences and talk across each other. Interspersed with these crisp exchanges are longer monologues and more lyrical scenes. In blue pen, someone has made annotations with directions ('Freeze – lights down', 'Ev sings off stage').

As the women leave the ship to explore the foreign soil, according to the script, their mood changes from 'abject to almost confident'. A matron (Claire) inspects the convict women's heads for nits, roughly dispenses flour and pork, and assigns them work in the Female Factory, where women comb, spin and card wool in exchange for rations. The women drink and fight over a bottle of gin. The matron calls the convicts trollops and threatens to cut their rations in half. Yvonne responds, calling her a 'slut'. The women start rioting as Evelyn sings a song, 'Convict Maid'. In the next scene, 'Courting Day', Vic inspects the women's teeth, breasts and 'rump' as if they are on parade. The cast pretend to be animals: a cow (Jude), a horse (Evelyn), a cat (Yvonne) and a dog (Helen). Vic dismisses them all – 'bad teeth', 'slack arse' – until he arrives at Yvonne, whom he chooses as his bride. Vic and Yvonne marry, the cast pose for wedding photos and Vic walks off carrying Yvonne over his shoulder. (Notes for this scene comment on the stereotypes through which women in early colonial settler days are viewed: 'breeders, prostitutes, servants, good-time girl, bushwife, slave'.)

The action moves to a pub, where the women play boorish men drinking, wrestling and fighting and miming sex. As the actors depart, Helen is left alone on stage reciting a speech, 'What is a woman?':

> ... I was an afterthought, a playmate, a second class citizen ...

> You want me to mother you, you want to worship me and make a goddess of me but I disgust you, you loathe me because of the dark wetness of my most secret place ...

> What is a woman?

You expect me to find meaning in my household tasks, my hands in water and children's shit, my back bent in your service, my mind flabby from constant distractions, but when I interrupt your recital of the day's woes or try to speak of my daily frustration or pleasure I must hear my work dismissed as trivia, and my concern for my children called an obsession ...

Helen's speech ends and the lights are turned off for the 'Knowledge Scene', as if to dramatise the way women are in the dark about the way their bodies work, about sex, the mystery of how they are turned into girls, and then women. The actors move around the stage asking the audience questions. 'Does it hurt to have a baby?', 'What's this blood, Mum?', 'How far can I let him go?' Another cast member answers: 'Just women's trouble dear' and 'You'll just have to get used to it'. Someone hisses the words: 'She fucks.'

While explicit language was not new at the Pram Factory when *Betty* was performed, the memory of the arrests at La Mama for obscenity was a recent one. Over the past two years, newspapers had covered multiple trials across the country that saw the publisher Penguin and booksellers charged with distributing and selling 'obscene literature' – Philip Roth's *Portnoy's Complaint*, the story of a young man's sexual obsession and masturbation. Yet here were a cast of women using words like 'cunt and 'slut' and 'fuck', talking about girls' unashamedly sexual bodies and women's naked desires. The sight of five women on stage fighting and cursing and liberally swearing must have come as a shock to audiences. For those watching, it must have been electrifying.

Throughout, the *Betty Can Jump* script seems to anticipate Anne Summers' feminist blockbuster, *Damned Whores and God's Police*. Released three years later, Summers' book argued for a history of Australian colonial settler society as one where women were consigned to one of two roles: a woman was either a whore or a saint. But even saints could be discredited. In a scene about Caroline Chisholm, who housed and educated women and children emigrating to New South Wales in the mid-1800s, Vic's character describes Chisholm as: 'Insane, you know. She left her family, she goes out into the streets of the town and gathers in young girls.' In her diary's production notes, Kerry muses on the way Chisholm was cast as either a saint or a lunatic. Her stage directions suggest that 'Vic's character could put her in a straitjacket' and then a 'minister/priest could narrate the Vatican criteria for sainthood and decide that she fulfils this – he could place a propeller-hat on her head as a halo and give it one whirl around'.

The following scene, the 'Bush Scene', depicts another kind of figure often cast as saintly in the historical imagination: the bush wife. The scene opens with the cast battling through a hot, dusty and scrubby land, but the mood is buoyant. The women talk about their work – rabbit trapping, milking cows, washing and feeding babies, chopping wood. But the atmosphere changes as the scene progresses and hardships pile up. It ends with Helen giving birth to a stillborn child and singing a mournful Henry Lawson poem 'Past Carin'. Kerry recalls the impact of this scene, pieced together from diaries of settler women, on audiences each night: 'Helen sang [Past Carin'] with true pitch and clear unemotional delivery. At this point in the show, every night, women in the audience began to sob, tears streaming down their faces.' Unlike other scenes that were improvised, the bush scene was structured before the actors developed it, Helen writes. 'An actor and a researcher worked together on the scene, starting from the idea of a progression from optimism through bewilderment, resignation and exhaustion to a final stage, expressed in the song, of blankness and emotional death.' This deliberate story structuring, writes Helen, helps explain why it worked. Night after night – including those nights when hostile men in the audience made comments throughout the show – 'there was always a moment of utter stillness in the theatre when the song was over'.

The collective wanted to juxtapose this scene with a scene from the present day, and when the bush scene ends, the action switches to the contemporary world. A couple is arguing over a lost baby. Evelyn plays the mother, and Jude plays a malevolent character who taunts her and throws a jug of water at her. This short scene is followed by another one where actors riff on the 'As a woman I feel like ...' phrase. Helen delivers a speech about feeling like a 'glittering blade':

With men I feel like a very sharp, glittering blade that's only partly out of its sheath.

It glitters and glitters.

They don't see it, but I don't dare to show that blade, to come right out of the sheath, because I'm afraid of how fierce and joyful it will be to stab – and stab – and stab. So I don't show it, I hold it, somehow I hold it back, but it's there, glittering.

Yvonne follows with her 'As a woman ...' speech. She feels 'like a great big mouth which has taken a great gasp of laughing gas ... laughter expressing a life's repression, each paroxysm hiding below layers of raw flesh wounds'. Yvonne ends her soliloquy imagining women's laughter turning back on men: 'I am laughing at you, laughing at your smug self-satisfaction, because now the laughter is against you.'

As Yvonne finishes, Evelyn enters playing Louisa Lawson, founder of the early feminist journal *The Dawn* and member of the Womanhood Suffrage League in Sydney. Louisa's polemic against women becoming 'what men make them' is taken from a column Lawson wrote for an 1886 edition of *The Bulletin*:

> Why, a woman can't bear a child without it being received into the hands of a male doctor; it is baptised by a fat old male parson; a girl goes through life obeying laws made by men; and if she breaks them, a male magistrate sends her to jail, where a male warder handles her and locks her cell at night ... if she gets so far as to be hanged, a male hangman puts the rope around her neck.

Evelyn's Lawson speech ends with an attack on 'Men's vanity ... especially when they're talking or writing about women'. Lawson mocks men who 'know so little about us. We see it,' she says, calling for women to join together in the laughter: 'Why don't women laugh right out – not quietly to themselves; laugh all together; get up on the housetops and laugh, and startle men out of their self-satisfaction?'

The stage directions suggest Yvonne returns to the stage at the end of Evelyn's speech to repeat her laughing-gas speech and burst into hysterical laughter. One night during this scene Evelyn leapt up onto the stage. 'A plank was loose, and it shot up,' she recalls. Vic remembers: 'Evelyn bounded up on this rostrum and it bloody collapsed underneath. She went through the top layer to the floor beneath and we all thought she'd killed herself, but she pulled herself out and dusted herself off and we kept going.' Evelyn says: 'I got stuck by the waist. And I remember saying something like "Do you know what it feels like to be a woman?" And the audience clapping me.'

The play concludes with a speech by suffragist Vida Goldstein (Yvonne) who protests 'against our sex being made a peg of men on which to hang the undesirable attributes of humanity ... We are everlastingly told of "feminine" spite and vindictiveness ... of "feminine" cruelty, vanity and superstition.' Vic, playing a 'mad-misogynist', delivers a speech against giving women the right to vote. Women, he declares, are

> largely guided by sentiment and often by the shallowest of senti-ment ... If the franchise were extended to women and political discussion were allowed to enter the home, I am quite sure that the bulk of women in Victoria, house-mothers and respectable matrons do not want this bill at all, or the power of voting.

The play that began with women mimicking animals ends with Vic comparing women to birds. 'As for the shrieking platform of women who do advocate it, I would as soon give votes to Cockatoos.' In this scene Vic is described as dressed in a 'diggers hat, a false chest with Vote Man 1 on it ... 2 football bladders for balls, yellow boots, and bag of "wild oats"'. Evelyn chastises Yvonne/Goldstein – 'A woman doesn't protest my dear' – and dresses her like a grotesque image of a housewife and mother. She places a giant wedding ring around Yvonne's neck, a gag with a smiling mouth painted on it over her mouth, and blinkers on the sides of her eyes. Yvonne wears huge high heels ten sizes too big, a rubber glove stole and a bra with a baby's milk bottle and plastic nipples attached. The scene ends with Vic and

Yvonne – married for a second time – dancing off stage to 'Strangers in the Night'.

The *Betty* collective used exaggerated characters and costumes in the show to satirise gender roles and mock heterosexual institutions such as marriage. Kerry, for example, remembers the group commissioning the artist Mirka Mora to create a larger-than-life puppet representing a bridegroom, not unlike the way the US-based Bread and Puppet Theater was using giant puppets and effigies during anti–Vietnam War protests. 'Yvonne was the bride married to this enormous male buffoonish sort of puppet. I think someone was inside the puppet or behind it. Some other people were operating the arms.' In the show's bar scene, the cast attached jockstraps and fake penises to their costumes. Micky remarks on how 'that scene was pretty shocking to an audience at the time. It worked very well as role reversal which became an important part of early feminist stuff to point out things to ourselves and to others.' Vic remembers how each night during the scene about women's votes, he strapped on a long salami as a penis 'and a big pair of inflated football bladders with pipe cleaners stuck in them dyed black to be pubic hair'. As the play's season entered its final weeks, the audience would not have failed to notice the rancid smell wafting from Vic's salami.

The costumes were designed to be confrontational, and they paralleled feminist theatre being made overseas at the same time. As they performed *Betty Can Jump* in Melbourne, feminist street theatre in the UK was using similar exaggerated shock tactics, such as a giant penis and a giant deodorant, to satirise gender roles. In a 1972 video recording of *As a Women*, the Caravan Theatre play that influenced the *Betty* women when Maggie Helmer came to Melbourne, one of the female characters, Aili, wears a costume of grotesquely oversized breasts when she marries. When I visited Cambridge, Massachusetts, to research the theatre group's archives at Harvard's Schlesinger Library, I met former Caravan members in the Harvard-Epworth Methodist Church where they rehearsed and performed shows while the Student Nonviolent Coordinating Committee operated from the basement below. Aili Paal Singer, the actor who first played the role that was named after her, tells me her costume was a comment on heterosexual family marriage and the way it distorts relations between men and women. The breasts, she explains, represented her character 'trying to crush and choke the husband who made me into the big mama'.

Vic describes how the *Betty* cast's basic costume of T-shirt and yoga pants, 'a sort of gender negating, shapeless thing', gave the actors room to move, and allowed them to add key props and accessories to signal changing characters. The show's short scenes meant there was no time 'to dress every segment'. Vic remembers doing the group dye, with a different coloured costume for each actor. Claire recalls wearing a sort of 'apricot orange ... I think Ev wore a green one'. Photos of the play showing the cast crouching, leaning into and away from each other, and flinging their arms wide, suggest a play that was full of intensely physical movement. Wearing bare feet for most of the performance, the cast look like they are ready to leap at any moment, as if they had understood the show's title not just metaphorically but literally.

In 'Pramocracy', John Timlin writes that the APG eschewed 'the conventional proscenium arch in favour of an open space'. When the actor was in the round, performances became three-dimensional: the audiences could see performers sweat, and actors relied more on their body, rather than voice and prop, to communicate with the audience. Audiences in the round, looking at each other's reactions, also became more aware of themselves as participants in the performance event. What was new about *Betty Can Jump*, though, was the way it addressed women in the audience. Photographs of performances show audience members sitting at floor level, on both sides of the stage, within touching distance of the actors, embedded within the action. From their seats they lean into the performance space. Mouths turn up into a smile or a laugh. Someone bends forward with a chin resting on closed hand, someone else turns a head towards the action and appears to bite on a knuckle.

Filling a small space in close proximity, the audience could take on a different character from night to night. 'Sometimes we heard people crying out loud,' Helen wrote in her *Dissent* article. There were nights 'when we couldn't raise a sound' from the audience, and nights 'when our voices were drowned out by shouted remarks from men, often hostile or sexually abusive'. In contrast, she writes, they only heard a woman call out once, during Helen's 'What is a woman?' speech. 'A girl yelled out "Right on!" which both embarrassed and delighted us'. The reactions of women in the audience, Helen adds, were mostly 'of the "shock of recognition" kind: at Claire's businessman saying patronisingly, "Why don't you try teaching?"; or at Evelyn teaching her blinkered daughter about "feline cunning"'. Sometimes the cast would hear women in the audience softly crying. And standing offstage at the beginning of the bar scene, as Yvonne, Claire, Evelyn and Jude lampooned chauvinistic men, Helen noticed older women were often 'convulsed with laughter'.

The *Betty* collective used consciousness-raising exercises to develop the show, and they wanted the performance to be a consciousness-raising experience for audience members too. Micky's poster for the show invited the audience to stay back after the performance to talk to the cast about the 'issues the play raises and tries to deal with'. Women ran up to the cast after performances. 'Some of them were weeping, others were laughing in delight,' Helen wrote in *Dissent*. 'Women we'd never seen before put their arms around us ... I couldn't count the number of women who said to us: "You've said things I never knew anyone else thought but me."' Women would 'fall about at parts of the show, or they would sit there ... tears streaming down their faces', Laurel recalled in her 1975 interview with Kerry. Evelyn described the production as 'an affirmation of being female and of reaching out ... to the women in the audience'. In 1984, Claire reflected on how the response was unprecedented at the APG: 'What was remarkable about it was the way it was received by women ... For the first time I experienced the sense of talking to women in the audience much more than to men.' Jane Clifton had not yet joined the Pram – she was a member of the theatre group Tribe, an even less mainstream group of improvisers who later swelled the membership of the APG. She recalls going to a *Betty* performance: 'all-female – that was new and exciting. I remember that it was strong, engaging theatre despite the fact that many of the performers were not actors in the regular sense of the trade.'

Creating an intimate atmosphere at Pram Factory shows and telling stories that reflected the audience's own lives and community were founding principles of the APG. But the company was nevertheless keen to receive positive reviews in both the mainstream and independent press. The group sent letters to prominent theatre critics, including Beatrice Faust (*Sunday Review*), Leonard Radic (*The Age*) and Leonard Glickfeld (*The Bulletin* and *Australian Jewish News*), inviting them to a media performance of *Betty Can Jump* on 2 February.

The critics not only came, they wrote overwhelmingly positive reviews that praised the show's collective approach, its experiments with form, and the way it tackled subjects previously considered personal matters. Reviewers highlighted the show's ensemble nature, only occasionally singling out individual contributions and performers. 'More than any of the Australian Performing Group's productions, this is a group creation,' Radic wrote. The anonymous *Melbourne Times* reviewer declared that 'no member of the cast merits being singled out', noting the production was a 'totally co-operative effort'. When reviewers *did* make special mention of a cast member, Evelyn was the actor most frequently named. Writing for *The Australian*, Tim Dare described her as 'the most active of the cast', but then quickly noted the contribution of the entire collective: 'We cannot afford to lose the skills that went into *Betty Can Jump*.' Faust too described Evelyn as 'superbly funny', while also giving a nod to two other experienced actors in the show, Yvonne and Vic. (Carmen Lawrence agrees with the critics' assessment of Evelyn's performance: 'She was the best of the actors in that whole bunch by orders of magnitude … more compelling in her presentation …

Acting's a funny thing; some people grab you and she was one of those who did that for me.')

Laurel singles out Helen's performance as memorable too: 'Her presence was really powerful in the play.' The show's success with both audiences and critics had something to do with the simple, direct voice the cast – particularly Helen – brought to the show, Laurel suggests now:

> The unadorned woman speaking directly to the audience was a very new thing and very powerful. It's almost like the simplest gestures were the most powerful because they were so unusual and new and you felt the absence of all those other trappings. They weren't women in high heels and corsets and period frocks and make-up and all the rest of it.

There was little rivalry over 'the amount of performing time each actor got', which came as a surprise to the more experienced cast members, Helen wrote in *Dissent*. There was no lead actor in *Betty Can Jump*, just as the women's movement, with its emphasis on collective actions and consensus processes, could be sceptical of stars. (While Germaine Greer was loved by many in the movement, she was also criticised for not being *of* the movement but hovering above it, too focused on being a celebrity, too heterosexual and too focused on individual liberation without having a collective plan for how to get there.)

The collective approach has its limits, however, and the lack of a writer handicapped the group's ability to develop an overarching structure. The collective was forced to strike a balance between radical democracy and finishing the play before the imminent performance date. 'I don't want to make any extravagant claims for the way we worked,' Helen wrote, 'but we did come close to a workable democratic method, at least till the approaching performance date forced us, in the interests of expediency, to abandon the search for ways of working each sequence up from its fundamentals, whether a document or an image or an actual experience.'

The collective process may have been painstakingly slow at times, but it was also responsible for much of the show's originality, which critics routinely praised. *The Bulletin*'s Glickfeld described the play as a genuinely radical break from the dominant school of staid Melbourne theatre, including the Melbourne Theatre Company's recent run of Noel Coward plays: 'Melbourne is altogether in the grip of reactionary theatre thinking … With so many pipes in the Melbourne Theatrical Club blowing old tobacco-smoke, one can be forgiven for wanting to get a bus back to the clean air of *Betty Can Jump*. Beatrice Faust similarly commented that the play's 'most remarkable feature' is its 'inventiveness', while the *Melbourne Times*' reviewer described the play as quite unlike anything that had come before: 'The sight of five adult women in jockstraps is sufficient to make the mind boggle and the chauvinists retreat.'

Numerous critics praised the show's comedy. The *Melbourne Times*' reviewer noted the play's 'compassion' and 'humour', concluding with the observation: 'If the audience is anything to gauge by, Betty could well jump into an extended season.' Critics frequently commented on the way the play simultaneously entertained audiences and connected with them emotionally. Some noted that the show's comic elements contrasted with the stereotype of doctrinaire and humourless women's liberationists (a stereotype that was, to be fair, in many ways a creation of the media the critics were writing for). Dare wrote that 'the production succeeds masterfully because it is overlaid with so much humour – much of it bitter, some of it bubbling'. Radic's review for *The Age* approvingly noted that: 'The company has resisted the temptation to preach the liberation doctrine in the shrill and strident tone often adopted by professional Women's Libbers. Instead the tone is subdued, with the play relying for its effects on humour and understatement.'

In *The Bulletin*, Glickfeld described the show as 'through and through entertainment' and, in a second review for the *Australian Jewish News*, as 'violent, rollicking and sometimes moving entertainment in the vaudeville-cum-Brechtian mode'. Faust ended her otherwise mixed review declaring the show was 'crash hot entertainment'. The

Herald's Gerald Mayhead singled out the bar scene that lampooned the ocker male: 'Five women hilariously parody the beer-drinking, forearm-flexing Aussie with sufficient truth to make a male flinch.' Radic, too, was a fan of this scene: 'The best bit is the bar scene, where they caricature the average hard-drinking insensitive Aussie male.' Interestingly, it was the lone female reviewer, Faust, who criticised the scene as lacking realism in depicting the way men talk: 'The scene was feminine in the worst sense, showing dismal ignorance about how men really interact.'

When I speak to her now, Evelyn recalls deliberately injecting a comedic note into the 'As a woman I feel like ...' scene. 'Instinctively I believe that when you get too heavy with truth ... it may be fabulous for what the group is going through, and it feels original and authentic and new, but when you put that out there on a stage, does it stand up?' Comedy, Evelyn says, 'is really important for bursting earnest bubbles and for revealing some really difficult truths about the world'.

Reviewers validated Kerry's determination to go beyond what she saw as *Marvellous Melbourne*'s superficial focus on great men in public life, and the cast's mining of their personal lives for material. Critics were almost unanimous that the personal, contemporary scenes about women's lives in the 1970s were more effective and powerful than the historical ones. Glickfeld wrote in his *Australian Jewish News* review:

> The second part of the play is more successful, because it is more personal. Here the girls [sic] recount and physicalise their own feelings and impressions of being a woman in the Australia of today. The sketches have a genuine, imaginative flair, the words are strong and graceful and one feels a quality of heart that has never been allowed to surface before in an APG play.

In his *Bulletin* review, Glickfeld called these scenes 'the moving and poetic climax of the play'. Mayhead wrote that 'the mainstream of the action is women passionately expressing themselves', adding that the contemporary scenes are 'where the piece begins to come alive'. The play's personal and contemporary scenes, while well received, nevertheless drew criticism from some reviewers for being underdeveloped. The *Melbourne Times'* reviewer wanted 'more time spent on the relevant contemporary issues', writing that material 'derived from the actors' own experiences came across with a great deal of commitment and feeling' but that 'each sketch was only long enough for a point to be made ... there is a wealth of material left to be more fully explored'.

The cast agreed with the critics' assessment that the play's personal, contemporary scenes were more successful than the historical ones, and that aspects of the play were undeveloped. Kerry acknowledged these criticisms in an end-of-season note scribbled in her production diary: 'Confrontation of audience not shocking enough we ... aimed at producing a consciousness raising event + possibly succeeded, [but] we didn't really delve deeply into the ideas.' In a recollection for the feminist journal *Lip*, Kerry recalled that

> the scenes where we merely tried to present facts (eg. the scene about Caroline Chisholm and the one about Louisa Lawson) were far less satisfying to us and to the audience than the ones where we had really created something from the beginning and from some deeply personal part of ourselves.

Claire reflected on the reasons the historical material lacked the conviction of the contemporary material: 'Maybe because we were too gawkish as performers, or perhaps because we needed a writer to structure the improvisations we did on the historical documents ... we didn't feel as committed to that stuff as we did to the very personal, private revelations of the second half.'

Evelyn described the historical scenes as an attempt (not always successful) to make a 'generalised statement about a specific time in history (from the convicts to Louisa Lawson) saying that women throughout history have had to struggle to maintain identity and a productive entity'. Those first historical scenes 'took so much agony', Micky told Kerry in 1975. While 'in some ways they were terribly important ... in other ways [they] failed so magnificently'. Helen summed up the problem in her interview with Kerry:

> We were side-tracked by the historical stuff. We tried to take on a grand project we were not equipped for. We tried to do the definitive women's show, which dealt with women in Australia since the beginning and for all time. I remember the personal workshops were terribly interesting and terribly instructive, but the connections seem vague now between that and the historical stuff we attacked.

The images developed in the consciousness-raising workshops created an immediate rapport with audiences, Helen wrote: 'One part of the show which never failed, which we knew couldn't fail, the impulse of which never weakened, was the sequence of images of ourselves as women'. Micky told Kerry that the show did things that 'hadn't been done before in theatre, like Helen's image of herself with intellectual men as a sharp glittering blade in a sheath, and Yvonne's image of herself as a hysterical laugh ... Women in the audience were engrossed in those things.'

While the show spoke to women, it spoke most directly and clearly to women from a particular class and social world. When Kerry interviewed her in 1975, Evelyn defended the show against accusations it was too narrowly focused on the group's own experiences as (mainly) middle-class women:

> I remember at the time that women would criticise us saying we didn't look at women as workers, and that we didn't show working women's struggle. And I said 'No, we're middle-class women and we have to deal with this ourselves first', and this was obviously true of the first workshop period.

Kerry uses similar reasoning when I ask her about the play's focus on non-Indigenous women, something that might seem a glaring oversight to contemporary readers: 'We were not so much blind to the lives of Indigenous women, it was more that we were catching up with ourselves.' They were trying to answer the question Kerry asked herself when she returned from France: 'Who are we?'

The visceral responses of audiences to *Betty Can Jump*'s contemporary scenes validated the cast using the specific circumstances of their own lives to make a show. When Claire spoke to Hilary Glow for *Meanjin*, she remarked on how unusual it was in 1972 to use their own lives as raw material for a play: 'It was completely new to go to ourselves as a source of the material, and we had all sorts of accusations levelled at us: we were told we were being self-indulgent.' But did it hold up as art? Claire now says the show made up for its lack of 'a conventional dramatic form' with 'an intense engagement with the audience'. But they didn't know what they had until the preview night. 'So there is that awkwardness [and questions] about "Is this going to work dramatically?", "Had this found its dramatic form?"'

Vic now describes the show as 'completely anarchic', while Kerry agrees with the critics' assessments that its pastiche nature, its lack of an overarching narrative and its often awkward melding of different time periods did not always work. She qualifies this point, however, by adding that *Betty* had a larger story to tell: 'What we had to do was bigger than a narrative.' This tension, between the dramatic need for a coherent story, and the many disparate historical, personal and political elements the play grappled with, was never resolved. Later in 1972 Garner wrote that in one sense their lack of theatrical polish was almost the *point* of the play: '*Betty Can Jump* might have been lacking in all kinds of professionalism, but we knew what we wanted to say and we said it in such a way that a lot of people understood.' It was 'amateurish', Helen tells me now. 'We really didn't know how to do what we wanted to do. And we were kind of groping around in the dark.'

Staging a women's show was a new direction for the company, and there were mixed responses within the APG (as I show in the following chapter). But *Betty* was also 'thoroughly in accord' with the 'ethos of the APG', an APG News editorial acknowledged – 'that theatre should spring directly from its environment'. In exploring subjects such as rape, sexuality, gender roles and women's feelings about their lives, however, the *Betty* women extended the range of subjects theatre at the Pram Factory could tackle. In a position paper written for the group the same year *Betty* was staged, Garrie Hutchinson and Graeme Blundell tried to theorise the APG's relationship to its community. Contrasting their productions to the imported theatre of the mainstream companies, they wrote that APG members instead wanted to make theatre that engaged in social and political issues and provoked audiences to 'change the way they see the world and themselves ... and demand personal or collective action'. They described the APG as a 'theatre of research' that used the 'collective workshop' to overturn 'preconceived notions ... of performance'. They differentiated this approach from 'pro companies where no risks are taken, and only safe and assured gestures are made'.

The company's openness to its community was echoed in the Pram's physical structure, a sprawling warehouse built flush to the street, with rows of cut-out windows on the upper and lower floors that could let light stream in. It was a club house, a rehearsal and workshop space, a venue for concerts and weekend flea markets, and a theatre for hire for other performance groups. But the APG also believed in movement in the other direction. The *Betty Can Jump* collective continued the APG approach of taking performances outside the four walls of a theatre space by introducing their consciousness-raising exercises to schools and universities. Members of 'the *Betty Can Jump* group have been visiting schools to talk about the play', one APG bulletin notes, including 'Germaine Greer's old school' (the Presentation Convent in Gardenvale). The article describes the visits as 'invaluable as a way of spreading information about the APG and about WL [women's liberation]', likening the visits to tours of radical new writing to alternative venues by the Portable Theatre group in the UK. Reactions at schools 'have so far been favourable', but the (anonymous) author offers a qualification: 'Apparently some mothers of the girls at Star thought that the school was attempting to indoctrinate them with insidious ideas about WL'. ('Star' is a reference to Presentation Convent). Some of the *Betty* group also went back to campus: in May 1972, Kerry led a workshop at the University of Melbourne about the possibility of creating theatre from consciousness raising, demonstrating some of the exercises they used to make *Betty Can Jump*.

After *Betty*, members of the group brought their sense of theatre to women's lib protests. In September 1972, Evelyn and twelve women walked into the public bar at the Young and Jackson Hotel opposite Flinders Street Station and demanded that the barman serve them drinks. When he refused and told them to leave, they stood outside, their colourful signs and theatrical chants delivering them the main photo spot on the front page of *The Age* the next day. In the centre of the picture is Evelyn, reading from a script and holding a sign in all-caps lettering: 'THIS HOTEL DISCRIMINATES AGAINST WOMEN'. She now recalls the demonstration as being equally directed at the woman who *was* allowed in the front bar: 'I was demonstrating against *Chloé* [a life-sized naked portrait by Jules Joseph Lefebvre] hanging in the front bar.'

The wider women's movement became part of the Pram's day-to-day politics too: delegations to Women's Day marches were reported in APG bulletins. A women's theatre group that formed later at the Pram took its shows to factories (footage of Pram Factory women dressed up as bosses and workers performing a show outside a factory can be seen in the 1975 film *Don't Be Too Polite Girls*, a documentary made by Sydney Women's Film Group member Martha Ansara). Like *Betty*, the factory tours and shows could fall into the same trap as the one that could snare the mainly middle-class Pram men when they celebrated the working-class ocker male. Claire later acknowledged their limitations as a group of largely middle-class women in making work that resonated with working-class women: 'We would take theatre to the masses and I think by and large it was patronising and elitist. We told them what we thought they should be thinking.'

In preparing for the play, the *Betty* women read books such as Kate Millett's *Sexual Politics* and Germaine Greer's *The Female Eunuch*, which explore how women's bodies and the category of 'woman' were constructed by culture and literature. The performance scholar and playwright Peta Tait, who researched later shows at the Pram Factory by the Melbourne Women's Theatre Group, notes that just as theatre needs an audience, 'gender needs to be performed for someone'. Theatre, Tait argues, can show us that gender is not something fixed or essential, but that it is made by 'doing', a script that we both learn and improvise or even rewrite. Although she doesn't cite Judith Butler, Tait's observation argument echoes Butler's now famous proposition that gender is not a 'noun' or a fixed identity, not 'a subject who might be said to pre-exist the deed', but rather a 'performance'; it is always 'a doing'. When the *Betty Can Jump* cast satirised gender roles with exaggerated clothes and behaviour, and adopted male personas, they too were suggesting that gender is a performance, and a performance that could be changed.

If *Betty Can Jump* did manage to speak to women across different ages and classes and cultures, perhaps it was because, as cast members told journalists, they highlighted the problems of male and female conditioning. A preview of the show in *The Sun* quotes Helen Garner ('29, of Carlton') saying that women today 'are without their due freedom. "They have been stereotyped into an image and forced into adopting what they consider a female role. In the play we're trying to point out the nonsense of it all."' The same article quotes Vic Marsh ('26, of Carlton') saying that men need to 'be liberated and stripped of all conditioning just the same'. (In the show, the cast performed a *literal* removal of layers of male social conditioning in the suffrage scene, when the rest of the cast surrounded Vic and removed his exaggerated costume props: a 'deliberate stripping of male myths from Vic at end – not hysterical – ie we liberate him from his trappings he finds he can move freely', Kerry wrote in her notes). In an interview the following year with arts magazine *The Living Daylights*, Evelyn also makes a point about women's social conditioning: 'Women are brought up to be emotional and to relate differently to men.' But she is careful to qualify her statement about women's 'social conditioning' with a recognition of individual women's differences, and the different stages of consciousness they might be at: 'The differences in our experiences/personalities and stages we're at are great enough to ensure that in the battle yr fighting, yr still very much on yr own [sic].'

Betty Can Jump was not a perfect show, but it arrived at 'the right place, the right time, and with the right voice', Laurel reflects now. When the show's four-week season sold out, it was extended for two more weeks. Measured by box office receipts, *Betty Can Jump* was the most successful of the thirteen plays in the APG's 1972 program. Across thirty performances some 4231 tickets were sold, producing a box office of $5805 (approximately $61,000 in today's figures). The APG News singled out *Betty* for mention in an item on the company's healthy financial situation, noting that it was only the scheduling of subsequent plays that year that prevented the APG extending the *Betty Can Jump* season, with 'its extraordinary popular appeal', any longer. The APG was flush with success during this period, the short item notes, and *Betty Can Jump* was a high point: 'Attendances have never been better, revenues never higher, critics never happier.'

When I tell Helen what I'd discovered about the show's success she looks at first surprised, then her face rearranges into an expression of delight. 'Oh! That's fun to know, I'm glad about that.' Perhaps her recollection of the men's response on that opening night had erased any memory of the show's extraordinary financial and critical success? 'The guys were very snotty about it,' she remembers. 'In those days ... everything that women thought was important probably wasn't seen as important by many of them. The whole thing about what you were supposed to write about, or do plays about, was completely male dominated ... in ways that are perhaps hard to imagine now.' But things *did* start to change at Pram Factory after *Betty* – slowly, and often in a piecemeal fashion. And in a way that brought new dramas to the building, including a spectacular announcement by one of the Pram's leading writers.

14

15

BETTY CAN

jump

presented by APG. carlton womens lib.
pram factory, 325 drummond st. carlton
26th jan. for 4 weeks, wed - sun, 8-45pm
bookings (pf) 349493

16

17

18

19

20

21

22

23

24

25

Chapter 6
Betty rocks the Pram

In the weeks after Christmas 1971, when cafés close down and swimwear is pulled out from the back of closets, members of the APG are invited to a house party in East Melbourne. When Claire arrives, she notices the two front rooms are full of Pram Factory members. In one room, the men are huddled together deep in conversation; she joins a group of Pram women in the second room. Her mind is buzzing with the kinds of anxious thoughts that have become familiar to her during the fortnight before a play she is performing in is due to open: 'Are we going to get it together? What are we actually doing?' The women are in the middle of an animated conversation. As the conversation continues, Claire feels increasingly excited about the possibilities of theatre.

Fifty years later, Claire recalls the scene clearly: 'We were all going: "Well, what if we did that? What if we did this?" As we were talking, I looked over and the guys were all looking at us, and I knew it was a moment.' Until then, Claire says, 'it was far more common for us to be hanging around and listening to what the guys were talking about ... to find out what was happening at the Pram Factory, what the plans were and what we might contribute to them ... I could see that had shifted. We [had] separated ourselves off and gone into another room.' For the first time, women at the Pram 'were doing *our* thing. And what I really remember is "We don't need to talk to them!"' It was at this party, Claire told Kerry in an interview 1975, that she 'had this rush of realisation that ... we were creating a culture for women'.

In the poster Micky made to advertise *Betty Can Jump*, she pictured a balding man sitting backwards on a chair and looking startled; red spot colour on the poster highlights his eyes and lips, making him look like a sad clown. Micky explains to me her thinking behind the image: 'It's a man being shocked that Betty can jump. That was the rationale.' Micky's poster, it turned out, was an astute prediction of the way APG men would respond to the show. Most of the Pram women were working on the show in one way or another, so the small preview audience was mostly made up of APG men. Kerry recollects that the men 'all stormed in' and sat in the front row while 'we were quaking in our shoes'. Helen describes the scene:

> there they sat, the APG heavies, directors, writers, actors staring stony-faced at us, as we paraded what had seemed so precious to us, months of wrestling with our feelings and experiences, trying to mould them into a theatrical form by methods none of us had tried before.

If Helen had shared Claire's growing confidence in the days leading up to the first performance, it evaporated on the preview night. In that one hour, the *Betty* women were 'back to square one' she wrote. After the preview the APG men 'got up and disappeared into the office without saying a word, and when we slunk in there to change our clothes, they were drinking and laughing as if nothing we'd said or done out there had touched a single one of them in any way at all'. Claire has similar memories of the night: 'When we held that first open rehearsal my heart sank and I thought, "Shit, we're right out of gear. Is it a dramatic form? Where's the dramatic action?"' When Kerry interviews her in 1975, Helen remembers they had desperately wanted men's approval, and that she had only later realised how 'we had been barking up the wrong tree in trying to impress the men'. She described her delayed reaction in *Dissent*: 'What the fuck had we been thinking of, the night of that shameful runthrough? We were women, making a play about what it was like to be a woman, and our first concern that night had been to impress men.'

The 'APG men were grim after the preview, but they managed to mutter that they were relieved we had a show,' Kerry wrote. 'Some were ashen-faced and shaky, others patronising, while Jack Hibberd dismissed it as "mawkish and sentimental", which I took as a compliment.' Micky describes to me the men's criticisms of the show: 'It was calling women's things sentimental and weak and not as important. They're not the serious things of life, are they?' In her story for *Dissent*, Helen describes how male audience members could also be savage in their reactions to the knowledge scene:

> The scene in which the actors moved around in the darkness, whispering or wailing questions to do with women's ignorance about their own bodies, brought forth interesting comments and reactions, mostly from men and of a brutal kind. eg Child's voice in the dark: "What's that blood on my pants?" Raucous male voice from the audience: "That's where Dad hit Mum with the axe!"' In contrast, women in the audience were often 'absolutely convulsed with laughter – how many of them had sat drinking in ladies' lounges or in cars outside pubs?'. During the same scene, men could yell out comments: "Get the one with the big tits!" or "Hey, big cunt!"'.

Although the APG men were not as crude as some of the audience members, many of them did not seem to know what to make of the show. Claire now thinks the Pram men were more perplexed than dismissive:

> They were out of their depth and they knew it ... Something had changed. They just didn't quite know what. They hadn't been to any rehearsals. They'd been locked out of everything ... I think they just thought: 'What is this? Is this the end of the known world? Is this going to be brilliant? Is this going to be the world's biggest embarrassment?'

The Pram men I speak to now can't recall being dismissive of the show (though, to be fair, no one I speak to can recall the particular details of the preview night, or if they were even definitely there). Bill Garner describes *Betty* as 'defiant and joyful', though he adds that some men adopted a 'defensive posture'; it was an era where they had to change from being 'totally unreconstructed' men of a pre-feminist era. John Timlin tells me that, contrary to the reports of stony-faced men watching the show's first night, he recalls the men being 'amazed and delighted' about the performance. But both Bill and Max admit that their memories might have changed to conform with a later feminist consciousness, or to align with other people's memories. How the men felt about the show and responded to it is impossible to know. I'm inclined, however, to trust Helen and Kerry's impressions and experiences, which they recorded in the days and weeks after the show ended. But I'm also inclined to believe Claire's assessment that some of the men were simply perplexed. Or Max's suggestion that perhaps, as can happen when you've 'just watched something by some close friends', some of the men simply just felt awkward and unable to articulate their reactions.

Claire tells me that in the group's early days it was the APG men who initiated projects at meetings and at the pub afterwards, but she is careful to add that this wasn't necessarily the men's fault. Women 'were quite at liberty' to come up with projects, 'but the point of entry for these discussions was not always clear. It often felt as if the key bonds and ideas were forged in the largely male domain of the pub.' After *Betty* the Pram women 'felt much more confident putting ideas forward'. They began to push to change the way the group operated.

Pram meetings could be ferocious and chaotic: John Romeril remembers that 'budgetary and programming sessions usually saw APG blood on the APG tiles'. Carmen Lawrence recalls the 'interminable' meetings at the Pram. While she never formally joined the group, she remembers attending one meeting where her newborn son provided a moment of levity:

> I rarely lasted through a whole meeting, but one occasion I had my fairly newly arrived son with me and Max, who's a wonderful comedian but could be extremely doctrinaire and tedious when it came to the collective meetings, was going on and on and on. And

at some point David laid out a very liquid fart sort of right in the middle of a major point. Everyone just fell about laughing.

Max, for his part, recalls Carmen's 'stoicism, the way she just put up with all this the way we were all carrying on'.

As women at the Pram joined the women's movement, the conscious-ness-raising practices of women's liberation began influencing the way APG meetings were run, recalls Robin Laurie: 'We introduced processes learnt from feminist consciousness-raising groups into running the meeting: like once you've spoken once you can't speak again till everyone else who wants to has spoken.' But adopting the horizontal group processes of women's liberation wasn't a magic wand that made all the informal power structures at Pram meetings vanish. And there were still problems of what to do when people – because of work or children or other commitments – couldn't attend meetings. US second-wave feminist activist and writer Jo Freeman, in a paper called 'The Tyranny of Structurelessness', argues that a lack of structure can hide the informal power relationships and alliances within a group or – even worse – it can generate a group with 'much motion and few results'. Helen didn't attend APG meetings, but she recalls reading Freeman's essay and being struck by the way it illuminated her experiences of living in share houses and working at the alternative newspaper *The Digger*. Fifty years after Freeman's thesis was first published, Helen tells me she remembers it clearly: 'If you don't have a structure that's agreed upon, then the most charismatic, powerful members take control. They get a grip, they're running it, and there's no formal way of challenging them.'

Betty helped raise a feminist flag at the Pram Factory, but conflicts about the quality and quantity of roles for women continued. In 1975, Micky reflected on the years that followed *Betty* at the Pram: 'There was the crisis (ever present, I might add) about roles for women, which grew into arguments about insufficient parts for women, and men not being able to write parts for women.' Slowly, women at the APG began to take on roles as writers or directors more frequently, and there were more (and more various) roles for female actors at the Pram. *A Stretch of the Imagination*, the play that immediately followed *Betty*, was a solo piece written and directed by Jack Hibberd and performed by Peter Cummins. With men doing the show's lights and music too, it seemed almost wilfully indifferent to *Betty Can Jump*'s success, and a return to the APG's blokey ways.

The APG's next show, however, saw women take on key roles. David Williamson and Jack Hibberd are credited as the main writers of *The APG Revue 1 or Sonia's Knee and Thigh Show* (the alternative title refers to a leg-revealing dress Sonia McMahon, the prime minister's wife, had worn to a dinner with President Richard Nixon the year before), but its nine-person cast included five women: Sue Ingleton and four of the *Betty* cast members – Evelyn Krape, Jude Kuring, Claire Dobbin and Yvonne Marini. Micky Allan created the set, Laurel Frank was a researcher and Lorraine Milne and Glen Tomasetti were in charge of music and songs. In her history of the APG, Gabrielle Wolf writes that *Betty Can Jump*'s influence could be seen in some of the *APG Revue* material: in one scene, written by David Williamson, a female student challenged a teacher to think about gender roles; another sketch was a gender reversal of a typical rape, with women blaming a man when he was raped because he said no 'but meant "yes"'. The latter scene reversed the earlier APG practice of women playing men's roles, and it prompted mixed reactions from some of APG men. Laurel later remarked that Vic Marsh 'couldn't imagine being raped, but Peter Green wanted desperately to try to experience [what rape would feel like]'.

Laurel told me that after *Betty Can Jump*, 'while there was that consciousness of trying to have roles for women and use women as designers and directors and devisers,' *Betty* didn't radically alter the programming immediately. APG member Geoffrey Milne told Wolf that while men still dominated the APG's playwriting after *Betty*, the group gradually began to take a more democratic and 'inclusive attitude' to casting and choosing projects. John Romeril describes the changes more bluntly (and more optimistically): he recalls the APG 'legislated for equality of employment opportunity, and policed it … we used our commissioning procedures to a) attract and employ women playwrights, but also b) to insist the quality and incidence of female characters in the work male writers tendered was up to scratch. If the story's about a cop – why not a female cop, and a fully rounded one?'

In 1973, Helen profiled two productions in rehearsal, at the Pram Factory and La Mama for *The Digger*. Both shows dealt with women's issues. The Pram show, *Mrs Thally F*, tackled domestic violence; it was written by John Romeril, with a cast that featured Kerry Dwyer, Evelyn Krape and Jude Kuring. Jude was also directing the La Mama show *Night Flowers*, a play about lesbians by New Zealand playwright Max Richards. The show's female cast substantially reworked Richards' script: 'It was just a lot of pervy generalisations by a man who knew nothing about lesbians,' Helen quotes Jude as saying. 'We got rid of fallacies like the idea that lesbians suffer from penis envy.' After performances, the director and cast stayed back to talk to the audience about the play's shortcomings. Graeme Blundell, who was directing *Mrs Thally F*, tells Helen that directing women was a different experience from the 'old La Mama days': 'Women have developed a kind of personal shorthand that men don't have – except for their *macho*, joking shorthand, punches and pushes, which relaxes them all right but isn't interaction.' He says a new 'woman's style' of theatre has emerged. 'As a director you throw in ideas or energy, and they're taken up and developed in a way men can't do.'

These two women's shows did not stop Evelyn lamenting, in a 1973 interview with *The Living Daylights*, the ongoing lack of women playwrights, and the scarcity of female directors. Part of the problem, she suggests, is that while women want to take on traditional male roles, men aren't as keen to take on mundane and domestic jobs that are seen as women's work: 'The only traditional female work is shit work and it's interesting that shit work is all we can share with the men.' But questions about who does the domestic work and who will care for children – issues that Kerry, Micky and Helen were grappling with in their relationships before *Betty Can Jump* – did begin to be renegotiated, if not always successfully, at the Pram Factory.

Reading through APG newsletters, I noticed items about cleaning rosters and childcare at the Pram Factory begin to appear more frequently after *Betty*. At a meeting held on the day of the show's final performance, the APG executive discussed the idea of a childcare service: 'Creche: most important, a service for the APG and possibly for audiences. Jack to investigate.' The minutes, however, also suggest some members felt ambivalent about the group's responsibility to share childcare duties, even if that ambivalence was sometimes wrapped up in a jocular tone: 'An idea that needs some more discussion: a policy of birth control for the APG, Max suggested compulsory contraception. This is not expected to go over too well at the next meeting of the collective.'

An internal bulletin in March 1972 reads: 'It is really nice to see that the total collective can now share the responsibility of making and serving coffee, and taking care of front-of-house jobs. All power to the collective.' While the APG had cleaning rosters from its earliest days, responsibilities slowly began to be more evenly distributed between men and women, albeit with some notable holdouts, Kerry tells me: 'Some people were better than others at pitching in … Tony Taylor was fantastic at cleaning. Some guys who were more just stars I don't recall ever doing any cleaning.' Pram member Rose Chong recalls that 'issues such as the toilet cleaning had such heavy political baggage'. She remembers 'Max Gillies cleaning the toilet the moment before he was due to go on and (I nearly said "star") *participate* in *The Hills Family Show* … It was meant to be a *leveller.*'

By the mid-1970s, one measure of how quickly the mood was changing at the Pram Factory and in the Carlton share houses connected to it is the way that Helen, in her 1975 interview with Kerry, appears to talk about 1972 as if it was another era. While the men were 'severely freaked out' by *Betty Can Jump*, 'now there is a higher consciousness about sharing childcare and housework', she says. Laurel tells me she too noticed changes at the APG after the show. 'No man would've dared suggest that women should do more [cleaning]. If anyone was thinking of suggesting that they would've been crazy. There was an adoption of the politics of the play and the men, if their game was poor before, they definitely lifted it.' There was 'a bit of friction in some things along the way, but [shared responsibility for cleaning became] a banner that everyone flew', she says.

More children were born into the Pram Factory world, and the collective began to talk about how they could support mothers to participate in Pram projects. Some of the Pram men took their responsibilities to share childcare seriously, Kerry recalls. 'There were some men who were then very cognisant of the problem,' she says, singling out Greig Pickhaver (now widely known for his comedic alter ego H.G. Nelson) and Graeme Isaac, two APG men who supported Helen when she moved into a group house with them after splitting from Bill Garner. 'Those two particularly were really good at looking after children. They were very gentle men.' Evelyn recalls she and Claire would mind Sue Ingleton's baby after she returned from a period in England and joined the Pram. 'It was difficult for Sue at home. [Her then husband] didn't want her to be working. And she had a baby ... I remember going to her place and helping look after the baby ... so that she could rehearse'.

Not all mothers at the Pram recall being a part of a helping circle, however: 'The reason I left [the Pram] was that I had Tom, my first baby,' Jenny Walsh remembers. She left her son Tom in the Pram office one day, only to return to find a screaming baby no one was watching. 'There was this myth that the collective would help look after everyone's children,' she recalled in her Pram memories. 'We used to take our children to the collective meetings,' Kerry told me. '[But] most of the people there couldn't handle having these three-year-old kids making any sort of noise at all in the collective meeting.'

There were, however, voices at the Pram who were determined to advocate for mothers. In a report of a 1975 executive meeting, APG member 'Michelle' worried that rehearsals for the Brecht play *The Mother* were causing problems for real mothers in the cast. 'Eileen and Rose were just holding it together,' she wrote, noting that rehearsals were changed to school hours and that other APG members had been assigned to help the women: 'Greig, Alan and Janet will help Rose;

Robert M. and Evelyn will help Eileen. Eileen still doesn't know how she will cope over the next two weeks with housework.' Someone at the meeting complained that the rehearsals and show timetables didn't accommodate 'married women with kids', arguing that 'while working adults can tolerate a disrupted household, kids cannot'. Someone else retorted that 'women with responsibilities to children' should not work with 'more available people'. But the pro-mother sentiments seemed to win the argument. The minutes dismiss the idea of excluding mothers from projects because this would 'perpetuate a social division based on a false and sexist understanding of what freedom to work means. It is not 'too bad' to be a mother. We need to come to terms with child-care in the APG and to solve it within programming.'

Genuine efforts were made within the APG to tackle discrimination against mothers, but according to Kerry the issue was never fully resolved. Sometimes it was other women who were the least sympathetic to the needs of mothers in the group. 'A lot of the women who'd been very politically aware of feminism and so on didn't approve of having children. Somebody came up to me [when I was pregnant with my second child] and relayed that another woman had said "how can she bear to have another parasite in her body?"'

While the APG was debating the question of motherhood offstage, it also began to treat motherhood as a subject worthy of dramatisation *on* stage too. In a play that premiered at the Pram Factory in September 1972, *The Joss Adams Show*, Kerry played Joss, an isolated and struggling young mother of a six-week-old baby dealing with postnatal depression. Written by the New Zealand–born feminist playwright Alma De Groen and directed by Graeme Blundell, it tackled 'a taboo subject at the time', the scholar Denise Varney writes. 'De Groen's play offered a jarring, theatrically innovative feminist play at a time when the collective was struggling to respond to and accommodate women's liberation'. Writing in the APG News, Helen Garner describes the play as full of sympathy for a young mother who is struggling to cope with the demands on her: 'Joss Adams begs for help. She doesn't know how she will bear what is going to happen to her when she has her baby.' Garner takes on anti-abortionists such as Ronald Conway, who she says misrepresents women's liberationists when he claims the movement equates 'freedom with an empty womb'. And in a passage that could be read as a riposte to the anti-child sentiment Kerry suggested some APG members held, Helen writes:

> Joss Adams doesn't want to get rid of her baby. She wants to have it, and to love it, and she wants to understand what's required of her, but she's on her own. It's not the baby, or before that the fullness of her womb, which drives her into her crazy trance of pain and cruelty: she is alone and no-one will answer her questions, and she doesn't know what is happening to her.

The success of *Betty Can Jump*, and the influence of the women's liberation movement, clearly contributed to a new feminist sensibility at the APG. But the changes were uneven, and they were not always welcomed by members of the group. In her 1975 interview with Kerry about her experience in *Betty*, Laurel recalled that 'there was a lot of tension within the APG about *Betty Can Jump*, and suspicions about CR [consciousness-raising] sessions within the APG'. Kerry remembers: 'There were men who did not want women to be directors ... they didn't change, but the situation changed ... They had to accept it.'

In May 1972, simmering tensions in the group came to a head, leading Max Gillies to issue an urgent nine-page internal APG bulletin; a short note on the front page says the next general meeting had been brought forward a week 'due to the evident concern of members over occurrences, happenings and the general running of the place'. In his note, Max admits to problems in the group's sometimes lax processes. He promises the executive has 'smartened up procedures', and that they will start to mail minutes of the last meeting and an agenda for the next one to all members a week before all general meetings. The bulletin's next item is a letter from member Bill Hannan about the 'shambles of the last group meeting'. He complains about the executive who 'failed entirely to organise for the meeting', members being presented with a 'surprise agenda' forty-five minutes into the meeting, and the way an item about upcoming programming devolved into brawls about other groups' bookings at the Pram and about play-reading dates.

There were clearly problems with Pram meetings – and with an organisational structure that could bounce between radical democracy and a freewheeling kind of autocracy – but an even more explosive reason for the urgent general meeting is revealed in the bulletin's next three pages: a letter from Jack Hibberd tendering his resignation. Jack writes that his resignations from both the collective and the executive 'are quite final', and lists his 'dissatisfactions and requests ... for examination by all members of the collective'. He names *Betty Can Jump* as the first in a list of ten complaints. Under the heading 'Low theatrical and intellectual standards', he describes the play as: 'Indubitably sincere but lamentably short on ideas, direction, dramatic skills and contemporary pertinence. Altogether sloppy, moralizing, escapist and mawkish. A good cause traduced. A theatre traduced.' He calls *The APG Revue*, which followed *Betty Can Jump*, 'a real shocker', and an 'utter embarrassment' full of 'self-indulgent acting'.

Jack's other concerns include the group's 'maltreatment of writers', demands for 'recipe-writing', the company's 'failure to be experimental', a 'misuse' and 'non-use' of people with 'special skills' and 'talent', directors 'abdicating' their responsibilities, 'autocratic control by power clique', and 'too much concern with petty ambition and the tedious and pointless intrigues of intra-group power politics'. Max published a response to Jack's letter on the bulletin's following pages. He writes that Jack's concerns deserve 'open exchange', but chastises his tone: 'You express yourself dogmatically, with verbal facility, careless of the random psychic assault on individuals (many of whom probably share your dissatisfaction).' He urges Jack to reconsider his resignation and suggests an internal debate to discuss his concerns.

Hibberd was one of the Pram's two leading playwrights in 1972 (along with John Romeril), and news of his resignation letter would have spread through the tables at Tamani's and Carlton's share houses like billiard balls after a break shot by a Johnny's Green Room regular. Jack's resignation from the APG would have been a main topic of conversation at the Albion bar and at Carlton parties over the following weeks. His letter, and Max's long reply (which alternately chastises and mollifies Jack) give some indication of the tense climate at the APG in the weeks immediately after the women's show. John Timlin writes in 'Pramocracy' that *Betty Can Jump* was a trigger for divisions that emerged at the APG: 'Successful though it was, and truly experimental ... a crisis developed about direction and control, casting and money.' But anxieties about status and skirmishes over money and power within the APG did not *suddenly* emerge with the women's show. Jack's resignation, and his multiple criticisms, were in some ways just the most recent and dramatic manifestation of more widespread grumblings in the group. And *Betty* was an obvious vessel into which people could pour resentments and discontent that had been brewing at the Pram from the beginning.

Claire Dobbin tells me she feels sympathy for the writers at the Pram. They were often sidelined in a group that, for all its pretence of democracy, was 'very much a directors' [and a] performers' theatre'. APG members would interrogate the playwrights' work and 'put it under scrutiny' in a way that was often hard for the writers, she recalls. 'The writers would write their work, and we'd all go: "Yeah, okay. We like that scene. No, we don't want *that*."' Jack Hibberd was not the only writer who could feel disrespected, Claire remembers:

> [David] Williamson left and still, I think, he regards it as the worst experience of his life ... I don't think any of us understood what it was like being a playwright ... Jack was a writer long before the Pram Factory. He'd always been a writer and what he wanted was a writers' theatre, and he wanted a space in which writers could develop.

This tension between writers, directors and performers is not 'a new argument', says Claire, who sees a parallel between the divisions at the Pram and the tension between composers and musicians who play by ear. 'I look at all the musicians who can't read music and who just sort of can make music in a completely different way, and it's very threatening to all the composers. So it's an old artistic argument.'

Not all the Pram writers preferred to work alone though. John Romeril 'would lope about the theatre with a portable typewriter tucked under his arm, hammering away at constant rewrites', Meg Clancy recalls. 'I really loved working with Romeril,' Carol Porter wrote in her Pram memories. 'He would go into the little room under the mezzanine and he would be in there all night going tap-tap on the typewriter, and come out with reams of stuff, most of which we couldn't use!'

If there were tensions between writers and the improvisers at the Pram from the beginning, they were compounded after *Betty Can Jump*. Working without writers *and* without men 'was seen as a dangerously divisive', Kerry wrote. In those first months after the production, many of the *Betty Can Jump* women were keen to repair the breach between men and women in the group. 'I didn't really want to just live my life with women,' Kerry tells me. 'I wanted to live a life with men *and* women. I didn't want to be a separatist.' In 1975, *Betty* collective members spoke in their interviews with Kerry of their desire to belong to the bigger group. Laurel recalled that 'most of the women who were chosen for *Betty Can Jump* were actually already members of the APG, so there wasn't really a pull to form a separate group [and] the idea of cells really threatened some people'. Micky added that 'Max also worried about a separate group for women, and there were great arguments about that. In the end we wanted to work out, sort out the morass that was in the APG.' (When I speak to him, Max agrees that he 'didn't want the women to hive off'. He says his theory of the APG was that it was 'an umbrella outfit [where] we could all argue about what … constituted theatre'. Like the economic union he belonged to, he thought it was important to constantly make 'accommodation with each other to get different kinds of projects on'.) Claire said that there were good reasons not to separate from the bigger group: the women at the Pram believed that if they could change, so could the APG: 'We believed the APG was where it was all happening in theatre and we weren't ready to commit ourselves to doing only feminist theatre. We believed we could bring a feminist approach to the APG.'

Helen told Kerry that she too never wanted to stop working with men, and that collaborating with Vic was one of the joys of *Betty*. When I spoke to Helen in 2021, she reflected on how her early naïve optimism that the women's movement would change *everything* was tested over time:

> Once I got the sort of basic gist of feminism – or women's liberation as it was called then – I thought, 'Oh, *now* I understand everything, and everything's going to change, because all we have to do is just say to men: "This is what's the matter, and if we could just do *this*, and if you could just do *that* ..."' And I really thought that was going happen.

By 1973, when Helen was writing regularly for *The Digger*, the idealism of the earliest days of the movement had begun to be replaced by a pessimism about the intractable nature of a male world. In her feature on *Mrs Thally F* and *Night Flowers* for *The Digger*, she quotes Evelyn, performing in *Thally* at the Pram, sounding a despairing note: 'Male reality is the norm in theatre ... The only way women can get any real self-determination is when they've set up the working group right from the start.' Jude agrees: 'If we get anything done, it's ... by doing it ourselves, in a venue like La Mama.' The *Night Flowers* cast tell Helen that women's style of working – trying to figure out problems together, rather than having a 'spearhead' at the top – was different from the more 'aggressive, manipulative, verbal style' of men in theatre. Jude concedes though that trying to reach consensus over every decision could be slow and inefficient; sometimes 'people scream for direction, when they think they can't work it out for themselves. They say, fuck democracy!' Helen captures the different positions of women at the APG, including Kerry and Evelyn arguing the merits of separatism: '"[Separatism is] loserism," says Kerry, "It's no good having separateness from men as your aim. Women must force men to change." Evelyn insists that working only with women makes total freedom possible. "But those women die out," Kerry protests, "and nothing changes. If *you* change, your men change."'

· Helen goes on to single out John Romeril as one APG writer concerned about the lack of roles for women, but then adds that 'a quick glance over the recent APG program' revealed three plays (two by Barry Oakley and one by Jack Hibberd) that had no roles for women. When Kerry interviewed the *Betty* women in 1975, Claire conceded the APG did not change to the degree they were hoping for 'because the playwrights wrote in ways which had been ingrained'. In 1979, in an interview with Suzanne Spunner for *Meanjin*, Claire reflected that women at the Pram Factory had been too quick to think 'we had achieved what we set out to do with *Betty Can Jump* ... we agreed with the general feeling around the APG ... that it should be a plural group, and that we would be wrong to cause a split'. A closed group was seen as potentially 'dangerous and destructive', Evelyn added. While women at the Pram wanted to assert their independence from men, for some it was complicated by not only a feeling of allegiance, but a sense of debt to the men behind the APG. 'I completely pay tribute to all those guys,' Claire tells me now. 'They had the vision to say, "We're getting out of La Mama, we're going to start an Australian theatre. It's going to be a director's theatre. It's going to tell Australian stories." They catapulted it out of La Mama, out of Melbourne [University] and into that world.'

Kerry has said one prosaic reason why a separate women's theatre group didn't continue at the APG after *Betty Can Jump* was that making the show involved an 'immense' and 'drawn-out workload' over a five-month production period. Laurel recalled that 'because *Betty* was such an ambitious beginning ... people just fell away afterwards because they were exhausted by it'. Kerry, meanwhile, gave birth to her daughter Nellie within days of the show ending. In her *Meanjin* article, Suzanne Spunner adds two other reasons for the delay in a women's performance group forming at the Pram: a lack of 'independent impetus from the women's movement', and the shortage of theatre space at the Pram Factory. In her 1975 interview with Kerry, Helen described how the growth of the women's movement solved the first problem, providing a 'groundswell' to develop a woman's group within the Pram Factory. To start a group in 1972, when the media was still crudely depicting the women's movement 'bra-burning', 'would have been a big sticking out of necks without a big enough groundswell to support it', she tells Kerry. The opening of a second, smaller performance space at the Pram Factory in 1974, solved the second problem. The 'Back Theatre' provided 'an important outlet for any cells that developed', Micky says. 'There was room for new things and they weren't a threat to the stability of the APG.'

Like *Betty Can Jump*, the Melbourne Women's Theatre Group (MWTG) grew out of local women's liberation groups; it started using the Pram Factory in March 1974. I first met one of the group's founders, Sylvie Leber, when we both contributed to an anthology about the #MeToo movement in Australia. Sylvie's story was about a traumatic assault in the early 1970s and its aftermath which, at one point, saw her dressing up as a harlequin so staff at a psychiatric institution would admit her. She told her story to *The Age* newspaper at a time when rape and sexual violence were still shameful. 'I think I might have been the first Australian woman to go public via the media about having been raped,' she wrote.

Sylvie was born in Paris to a Jewish family with a history of fighting for social justice. Her paternal grandparents were member of the Jewish Labour Bund, a revolutionary workers' party in Poland, and her father had been a member of the French Resistance. Her parents migrated to Australia in 1952 when she was two, and she later studied at the University of Melbourne. She met Graeme Blundell there when she was an extra in an Alfred Jarry play, and later joined the La Mama workshops. When *Betty Can Jump* was being made, she was travelling through Papua New Guinea and communes in Queensland. Her attacker was a man she had hitched a ride with on her way back to Melbourne and her share house in Carlton. The media sensationalised her story, she says now, and in her #MeToo chapter, she writes about how her involvement in the MWTG – telling women's stories and finding an outlet for her creativity – was both a process of healing and a form of activism.

Sylvie says the MWTG began when a feminist group she belonged to asked the APG for space to put on some shows. 'We had a good contact [at the Pram] because one of our members worked in administration in the office ... and we were basically given free rein to use the Back Theatre whenever we wanted to.' Women from the APG also joined the group or performed in shows the MWTG staged, including Kerry Dwyer, Evelyn Krape, Claire Dobbin, Yvonne Marini, Sue Ingleton, Carol Porter, Jane Clifton and Ponch Hawkes (although Kerry now says she doesn't think she ever formally joined the MWTG). By the mid-1970s, women within the APG were tired of 'trying to theorise in feminist terms within the company', Evelyn told Kerry. It was becoming clear that instead of 'directing energies into putting on a show', they were wasting valuable energy convincing 'the [APG] men of the need to get the show on' in the first place.

The MWTG, like the *Betty Can Jump* group, mostly devised plays collectively, using a mix of workshops, consciousness raising and research to develop plays about issues such as abortion, mental illness and women in prison. (They also put on one show called *Women Times 3*, staging the three winners of a national callout for women's scripts.) The group's productions were often satirical and performed as cabaret- and revue-style sketches. They took shows on tour and onto the streets. The MWTG constitution describes the group's goals as 'the performance, encouragement and promotion of drama, music, art, literature, film production and exhibition and such other cultural activities, within a feminist framework'. It was to operate according to the 'principles of group democracy'.

If *Betty Can Jump* hadn't transformed the APG in the way some women in the collective had hoped, the MWTG can be seen as having taken up the baton of political theatre at the Pram Factory. Writing in 'Pramocracy', John Timlin says that while APG shows became 'less issue-based, less polemical, less didactic in the mid-1970s' (a time when the Labor government was in power federally, Australian troops had long been withdrawn from Vietnam, and the APG had become increasingly reliant on government funding to stage productions), the 'semi-affiliated Women's Theatre Group' was the exception. In

1976, the group toured schools, factories and community centres with a multilingual production called *She'll Be Right Mate*, a show about migrant women's experiences in Australia. The short play highlighted the 'double jeopardy' of a migrant woman who works full time while managing her home and negotiating a sherbet-loving teen daughter who roams the streets and wants to go to a co-ed school camp, Suzanne Spunner wrote.

The mother–daughter scene 'was really close to my heart', Sylvie says. 'My mother was over-protective: "You can't go and do this and that with your Aussie friends, you can't do all that fun partying" ... I couldn't go out with non-Jewish boys.' In Australia, Sylvie's father found work in factories and her mother was a pieceworker sewing garments at home; the production's poster 'has got a big picture of my mum at her sewing machine'. Of the eight women in the show, only two were born in Australia. In developing the work, the group drew on a research report about migrant women in the workforce, they interviewed migrant women, and they translated parts of the show into Italian, Turkish, Greek and Spanish. 'We had members of different multicultural communities training us to speak in their language,' says Sylvie, who performed the Spanish parts. 'We were actually very culturally sensitive to the different cultures, [and] our contacts were connected with the commission flats in Fitzroy in Napier and Gertrude Streets.' The production toured South Australia and Sydney and Newcastle, mostly performed in factories. In one factory in the Newcastle Docklands, migrant women who packed the large dining hall area for the show had tears in their eyes afterwards. 'They were kind of laughing and crying and everything,' Sylvie remembers.

The MWTG made the most of the funding that Elizabeth Reid set aside for feminist film and cultural festivals during International Women's Year in 1975. In a January 1975 meeting, the group discussed funding applications to the International Women's Year secretariat worth $37,356 for several works, including developing a play about women and madness. The following month, the group planned guerrilla street theatre, including 'some street theatre on women being retrenched from jobs (e.g. Everhot Factory)', and a women's festival, with activities ranging from puppets, skywriting, concerts, theatre, a film workshop and talent shows to classes on self-defence, car maintenance and woodchopping, and stalls for rape crisis and legal services and an ecology group. They held a mock fashion parade, 'where everyone dressed up in corsets and bras over their clothes', Sylvie recalls. When they heard that Oscar-winning actress Glenda Jackson was in town, they invited her to become part of the program. 'We had a giant tent but we didn't fit, so we sat on the grass in a big circle chatting with her.'

A number of the *Betty Can Jump* group reunited in 1975 in the women's show *Add a Grated Laugh or Two*. Directed by Evelyn Krape and Yvonne Marini, the show's all-female cast of nine performers included Claire Dobbin, with Kerry Dwyer involved in the show's 'discussions'. A press release issued by the MWTG describes the show as 'about what happens to women who step outside their rigidly defined roles, the fantasies which sustain an often empty existence, and the fate of those women who are cut adrift and who react by going mad'. The women's shows attracted a regular Pram crowd, as well as a new audience of women from the growing women's movement. Ponch Hawkes recalls a renewed excitement and energy at the Pram in this period, when amateur and completely inexperienced performers clamoured to work with more experienced actors from the Pram on the women's shows: 'Everything we did was selling out every night! People were flocking to the Pram Factory, the whole joint was completely revitalised.'

Robin Laurie, who performed in the *Women's Weekly* revue show (feminist shows that satirised women's magazines and myths of heterosexual romance), says they 'were a sensation and a huge success ... People (men mostly) kept saying patronisingly what a relief it was that feminists could be funny.' She recalls a small group of women – Jenny Walsh, Carol Porter, Evelyn Krape, Claire Dobbin – developing a show in 1974 called *Women and Children First*, which looked at 'women's lives, mothers and daughters, fertility, violence and sexuality'. Carol Porter made 'beautiful, Japanese sliding screens ... out of dressmaking patterns on wooden frames, which enabled shadow play' (Porter's set is still cited by APG members as one of the most visually stunning designs created for a Pram show). In her history of the group, Playwright and theatre scholar Peta Tait describes the audience reactions to the women's shows: 'They spontaneously cheered, yelled, clapped and whistled to show their approval.' Sylvie recalls how a 'young girl' in the audience who had been in Larundel Psychiatric Hospital came up to talk to performers after *The Travelling Medicine Show* about her experience and the abortion she had there. 'Many of the women in the audience felt they experienced these productions in a sort of conspiratorial partnership with the performers,' Tait writes.

The relationship of the MWTG to the APG and the Pram Factory was never completely settled. Some members of the women's group saw theatre as simply another way to explore feminist ideas and activism, while more experienced actors in the group wanted to develop professionally. Conflicts developed, and many of the 'Pram Factory women left [the MWTG] after about a year because they felt that theatrical standards weren't high enough', Claire later recollected. 'They felt there wasn't enough tough criticism about good scripts and performance, and that the politics had become more important than the theatre.' Although she performed in many of the women's shows, Claire said the group 'took a more polemical line than some of us were prepared to follow ... I didn't want to do theatre which was political at the expense of being theatrical.'

If the women's shows didn't always succeed artistically, the group succeeded in other ways. It gave women confidence and, as Peta Tait writes, the chance to take on qualities designated as masculine, like 'strength, aggression, and creation'. And the shows – which often involved nudity, playing men's roles and wearing men's costumes – were a place where women's bodies were allowed to mean all sorts of new things. 'The depiction of images of the female body in MWTG performances was a process of reclaiming and repossessing the female body,' Tait argues.

Ironically, the group's examination of gender went hand in hand with, at times, excluding men from audiences. Pram member John Smythe recalls a day when he was quietly colleting dirty glasses and coffee cups to wash while, behind heavy red velvet curtains, rehearsals were in progress for one of the women's revue shows. As he went about his work 'an improvising performer rose into view over the back of the seats, climbing into the bio-box in the process of exploring some performance dynamic. She saw me and screamed. I was discovered and roundly harangued for invading their sacred space.' There were frequent debates over the MWTG's practice of excluding men from the audiences of some shows. Robin Laurie recalls APG actor Robert Meldrum attended a women's-only performance of *The Power Show*, a 1977 production staged when the group moved to new premises in Faraday Street. When I ask him about it, Robert laughs with the deep, full chuckle of an actor in demand for his voice work: 'I came in drag. I had some cohorts, and we got together and we concocted a plan. We decided I'd dress up as a woman.' To their credit, Robin recalls, the women running the show had a discussion about whether to allow him in and in the end decided to because 'he had made an effort'.

Evelyn, for one, was never completely convinced that 'a women's theatre' could 'produce a new kind of female voice' through combining women's liberation and experimental theatre practices. 'I think if you've got skills as an actor, you will find that.' Sylvie did not join the separatist push within the women's group, but she believes the move to exclude men from audiences was 'the beginning of the end for the [women's] theatre group'. Robin Laurie recalls that towards the end, the MWTG women 'wanted the APG women out, and as the Pram women left the group the WTG made the move down to Tilley's Space [the Faraday Street warehouse]'. (The lines between the groups were not inviolable though, Bill Garner wants to make clear: 'I had a girlfriend who was one of the separatists ... and she would sneak me into the separatist house to stay the night.')

The MWTG lasted until 1977 after staging at least twenty-five original shows. Sylvie continued her activist work, including helping to establish Victoria's first rape crisis centre. She produced a women's music radio show called *Give Men a Pause* on 3RRR, and she was one of the founders of the women's band Toxic Shock, whose lead vocalist

Fran Kelly later became an ABC journalist and presenter – 'she was working as the events organiser at La Trobe uni; [that] helped us get lots of gigs,' Sylvie recalls.

By 1978 in Melbourne, you could watch women performers and hear women's stories almost any night of the week, Suzanne Spunner writes:

> Everywhere you turned it seems there were plays by and about women: *For Coloured Girls When The Rainbow Is Not Enuff* [sic] was playing to packed houses at the Comedy Theatre and at Russell Street *Dusa, Fish, Stas and Vi* was playing to capacity audiences, while at La Mama *Savage Sepia*, a locally written, all woman production, was also enjoying good houses and sympathetic reviews ... two of the most successful shows staged by the APG were Kerry Dwyer's production of Fassbinder's *The Bitter Tears of Petra Von Kant* and Fay Mokotow's production of Susan Griffin's *Voices*.

Kerry recalls now, however, that the women's shows 'were always in the Back Theatre and they were always late at night'. She wonders why they didn't get more backing and 'morale-boosting support' from the APG. But women were starring in APG shows too. Jack had long returned to the group by this time. And so had Kerry: 'The APG had this sense of being a *vortex*, and once you were in you couldn't get out. If you got out, you just got ripped back in again.'

Chapter 7
Betty's legacy

When I visit Kerry at her home, the ground floor of postwar duplex on a steep hill that leads down to a beach in Sydney's eastern suburbs, I ask her about *Betty* as we sit at her kitchen table, the place where consciousness-raising groups often met to talk about their personal and political problems. Kerry tells me that while the *Betty* collective didn't mean for the play to be a personal therapy exercise for the cast and crew, 'we *were* doing it to understand ourselves'. And so while the collective staged the play to be a consciousness-raising event for audiences, it was also a transformative experience for the women who made it. Yvonne would later write that doing the show was like a 'therapeutic act', one where they discovered new skills and abilities. 'It was definitely all about us changing,' Claire says now. 'That's what it was. It was about us.' The consciousness-raising sessions continued when the play ended, Kerry says: 'There was quite a strong group that kept on. Gradually, people thought, "Oh, I've unburdened myself."'

When Kerry interviewed the *Betty* cast and crew in 1975, they described the play's impact on their lives. Laurel recalled it as a time when 'everyone was extended in their sense of themselves'. Helen described the show coinciding with a 'whole lot of' changes in her life: 'I didn't know what I was in for. Once there, it made sense. It was exhilarating and it was a real opening up.' Micky described being involved in *Betty Can Jump* as 'the beginning of my being able to find my emotional and intellectual life as a woman ... In a way it was my coming out into the world ... I remember feeling really alive

149

at the time.' Being a part of *Betty*, Micky told Kerry, was a kind of 'acceleration of what happens to most people when they join the women's movement'. The combination of consciousness raising and theatre, and working to create something together, proved to be a powerful and 'especially explosive combination'.

Nearly five decades later, when I speak to Micky at her home and studio, hidden behind gum trees and another property down a twisting driveway outside Daylesford, she reiterates these sentiments unprompted. She recalls not so much specific details of those months, but instead a *feeling*, 'a sense of enormous enthusiasm and exhilaration'.

Evelyn had grown up in the tradition of Yiddish music and theatre, and then at the Secondary Teachers' College her stage persona and clear, strong voice made her a natural fit for American musicals. 'But it was at the Pram Factory that I really learnt about what was happening in contemporary theatre with Grotowski and Brecht and Pinter,' she says. 'And as I got to understand what the Pram was on about, I found ... my home.' Evelyn was committed to the Pram's vision of creating an Australian theatre, and she was surprised when a *Marvellous Melbourne* reviewer commented on her character's Jewishness. 'I played the madam of a brothel and – I don't know why – I thought I was playing her as a Russian ... but a review in the paper said my "Jewish madam of a brothel". I thought "Really?" I didn't think there were any Jewish madams of brothels, and then I thought, "Is my Jewishness showing so much?" At that stage, I was kind of keeping my Jewishness under wraps,' she says.

Evelyn is now the director of Kadimah Yiddish Theatre in the Melbourne suburb of Elsternwick, part of a Jewish cultural precinct that includes the Holocaust Centre and the Yiddish college Sholem Aleichem. Kadimah's shows, such as the *Ghetto Cabaret*, a story about the Jewish musicians, singers, dancers, acrobats, opera and theatre performers in Europe in World War II, combine Yiddish and English. She sees her work there as bringing together her Jewishness and the Pram's exploration of what it means to be Australian. Now, at the

Kadimah, 'my Jewishness … is foregrounded, and the underbelly is my Australianness', she says. When I talk to her on the phone from Sydney, in the middle of the Melbourne lockdown, Evelyn is working on a story about the Polish poet Melekh Ravitsh. 'He came out here, before the Holocaust, looking to see if he could create a Jewish Homeland in the Kimberley.' She has recently finished recording the audiobook of writer Arnold Zable's fictionalised story of Carlton in the 1950s, *Scraps of Heaven*. Evelyn enthuses about the novel, which imagines Carlton as 'a melting pot of Italians and Greeks and Jews and Australians', as Australia's 'answer to the Lower East Side in New York'.

Being both Australian and part of the Jewish diaspora have been constant themes in Evelyn's work, but so too is her experience as a woman in this world. Her stage work has consistently developed the themes the collective first explored in *Betty*. 'All the major work that I've done has had women's issues at its core … women trapped … women abused.' In the 1980s, she performed the one-woman show *Female Parts* in Melbourne, Sydney and Adelaide. The show, by Nobel laureate Dario Fo and his wife, actor and activist Franca Rame, is made up of four short plays about young women dealing with domestic violence, babies and struggling with work and life. Thirty years later, in a 2015 season at the Melbourne Arts Centre, she performed *More Female Parts*, an update by playwright Sara Hardy exploring women in their sixties tackling divorce, violence and control in relationships.

After *Betty*, even as Evelyn was increasingly outspoken about the number and quality of roles APG playwrights wrote for women, she also developed possibly the most significant relationship of her personal and professional life. When they were rehearsing the 1972 revue she confronted one of the show's writers, Jack Hibberd, about the 'meter maids' featured in *Sonia's Knee and Thigh Show*. 'I rang [Jack] up and said there were Queensland meter maids [in his skit] that offended me … We needed to be more than just playing meter maids, dressing up.' Another scene in the show involved a mother in a high rise who took a hot iron and put it on her baby. 'It was so shocking,' Evelyn says now. The show 'caused huge conflict with me and Jack', Evelyn recalls. '[He] was really angry with me and didn't talk to me for a year.'

When they did start talking again, the pair became a couple, but the arguments continued. Sue Ingleton recalls Jack and Evelyn 'occasionally sat together [at meetings] but not often, probably because Evelyn liked best to shout her tirades of feminist abuse against his chauvinistic tendencies from across the room.' (Max Gillies described Evelyn to me as 'fearless in most social occasions. I can remember once when Gough Whitlam was in the audience, and she made a spectacle of him.') To Sue's mind, the dynamic between Evelyn and Jack 'enhanced their delight in each other'. Bob Thorneycroft recalls the couple 'screaming at each other' in the middle of a collective meeting too:

> Ev [was] having a go at Jack's lack of feminist awareness in his writings. A few minutes later, on the way back from the Men's ...I thought I'd nick through a large storage space as a shortcut back to my hard wooden seat. There were Jack and Evelyn, going for it.

Evelyn might have found the way Jack wrote women's parts wanting, but she now credits him as 'one of the people who influenced me enormously in terms of developing my sense of theatre, and what theatre can and should do'. Performing in his plays was 'immensely liberating for me as an actor'. She played Mousey in Hibberd's *One of Nature's Gentlemen* – a role Graeme Blundell had earlier played at La Mama – and Nellie Melba in his 1976 work *A Toast to Melba*.

Evelyn names Lois Ellis, her director in *Female Parts*, as another important influence. Evelyn describes *Female Parts* as a continuation of the themes *Betty* explored: 'serious issues about the world, about women ... what's happened [to me] as a Jewish woman and as an Australian Jewish woman'. The theatre she is drawn to is the theatre of humour and black comedy. The 'Pram has been an enormous influence on my attitude to creating theatre that really shocks and disturbs and confronts'. The longevity of Krape's career can also be attributed to her range, and her ability to cross over into mainstream roles, including film and television roles. She has performed with the Melbourne Theatre Company, Playbox and the Victorian Opera Company; in the movies *Babe* and *Babe: Pig in the City*, and in the television programs *Flying Doctors*, *Blue Heelers* and *Homicide*.

When Claire reflected in 1975 on her *Betty* experience, she told Kerry she thought the *act* of staging a women's show 'was stronger as a statement than the actual *content* of the show'. She described *Betty* as a 'turning point' in her life, one where she learnt to let go of her 'inhibitions as an actor' and 'barriers of self-consciousness': 'Betty was mind-blowing in that it was through the work we did and the CR groups we formed that we realised that the personal is political.' She directed, performed in and made costumes for many more APG and MWTG plays. In 1974 she toured hospitals, prisons and wharves with *The Sports Show*, a play written by Hibberd in collaboration with the cast about an Australian sporting hero who, as the show progresses, turns out to be a woman. The following year, Claire played the titular role in *Mary Shelley and the Monsters*, a show that was partly improvised, partly scripted by Pram member Tim Robertson (Evelyn played Mary's stepsister Claire Clairmont).

By this time Claire was becoming increasingly involved in running the APG. In his history of the group, Robertson recalls Claire's energies being split between performing on stage and the Pram's administration behind the scenes. He describes Claire as 'an excellent convenor of workshops, and energetic teacher and committee person'. Claire's teaching and organising skills, and her ability to manage the Pram's spectrum of personalities and agendas, meant that 'At some point ... I became the chairman of the collective.' Having a woman as chair of the group was no insignificant event, Claire says now. Later she established a career in the film industry as a script editor and consultant. And she was appointed to another role chairing an arts organisation, the Melbourne International Film Festival, a position she held until she stepped down in 2019.

Women's liberation might have raised Yvonne's consciousness, but she was interested in another form of higher consciousness: that of

153

'the soul and the psyche', says Albert Rotstein, who was married to Yvonne until her death in 2001. 'She was into the group [work], but it had to be to the elevation of the soul,' he tells me over a grainy Zoom interview. In her Pram memories, Yvonne describes beginning a daily meditation practice in her quest to explore her 'spiritual self'. In 1974 she attended an acting workshop run by Grotowski in Sydney. Like Kerry seven years earlier, the experience challenged her to rethink her relationship with theatre. 'I remember ... suddenly realising there was a world that it was possible to contact through theatre,' she wrote later. 'After that revelation I just couldn't do the Pram Factory style stuff anymore ... it didn't reach deep enough inside.' Stanislavsky's approach to theatre was psychological, Brecht's was intellectual, 'but Grotowski was into the intuitive', she wrote. Yvonne had cycled through different stage personas: from the wholesome comedienne to the feminist performer of *Betty Can Jump* and the avant-garde performer who cartwheeled on stage without wearing knickers, but after she returned from the Grotowski workshops she took on a backroom role as the group's paid administrator.

In many ways Yvonne was the 'soul of the APG', says Rotstein, who had known many of the Pram figures from his years as a medical student at the University of Melbourne, and who was a regular at La Mama and Pram shows. Yvonne was 'funny, animated and good-humoured ... her enthusiasms often knitted some of the other players together', he remembers. 'She was very fond of John Timlin, and he was fond of her.' (Timlin remembers Yvonne fondly too. 'I fought for her to be paid as, effectively, the APG secretary assisting me when I was administrator,' he says). Rotstein had unsuccessfully tried out for a role in the David Williamson play *The Removalists*, and he admired Yvonne's performances from afar, but she had settled on a spiritual life by the time they met again in 1979 on the corner of Smith and Johnston streets in Collingwood. They began living together, and he remembers Yvonne's fascination with the religious teachings of Theosophy: 'She read Blavatsky [Helena Blavatsky, co-founder of the Theosophical Society] very widely, and she had a lot of friends who were into Theosophy,' Rotstein says.

When Yvonne left the Pram, she joined the Divine Light Mission, a religious sect first founded in 1960 by guru Hans Ji Maharaj. The Divine Light gained popularity in the West when Prem Rawat, his teenage son and successor, established the church in the UK, the US and, by the early 1970s, Australia. Yvonne reflected years later on the 'crossroads' she reached when she could no longer see how her life on stage could be integrated with her spiritual path. She writes that when she – along with Vic Marsh – chose the Divine Light, 'most people thought we were probably a bit nuts [but] no one touched their inner selves at the Pram Factory, it was very intellectual'.

Yvonne's parents had been supportive of her early rebellions – leaving home as an unmarried teen for NIDA, and then moving into the inner city when she joined the APG. But when she attached herself to the Divine Light, Yvonne's father broke ties with her. Just as they had for Helen and Micky, the new ways of living and thinking that had become possible in the 1960s and 1970s created a fracture with her parents. Yvonne's sister Athena joined the Divine Light too, and both sisters wanted their father to join: they kept trying to get his attention but he wouldn't support it, Albert says. 'It caused her father to disavow them and go back to Greece', to a circular village near Corinth where ancient feuds continued between 'families that radiated off up the hill, in segments of their holdings'. Yvonne briefly worked in the public service in ethnic affairs, 'but she wasn't cut out for it', Albert recalls. Towards the end of her life, she discovered that she could sing. Not holy songs, but soulful music, Billie Holiday songs and Ella Fitzgerald songs.

Yvonne began having what she describes as 'cosmic experiences', an awareness of what she called 'this other dimension in us'. Rotstein tells me a story when I ask what she might have meant by this other dimension. 'I'm pretty sure one day, on the back veranda, she turned into a bird and flew off. I was talking to her, and something strange happened and it seemed to me that that's what it was. And then she was standing next to me again.' If he had asked Yvonne if that's what had just happened, Albert says she would have simply said, 'Yes. Anything's possible.' He adds: 'What I'm trying to say, is the powerful,

powerful nature of theatre was not unknown to her.' (As we talk about Yvonne, Rotstein keeps gazing skywards, somewhere off the screen, as if he might catch a glimpse of her.)

After *Betty*, Vic spent two years at the Pram performing in *The APG Revue* and plays such as Katharine Susannah Prichard's *Brumby Innes*, a co-production with the Nindethana Aboriginal theatre group, starring Jack Charles. But while he was assuming different roles on stage, Vic was struggling with his identity offstage, as a new father in a heterosexual relationship. 'I was performing an identity. You know, in a theatre, how clichéd is that?' he says now. Max Gillies remembers the shock of Vic and Carmen's relationship ending. 'I never forgot when she had the baby. They'd been living together here in Carlton and virtually the day after the baby was born Vic came out and left her,' he says. 'I was a monk for eleven years when trying to sort out my sexuality got all too hard,' Vic says now. 'I abandoned Carmen [and left her] holding the baby ... But I'd be dead three ways by now if I hadn't done that. I escaped into a celibate Ashram life.' Looking back, Vic says he sees a pattern of meetings with inspiring women throughout his life. He's now writing about these women in the follow-up to his first memoir, *The Boy in the Yellow Dress*. 'I realise now that I've had the most incredible encounters with women all the way through [my life] ... women who inspire me or correct me or inform me or support me, ever since the days of *Betty Can Jump*'.

For Kerry, the birth of her daughter Nellie in the days after *Betty* was in many ways more life-defining than anything else that had happened to her. 'I lay in bed for a few weeks, panting from the enormous changes that I'd experienced,' she later recalled. She wanted her next play at the Pram to be about death – 'I knew in the moment of Nellie's birth that my death was inevitable,' she wrote – but no one else at the Pram was interested. At the same time, Graeme's television and film career was taking off. He was already a regular on the television series *Homicide*, produced by Hector Crawford's company. Graeme describes how, when the Pram Factory started, he was building a parallel career on the small screen 'as a petty criminal with a bad Tony Curtis haircut'. He also had films roles in *The Naked Bunyip*, a

1970 mockumentary where he played an unprepossessing employee of an ad agency hired to interview Australians about sex; and in *Stork*, a 1971 film directed by Betty Burstall's husband Tim Burstall, with Bruce Spence in the title role. While Kerry was busy with *Betty* and then Nellie, Burstall offered Graeme the title role in his next film. *Alvin Purple* told the story of a waterbed salesman (Blundell), an unremarkable man in almost every respect except that he inexplicably turns almost every woman he meets into a state of sexual frenzy: schoolgirls, his high school teacher's wife, and the bored housewives whose waterbeds he fills.

With his Dudley Moore–like appeal and little-boy-lost eyes, Blundell played Alvin as a sympathetic character, a man whose effect on women's libidos is so powerful his life is a chaotic comedy of pratfalls; orgasms are on tap as surely as the water that he uses to fill his waterbeds. Featuring full-frontal nudity (of both Graeme and his co-stars, including Abigail Rogan and Jackie Weaver), Burstall's film took advantage of the Classification Board's recently issued 'R certificate', which allowed explicit films to be screened to audiences over the age of eighteen. The film was a huge success, taking in more than $4 million at the box office. It's possible to see *Alvin Purple* as a film that dragged the naked bodies of avant-garde theatre and 1960s radical counterculture into an increasingly liberal mainstream culture. But as Graeme has written, the film's success had another, more prosaic reason: simply 'that a huge group of people also loved watching sex on the screen or on stage'.

Viewed another way, Burstall's movie can be read as a chauvinistic response to a sexual revolution the women's movement embraced: *Alvin Purple* played both on men's fantasies *and* men's fears. The film depicts Alvin as a man tormented by women's out-of-control libidos: as a schoolboy he has to leave school early because of a menacing pack of schoolgirls, their lascivious legs powering the pushbikes they use to chase him; as a salesman, lustful clients make his work impossible, and in a scene where a waterbed client reclining in a negligee turns out to be a transwoman, he picks up his clothes and guards his penis as if his life is in mortal danger.

Throughout, the film's other male characters regularly make reference to the size of Alvin's penis as the secret to his appeal to women. It's as if the movie is enacting the worst fears of the Pram Factory men who worried about what women were discussing at their consciousness-raising sessions. The film was loosely based on a story by writer Alan Hopgood, and Graeme tells me he 'only saw a couple of pages of the script' before signing on to the film. Like many of the Pram shows, scenes and dialogue were improvised on set. He had some early 'misgivings', he says, but he liked Burstall's company and 'enjoyed his method of filmmaking, which was a bit of roughhouse as well'.

Graeme's film and television career was seen as too mainstream for the Pram crowd, and it became a source of tension in Graeme and Kerry's relationship. 'Graeme's agenda was totally different from mine,' Kerry has written. 'He was more interested in fame and other women.' During this time, she signed up to perform in a La Mama play that, too late, she found 'misogynist nonsense'. 'My marriage became a nightmare and I lost kilos, performing in a play that battered me about and trying to look after two babies on my own.'

Betty was, in its own way, bawdy and explicit too, but it wanted to critique male control of women's sexuality and women's bodies. *Alvin Purple*, for all its taboo breaking, was a film that seemed to want to reinstate men's authority over women's sexuality. When a psychiatrist notices Alvin's effect on women, he concocts a plan to send his repressed and dysfunctional female clients to Alvin for him to 'fix'. After listening to their problems on a cassette, Alvin walks through pink latex curtains – as if he is parting a woman's labia – to begin his work unlocking their neuroses. The authorities shut down the illegal operation, a court case follows, and the film ends with an extended car chase that reinstates a manly order. The tinnie-drinking Alvin, realising he's lost his true love to a nunnery, ends up as a gardener at her convent, the only place where he feels safe from predatory women. *Alvin Purple*, in other words, ends up reproducing the very saint-and-sinner dichotomy of Australian womanhood that *Betty* wanted to expose. While audiences queued to see the film, women's liberationists protested outside screenings, chanting 'Fuck Alvin

Purple!' Kerry, meanwhile, recalls enduring 'countless inane press interviews focused obsessively on how it felt to be Mrs Alvin Purple'. Kerry and Graeme's marriage didn't survive her new role as Mrs Purple. 'We limped along in our marriage for a while, until I began to move back into the APG,' Kerry has written.

Kerry began to perform in Pram Factory shows again at the end of 1972, at first acting in Alma De Groen's *The Joss Adams Show*, and then increasingly directing Pram shows. She remembers the 1978 production of the *Bitter Tears of Petra Von Kant* by R.W. Fassbinder as a breakthrough. She had initially been cast in the play's lead role, but (in an echo of her early experiences of student theatre) when the woman who was originally going to direct dropped out, Kerry recast her title role and directed the show herself. She compares the experience to an epiphany: she could see a 'blue laser beam' on the stage that 'gave me accurate intuitive knowledge of how to direct the show ... the work unfolded effortlessly'. The show was an artistic and financial success, one that led her to realise 'that directing was my path, affording me a far greater emotional, spiritual, mental and physical scope than performing'. At the same time, Kerry began exploring her interest in cinema, organising a festival of eighteen women's films – Reel Women – at the Pram Factory in 1978. The films included a number of works made by the Sydney Women's Film Group, which had been working since the early 1970s, in parallel with the theatre productions women had been staging at Pram Factory. Sydney filmmaker Martha Ansara contributed a documentary about women and work that featured footage from a factory performance of the *Women and Work* show.

When she was accepted into the Australian Film and Television School's Stage to Screen training course for theatre directors, Kerry moved to Sydney. She directed *The Wedding*, a 25-minute film starring Geoffrey Rush, Noni Hazlehurst and Robert Meldrum that opened the Feminist Film Festival in Sorrento, Italy in 1980. The long hours of filmmaking were not compatible with being a single mother with two small children, however, and she also discovered that in filmmaking, where 'you have to make these permanent decisions early on', she missed the improvisation she had enjoyed so much in making live performance. Kerry returned to theatre, and worked as a freelance director in theatres and companies such as the Belvoir St Theatre, Griffin Theatre, Sydney Theatre Company, Perth Playhouse and Malthouse Theatre. The connection between the physical and the spiritual remains an important part of Kerry's life. When I speak to her one morning in 2021, she has just returned from a two and a half hour yoga class across town after waking up at 4.30 am.

In more recent years she took another direction, becoming an interfaith minister and celebrant. But it was a direction that grew out of her experience with theatre and Grotowski. 'I had become very interested in the whole notion of ritual, and the essence of theatre is a sacred ritual,' Kerry tells me. Her interest in the mystical took her to India and Europe and to 'Ireland, land of my ancestors.' Being a celebrant, she tells me, was 'very much about a ritual that helps people go through big personal transformations.'

After *Betty*, Micky continued working at the Pram, designing sets, costumes and posters. For a while she was one of the APG's unofficial resident photographers – a role she shared with Ponch Hawkes and others – and she held her first photography exhibition at the Pram in 1974. She was a graduate of the National Gallery of Victoria painting school, and while she did run off with an artist, she left him to chase her own muse. And she did not relinquish her love of paint in deference to her first husband: because she had no sense of a 'pure print' when she started to explore photography, she began hand-colouring her images. On their overland trip to London she'd taken note of colours everywhere. The blue of men's clothes in India, the magenta of corpses burnt on pyres in the holy city of Benares, mosaics in Istanbul, the streams of lights like strings of coloured jewels decorating the densely populated continents as she flew home to Australia. In 1975, her exhibition *Laurel* (named for Laurel Frank) was Australia's first contemporary exhibition of hand-coloured photographs.

Micky's work at the Pram wasn't paid, and she found a part-time position in the slide department at Melbourne University. 'I was called assistant curator of visual aids and I put away the slides basically,' she says. In 1977 she moved to Sydney and into a household of people involved in *The Digger* newspaper. She also joined an 'anarchic feminist' theatre group called the 'Lean Sisters', performing in their *Krunk Book Christmas Show*. 'The story was Santa's workers rebelling against Santa ... I think I was Drudgeleen to begin with and I became Triumphaleen through this strike action of Santa's workshop.' In 1978, in an exhibition at the Ewing and George Paton Galleries titled *A Live-in Show*, she displayed photographs, drawings, paintings and poetry. It also incorporated a two-week performance, where she moved a bed, a television, and tables and chairs into the gallery. 'The idea of recreating a domestic environment within the gallery is now a familiar trope,' curator Yvette Dal Pozzo writes, citing works such as Tracey Emin's 1998 *My Bed* and Destiny Deacon's 1996 tableau *My Living Room, Brunswick 3056*, but when Micky created her work 'it was a revelation'. Like *Betty*, Micky's show insisted on rejecting the divisions between the private and the public, the personal and the political. People lingered, children drew at tables and played among leaves. In many ways Micky's show, which was both an art exhibition and a performance piece, synthesised her art practice, her feminist consciousness, and the Pram ethos that said the divisions between life, art, politics and performance were permeable.

Over the following decades Micky built a career in photography, painting and installation; her work has been exhibited in the British Museum, and in galleries and museums in Lisbon, San Diego, Jakarta and Manila. And her art, including images of Pram Factory shows, is now held in the National Gallery of Australia and the Museum of Contemporary Art in Sydney. They are a final riposte to her father's suggestion that a woman could not invent anything original.

When Laurel joined the *Betty* collective, her life as a recently graduated university researcher took a completely different direction. But in many ways, her working and creative life since can trace a more direct line to the Pram Factory than any other member of the *Betty* collective. When I meet Laurel in her small, neat home in Melbourne's inner north in 2018, a space decorated with carefully chosen fabrics and furnishings, she is still working as the costume designer for Circus Oz, a group she co-founded and that grew out of the Pram Factory. *Betty* was her first experience working in a group. At La Trobe she had spent most of her time with men – 'that's where I thought the intellectual action was' – but working on *Betty* was a process of 'throwing [all her stereotypes of women] off'. When Kerry offered Laurel a job at the Pram for $60 a week after *Betty Can Jump*'s run, she decided to stay on: 'I had no idea where she found [the money] there wasn't even a job description. She just opened things up for me'.

True to the APG's anti-star system, Laurel performed in a number of Pram productions, but her name appears most frequently in the credits of Pram plays as a designer of lighting, sets and costumes. Occasionally she is named as a stage manager. Laurel describes how

> there was excess of actors, writers and directors ... but no one was prepared to do the practical things. Two men who worked on the technical side, Ian McKenzie and Graeme Leith, taught me about lighting design and rigging, and this became my major work for the next five or six years.

Pram Factory members recall Laurel as one of the most affecting, and effective, members of the group. Bob Thorneycroft declares that 'Laurel Frank was my number one inspirational figure. She got on with the job and she's still getting on with it.' Yvonne Marini described Laurel (along with Fay Mokotow) as 'very quiet, very centred and focused – they seemed to hold a detached or rather impartial opinion of things without being swayed.'

After *Betty*, Laurel began researching puppetry and started a small puppet group at the Pram with Claire Dobbin. It attracted APG members and people 'from other fringe groups wanting to break into the collective'. In the beginning, the group focused on children's theatre – 'We did a version of The Owl and the Pussycat and toured schools and festivals,' Laurel has written – but at some point the puppet shows morphed into an exuberant, anarchic late-night show after the show in the main theatre. 'A kind of craziness broke through and we wrote scripts and devised new approaches to the visual element and added music,' Laurel writes. 'A lot of actors who were attracted to our little sub-group drifted through. Jane Clifton directed, Bob Thorneycroft and Hellen Skye choreographed.' At the same time Laurel was learning Tai Chi and yoga, and becoming increasingly drawn to the physical element of performance.

Laurel tells me her 'big, exciting change of direction' came with the creation of a circus project at the Pram in 1976. The Soapbox Circus fused many of the Pram's disparate influences and factions: the APG's political theatre tradition, Laurel's puppet group, a highly physical style of performance, live music (by Mic Conway's Captain Matchbox Whoopee Band) and a surrealist aesthetic (as opposed to a circus that used live animals, cast members dressed up as kangaroos and elephants). 'Soapbox Circus ... wanted to use circus and physical imagery to talk about politics,' Laurel explains. The group toured factories, schools and community centres with shows protesting uranium mining and Indonesia's invasion of East Timor. Laurel's own performing career ended when she fractured her coccyx during an acrobatic manoeuvre in the middle of a pantomime. 'I also had small accidents on ladders and carrying lighting gear, but I think mostly we all suffered in silence and there was not a great sense of occupational health and safety.'

Circus Oz was formed in 1977 when Tim Coldwell, Sue Broadway and other performers from Adelaide's New Ensemble Circus came to work out of the Pram Factory and merged with the Soapbox Circus. There was a productive tension between the Melbourne and Adelaide groups from the beginning, Laurel remembers: 'the Adelaide crew wanting our resources – being tired of working off the back of a truck – and ... the Pram Factory crew wanting the traditional circus skills and experience that they had.' The combination of the APG's politically engaged theatre and the Adelaide group's physical skills – well beyond the basic juggling and acrobatics the APG group had developed – became the defining feature of Circus Oz. Laurel recalls making their first tent in the basement of the Pram Factory. 'It was freezing and we had miles and miles of incredibly heavy canvas to feed through the industrial sewing machine. Tim had designed the tent and we did everything, putting in every eyelet and sealing every rope end'. They used the same 24-hour roster system on the sewing machine that the group had used to sand the floors when they first moved in, according to Meg Clancy.

Unlike many circuses, Circus Oz has always had a strong tradition of women performing the most daring aerial acts, acrobatics and fire-eating segments. Circus Oz's 2018 production, *Model Citizens*, was a showcase of women's strength. An arts website I was reviewing for sent me to the show's run during the Sydney Festival, just as the #MeToo movement was cresting, and I was struck by how the women in the cast shone in almost all of the evening's most dazzling tricks. They were also responsible for the night's most impressive show of strength. In a propless scene, the five female cast members elegantly walked over and down each other's heads and shoulders and arms. The act ended with Freyja Edney singlehandedly suspending the four other cast members above her.

Peta Tait argues that Circus Oz is one of Australian feminist theatre's most important innovations: a style of physical theatre that 'restages' and subverts cultural representations of the female body as passive, weak and the object of a sexual gaze. When we meet, Laurel tells me she can 'see a clear line back to *Betty Can Jump* from what I'm doing with Circus Oz ... As a springboard, I think *Betty Can Jump* was really important'.

After *Betty*, Jude had a successful film and television career, working on feature films such as *Newsfront* and performing the long-running role of Noeline Bourke in the television series *Prisoner*. Produced by Grundy, *Prisoner* became one of Australia's most successful television exports, reversing the one-way flow of screen culture that had fuelled the Vincent Report and the push to develop an Australian entertainment culture. Like *Betty Can Jump*, it was notable for being a story dominated by female characters. But ironically, like the convicts in *Betty*, the main characters in *Prisoner* were criminals (the character Noeline was in and out of Wentworth gaol for bungled robberies). I tried to send messages to Jude asking for an interview for this book, but I've not been able to reach her. None of the Pram people I spoke to are in contact with her now. It's as if she continues to hold herself apart from the group. Max describes Jude as a 'lone wolf' who was drawn to the puppetry group. Helen remembers that at one point Jude adopted a kind of 'ventriloquism when she'd only talk to people via a puppet'.

At some time in the mid-1970s, Kerry visited Sydney to audition for a film, and stayed with Jude at her home in Elizabeth Bay. When she left, Kerry sat in a room at Jude's place sipping iced peppermint tea and typing her a letter. She wondered where Jude was ('How come you are never there when I need you?' she wrote), wished Jude a happy birthday and thanked her for the use of her Gregory's street directory. Kerry left a copy of the questions she had put to the other women about their *Betty* experience behind for Jude, and then packed her bags and drove off to put her car on the train and return to Melbourne.

And what of the others who played cameo roles in the story of *Betty Can Jump*? In 2019 I stood outside a Starbucks on California Boulevard, Walnut Creek, a city in the eastern San Francisco Bay area, waiting for Bobbi Ausubel to pick me up. You may remember Bobbi as the woman who co-founded the Caravan Theatre, and was behind the first women's liberation show in the US, *How to Make a Woman*. The play was a huge success and the company performed the show on and off for half a dozen years, often changing the script after audience feedback – sometimes Bobbi would loiter in the toilets after performances to eavesdrop on women who had seen the show. Bobbi, now in her eighties, picked me up in an old-model sky-blue station wagon – the kind of vehicle that you can imagine being filled with costumes, sound systems and handmade signs for impromptu demonstrations – and immediately started telling me about her morning running an acting workshop for seniors, helping them tell their life story through drama. Over lunch in a nearby mall, she explained that she had separated from her husband Stan Edelson in

1976. She lives with her partner Cecelia in California, and cares for her and Stan's now adult daughter, Rivka Solomon, with whom she writes feminist books and plays.

Bobbi now campaigns on behalf of sufferers of myalgic encephalo-myelitis (chronic fatigue syndrome) such as Rivka. When the Caravan Theatre folded, Bobbi worked with many of the experimental and feminist theatre groups that formed a thriving movement in the 1970s, thanks to a healthy National Endowment for the Arts scheme. 'All that got wiped out with the whole Republican administration. It was no longer fun', Bobbi tells me. 'The world had changed, the 60s and 70s were finished or finishing and most of the theatres like ours, the experimental theatres, were finishing.'

In 1980 Bobbi reunited with Maggie Helmer when she directed Maggie in the one-woman play *Silkwood*. Maggie had by then renamed herself Jehane Dyllan, remarried and moved to Washington DC, where she had become involved in the labour movement. *Silkwood*, a dramatisation of the life of the whistleblowing Oklahoma nuclear plant employee Karen Silkwood, predated the Meryl Streep movie of the same name by three years. The play told the story of Silkwood's life, which ended when she died in a suspicious car accident after she began raising questions about health and safety at the plant. 'We did improv, improv, improv, to make a one-woman show out of Karen Silkwood's experience,' Bobbi explains. The play, funded by labour unions, toured around 200 venues. After the show, Jehane would stay to talk to audiences, some of whom had attended the first stage play of their life that night. When Jehane died at the age of forty-six in 1991, Claudia Levy, in an obituary in the *Washington Post*, wrote about the effect of the *Silkwood* tour on audiences. 'Often they were eager to testify about hazards in their own jobs, and they came bearing documents, as if she were an investigator, and asked how to join or organize unions.'

While *Betty* uncovered stories about Australian women's history-making battle for the vote, Carmen Lawrence was making her own history as one of the twelve women at the first Women's Electoral

Lobby meeting in Beatrice Faust's lounge room. She now says it is 'very hard to know' how decisive WEL's campaign was in the election, but 'the general sentiment that women needed more of a place in the sun would certainly have influenced some women's vote [and] the growth of Women's Electoral Lobby was exponential ... from ... us sitting around in Beatrice's lounge room to having branches in every state, and enough women prepared to go out and interview candidates'. When Labor was elected, WEL play an influential role in the Whitlam government's adoption of its policies in childcare, equal pay and anti-discrimination legislation. 'The Whitlam government didn't really have an agenda for women. It was sympathetic and broadly well disposed, but it didn't actually have an agenda, so we were trying to set one.'

The make-up of the Australian federal parliament took an inordinately long time to start reflecting the changes women's liberation had brought about in other parts of society; no women were elected to either the House of Representatives or the Senate in 1972, but women who were active in WEL were part of an influx of women into parliament in the following years. WEL member Susan Ryan entered federal parliament as senator for the ACT in 1975, becoming the Minister for Education and Youth Affairs, Minister Assisting the Prime Minister for the Status of Women, and Special Minister of State. Carmen left her academic career when she was elected to the Western Australian state government in 1986 to represent the seat of Subiaco in Perth's inner west. She rose quickly in the Labor state government, becoming Australia's first female premier in 1990. She entered federal parliament in 1994, in a by-election for electorate of Fremantle, and served in the Keating government as Minister for Human Services and Health, and Minister for Women until the government's defeat in 1996.

In 2020 I phoned Carmen at her home in Perth (an hour later than our planned call because I messed up the time zones). She has returned to teaching and research at the University of Western Australia, and is still thinking about the connections between the personal and the political. She's interested in the enduring problem of how political movements based on identity – sex, gender, race, culture and so on – can open up ways to be political and activist without closing down the connections needed to make a broad-based movement.

'I've been lecturing students for the last ten years in psychology applied to contemporary social problems. One of the big social problems [in my teaching] is the identity dilemma ... you want people to feel as if they belong somewhere, but not so powerfully that they can only belong by excluding others.'

'And it becomes a very fixed idea of identity?'

'It does, it becomes prescriptive. And the very essence of what we were trying to do in the 60s and 70s was to kind of release that pressure. The sort of conservative, conventional stifling role requirements, for women in particular. But some people, they flipped almost immediately to the opposite, which is that there was only one way to be a women's libber, and there was very strong disdain sometimes expressed for people who were more moderate in their approach to the issues, and vice versa.'

Carmen was talking about the battles between women within the women's liberation movement. The filmmaker Martha Ansara and writer Anne Summers have both talked, for instance, about attending early women's liberation conferences and being abused for wearing make-up and feminine clothes. But there were other, deeper divisions, both tactical and philosophical. Over the merits of separatism, and whether it was possible to be a feminist and heterosexual. Over whether you should – like Elizabeth Reid – work within the system to create change or agitate from outside. And whether indeed a capitalist system, reliant on women's unpaid labour, would need to be overthrown completely before women could be liberated.

For Helen Garner, feminism was a great liberation, but from the movement's earliest days, she saw that women's liberation could preclude other possibilities. How can you be an artist *and* committed to political movement? Can you simultaneously be creative and true to yourself while staying loyal to the group?

26

27

28

29

30

31

Chapter 8
Betty and Helen

'That's the other problem we don't know how to solve,'
says Kerry. 'We just don't know any women writers.'

Helen Garner in The Digger, 1973

It's one of the coldest November days for years when I arrive at the Melbourne Town Hall for the opening event of the Broadside Festival. A line begins at the entrance and continues further than I can see. I always pack either too few or too many clothes when I visit this town – almost as if I don't want to be comfortable in the city I left twenty-five years ago – and the wind is blasting my exposed legs. The fit of my wedge shoes is just wrong enough to irritate. I enviously eye off the locals who had pulled on pairs of black boots for city walking that morning. There are small groups of older women, younger women in pairs and threesomes, a few mother and daughter couplings. I walk south down Swanston Street and turn east along Collins Street looking for the end of the line. I pass St Michael's Church (where a large group of women had gathered to quietly farewell Dr Wainer thirty-two years earlier) before turning left up Russell Street. I'm halfway around the block when I text my friend Nici (the best read of all my friends, save for a professional book reviewer) to tell her I'm outside Westpac, at the end of the queue waiting to hear Helen Garner talk about *Yellow Notebook*, the first volume of her diaries. It's the opening event of the 2019 festival of feminist talks. Tickets sold out weeks ago.

Garner's first diary begins in 1978. It covers nine years of more and less ordinary days, of conversations she had, of things she saw and heard and felt, of thoughts and insights about love and family and friendships, the craft of writing and what success means. She writes, for instance, about walking her dog on a 42-degree night 'when a great wind swung around behind me, coming from the south-west. The temperature dropped ten degrees in seconds. Dust flew. I had to cover my eyes. The air stank of burning and was full of smoke, the small trees whipped about.'

As she walks, 'a huge sheet of paper rose vertical and danced there'. Through a window she spies 'a table set formally for a dinner party, white cloth and red candles, and a beautiful young woman with thick black hair, wearing a red dress, standing at the table talking to her husband who is a shoulder in a brown suit'. At first, I misread 'rose' as a colour, not a movement. I pictured a pink paper ascending in a dusty twilight. When Garner introduces red candles, a white tablecloth, a red dress and a brown shoulder, it's as if she is not so much writing as painting.

So much of Garner's writing, her watching and observing, involves walking. I don't think it is unrelated that there are shoes are everywhere in her books and essays. She frequently introduces characters by describing their shoes, like actors in a play walking on stage. In *Monkey Grip*, her first novel, someone is 'flying up the path on her high heels', someone else is 'wearing a brand-new pair of blue and white brogues: spiv shoes', another character 'plunged along in front of me in his stolen Paddy Pallins'. In another novel, she writes that a woman 'flung the pink quilt out to air over the windowsill and went into the city to buy herself a pair of shoes'. A different character's 'toes were so cold that they felt like rows of marbles inside her shoes.' In *Yellow Notebook*, Garner is crossing a road when she notices a girl whose outfit is finished off with 'red stockings, brown flat shoes, green gloves and a little red knapsack': she looks 'terrific' ('terrific' is a very Garner word. 'I think you're terrific', 'You've got to read this, it's terrific', characters say to each other in *Monkey Grip*).

One day, during a week I'm reading one of Garner's works, I pass a mini schnauzer running up the footpath outside my house. Behind the dog is a man at least six foot three, with a neat small head, shaved to a buzzcut, that juts out in front of his broad shoulders. His right arm is outstretched holding a lead. A fluffy cloud pulls him along. It's as if he has chosen his dog to say: 'Don't be afraid of me. I'm the kind of man who can barely control his mini schnauzer.' When you read Garner for long enough, the world can start to look like scenes from a world she has already written.

Garner's eye for luminous and illuminating observations is just one of the reasons she attracts rockstar-like crowds. Another reason, I think, is she way she tackles the chaos of life, the moments of shame and humiliation, the hurt that people inflict on us, and that we inflict on others. She writes about the daily wreckage we leave behind when we clash and crash with people we are meant to love. Husbands betraying wives, women hurting their friends, sisters betraying sisters. In her non-fiction work she's drawn to the way this ordinary daily damage can become great catastrophes and tragedies. A young woman who dispenses a cocktail of drugs to her boyfriend and then watches his life slip away, a father who inexplicably drives his small children into a dam one night, a mother who turns off the road with her own car full of children and steers into a lake.

Garner writes about all the large and little explosions of anger we want pull from ourselves and hurl into the world, teetering daily on the edge of going 'berserk' (another very Garner word). In one story (one of her true stories) she writes of a day she sees a schoolgirl taunting an older lady in the street. Garner seized the girl's ponytail and gave it 'a sharp downward yank. Her head snapped back. In a voice I didn't recognise I snarled, "Give it a rest, darling."' Her third and latest diary is full of people smashing and breaking things. In one climactic scene, in a rage over a great betrayal assembled through hundreds of little lies, she tips a box of her then husband's cigars into a pot of soup, then takes a pair of scissors and slashes a straw hat that belongs to his lover, stuffing the remnants in his 'big black ugly shoes'. In the middle of this kitchen sink carnage, she goes to her husband's study and finds the 'proof copy of his fucking novel'. 'I wrench the cap off his Mont Blanc fountain pen and stab the proof copy with the nib, gripping the pen in my fist like a dagger. I stab and stab, I press and screw and grind.'

The scene comes as a relief to the reader. In the previous dozens of pages, we watched on as Helen – the great observer, the noticer of the smallest details – carried on her days blind to what is staring her (and her reader) in the face. When I read it, it was as if she was finally re-enacting her 'glittering blade' scene, the one that gripped *Betty* audiences. But this time, the knife was finally out of its sheath:

> With men I feel like a very sharp, glittering blade that's only partly out of its sheath.
>
> It glitters and glitters.
>
> They don't see it, but I don't dare to show that blade, to come right out of the sheath, because I'm afraid of how fierce and joyful it will be to stab – and stab – and stab. So I don't show it, I hold it, somehow I hold it back, but it's there, glittering.

Helen's third diary is set in the mid-1990s, yet her domestic life eerily recalls the scene her good friend Micky played out twenty-five years earlier with her artist husband in London. Leaving the house to him and his art. Shrinking herself, making his large canvases appear more substantial, more significant. Here we are, back at the beginning, where men rule not only the public spaces but the private ones too. Helen's husband in her third diary, a novelist who regards literary fiction as the highest of the arts, spins endless fictional stories not just to her, but to his lover. You want to scream as Helen leaves the house each morning, ceding to his demands for total solitude during the day so he can work. You scream again when she returns home in the evenings from her own writing labours, with food and hours left in her day to cook for the both of them. Your jaw drops when he belittles her non-fiction writing as a lower-order craft, when he criticises her close relationship with her daughter, and when he dismisses her anxieties and makes light of her worries.

'What is a woman?' Helen had asked in 1972. 'You want me to mother you, you want to worship me and make a goddess of me but I disgust you ... You expect me to find meaning in my household tasks ... [but]

when I interrupt your recital of the day's woes or try to speak of my daily frustration or pleasure I must hear my work dismissed as trivia, and my concern for my children called an obsession.' As I read Helen's third diary, the moment she raged and slashed felt both right and righteous.

There are so many knives and blades and Garner's work. Some sinister, some seemingly innocent, like the knives she or someone else sets on tables for life-sustaining meals. In *Monkey Grip*, after a perfunctory encounter with her careless lover Javo, Nora grabs a bowie knife and fantasises about 'plunging it into the famous handsome picture of him in Cinema Papers'. She drops the knife and writes him a letter instead. In Helen's most recent diary, she recounts taking her latest book to her parents. Her father criticises her photo (it 'made me look old') and then takes his blade and turns the book on its cover to demonstrate how to sharpen a knife against a stone. Words and knives and men keep close company in Garner's writing. That's not to say that she doesn't like – and sometimes passionately love – men. 'I like men. I *just* like them,' she records in her *Yellow Notebook*, almost a decade after she told Kerry of her fondness for Vic: 'I liked him. I like men.' It's just that her like can sit on a knife edge.

Literary critic James Wood, in a 2016 essay, describes Garner as a 'savage self-scrutineer', one who 'relishes complicated feelings' and is 'unsparing, in equal measure, of her subject and of herself'. He's right, but there is nothing arid or unrelenting in her work. There's too much appreciation for someone's perfectly put-together outfit, for a piece of music at a concert, for a lemon harvest from a backyard tree. And her writing shows us a woman with a powerful awareness of her own longings and desires, and an almost equally strong will to fulfil them. When her third husband doesn't share her desire for holidays, she takes them anyway. On a solo trip to the coast, as she looks out to the sea, where boats and black-finned creatures tear rips in the water, she has a 'sudden wish to be wearing a soft and billowy skirt'. Twenty-six pages later she writes, 'I bought a diaphanous black skirt at a sale.'

Inside Melbourne Town Hall I look around at the Broadside crowd. There are so many women in their twenties and thirties. And more than a few teens. Feminists have never stopped working on the ground, inside nooks and crannies, and balancing on the last rungs of ladders that bump up against glass ceilings, but in 2019 feminism has returned as a mass movement, something to gather together for. Two years earlier millions had joined women's marches in cities across the world. Knitted pink hats popped bright against skies blue and grey, heavy hearts becoming somehow both lighter and fuller with each step. Later in 2017, the actress Alyssa Milano tweeted the grassroots activist Tarana Burke's #MeToo slogan, and millions more joined a movement that had gone online, and back offline again into workplaces and public spaces.

In Australia it felt as if the moment had been building for some years. A long weekend of talks at the Sydney Opera House had been attracting ever bigger audiences each year since its launch in 2013. By 2019, young feminist writers were everywhere: in daily newspapers, running literary journals, writing blogs and blockbuster books. Like a literary pyramid scheme, the growth of feminist readers and writers spawned its own boutique festival in 2016, the Melbourne-based Feminist Writers Festival. When #MeToo arrived on Twitter time (that is, in no time) the number of women writing and publishing feminist stories exploded. Tales of the small and bigger ways women navigate little aggressions and bigger assaults were everywhere. Like one worldwide, round-the-clock consciousness-raising exercise.

In 2016, I was wondering about how women telling their most personal stories seemed to be becoming an almost compulsory rite of passage for aspiring writers. Online magazines and feminist sites would pay as little as $50 – or offer payment in the form of 'exposure' – to women telling their stories of sadness and trauma. I had started noticing that stories of women's suffering seemed to be everywhere. In newspapers, in literary magazines and online. Men, as they long have, dominated reports about big issues and essays about big ideas (and, research shows, men not only dominate media jobs worldwide, but in news stories they dominate as experts, while women dominate as witnesses and victims). Women, on the other hand, had well and truly cornered the personal story market.

In the middle of this trend, I read about an artist announcing a performance piece where she would stage and film her own rape by a stranger. At the time, I was teaching young journalism students. I began thinking of the advice I might give to women in my class if I threw out all the usual instructions about the inverted pyramid, about news values and objectivity, about keeping themselves out of the story. If I was honest and said: 'You know what, there is this huge market for personal stories about your suffering.' But I also thought about how a personal story can come to define you. It can take you down career and creative cul-de-sacs. And continually writing about your own life can be both exhausting and exhaustive. It seemed to me that for women, the liberation of personal revelation was becoming a burden of compulsory disclosure. I hastily wrote an opinion piece for a daily newspaper, beginning with reference to a scene from the series *Girls*, where the main character, the writer Hannah, meets with her editor, who presses her to write about her most personal, shocking and titillating stories to make her book more compelling. 'Did your hymen grow back?' her editor complains after reading a draft of Hannah's too-tame exploits.

I talked about the rape art piece, our appetite as readers and audiences for stories about women's trauma, and the pressure on young writers and artists to constantly up the ante with their most personal, salacious or traumatic stories. I also – disastrously, it turned out – linked to a couple of pieces I'd read recently that seemed to demonstrate this trend. When the piece came out, many writers contacted me and tweeted to admit they recognised this self-revealing phenomenon with a kind of cringing recognition. One friend, a fiction author, told me she resented the expectation when she marketed her books that she should reveal her own personal stories. But within a day, one of the authors I had linked to read my piece and tweeted angrily about it. Within hours, it seemed, hundreds of people joined in to express their outrage, fury and indignation. For two days – but what seemed to me like a year – people on Twitter told me I was silencing women and shaming them, that I was a disgrace to feminism. I walked the streets shaken, wishing I could disappear between the pavement's cracks. I phoned a few trusted friends, a writer and a podcaster. Was I a terrible person? Was I really trying to shut other women up?

In the middle of all this I had a strange realisation. So *this* is how Helen Garner must have felt when she released *The First Stone* in 1995 – except that that in her case so many more voices were shouting in anger, and the raging went on for an *entire year*. People called her a traitor to feminism, acquaintances turned the other way in the street when they saw her. They condemned her not on a non-existent Twitter, but it columns, in letters, on the radio and in books. She was not cancelled – any more than I was being cancelled two decades later – but she was the target of an onslaught that was, to use the second-wave feminist terminology, a 'trashing'. Jo Freeman, who wrote the article, 'The Tyranny of Structurelessness', that resonated so much with Helen, wrote another article where she explained 'trashing' as criticism so extreme, personal and relentless, it set out not to engage someone in debate, but to destroy them. I don't want to go back and prosecute the story of the Ormond College case and Helen's book about it. So many words have been written already. But it's worth a brief detour back to those events. If only to understand where we all stand, or stood, and where we might stand alongside each other as generations, as feminists, today.

When I arrived back on campus early in January 1992, the university, still in summer break, was like a ghost town. As I moved with my two newly elected co-editors into the *Farrago* office to put together our first edition, rumours that the master of Ormond College had been sexually harassing multiple students soon arrived via one of my co-editors, a law student who knew one of the complainants. She wrote about their attempts to have the complaints dealt with at the college, and then by the university. We also heard stories about a famous author who was writing a book about the allegations and the students. Helen Garner, I was told, was going around the college 'banging on doors' and 'trying to dig up dirt'. She'd written a sympathetic letter to the master. I chose a side. The girls. In our first issue, and in issues afterwards, the university censored our stories about how the girls' attempts to be heard at Ormond and then at the university were being brushed off. We published instead an image of a woman with a gag over her mouth (not a million miles away from the gagged Yvonne on the *Betty* stage, I think now) over our censored stories.

When Helen's book about the saga was released three years later, features were published in the *Sydney Morning Herald* and *The Australian* with great fanfare, trumpeting the story as a tale about two warring generations. My own punishing, 'priggish and pitiless' generation, and Garner's, an older, humane one that could see complexity, that understood the power of younger women, the weakness and pathos in older men. Anne Summers, then editor of the *Good Weekend*, meanwhile, wondered where all the young feminists were. When I read Garner's story, I bristled – and then went a little bit berserk – when she described my co-editors and me as the 'puritan feminists' who were running *Farrago* in 1992. And I was disturbed that she had made the decision – on the advice of her publisher's lawyer – to split the character of one woman at the college who supported the two young complainants into multiple characters in the book, giving the impression of a feminist conspiracy.

When I reread *The First Stone* recently, I read a different book. I can certainly see how Helen was grappling with a generation that seemed foreign to her. One that seemed obsessed with rules and retribution. Now I see more ambiguity, and much less certainty, in her text than I remembered. The uncertainty and ambiguity was part of the reason the book got her into so much trouble. 'There's a phantom version of the book out there. People can pin on it anything they want,' Helen wrote in her diary when the book was released.

The First Stone seemed to divide people along lines not simply generational, but between those who loved her words and her relentless examination of the story and its characters, and those who believed art and nuance had no place in this story of institutional power and gender. But Garner's writing lets in multiple meanings; it's often full of doubt and it is certainly full of questions. She is frank and sometimes brutal in her opinions, but never hectoring; there's an opening-out to other views, other possible ways of seeing things that leave enough escape hatches that the reader is never in danger of feeling the claustrophobia of being locked in someone else's closed room. Political writing, meanwhile, sits on certainty, on singular meanings. And now, increasingly, on a focus on the self and the harms done to it.

In 1975 Helen was already thinking about the tension between art and politics when she spoke to Kerry about her experiences with the MWTG. She said she thought women with experience and talent 'have drifted away from feminist art, mainly from boredom at not being able to extend themselves'. She gives as an example the MWTG political shows with messages that start with a political position, one that says they must 'say X'. When they do this, 'they are cutting out subtleties of which they are capable, and which the audience is capable of picking up', Helen tells Kerry.

In the interview she goes on to describe her experience working at the Women's Liberation Centre. The centre was a large office accessed by climbing a steep set of stairs behind a purple door on Little La Trobe Street. It brought together loosely connected women's liberation groups from across Melbourne to plan campaigns, publish a newsletter and run a switchboard that operated as an advice and referral centre. Helen helped paint the centre and was a member of its coordination committee. But she found the kind of art she wanted to do – 'writing that is not merely journalism'– at odds with what she saw as an 'anti-intellectual strain' at the centre and with its politics. Helen tells Kerry she thinks 'the nature of the function of art is to go further than crude political action ... because I don't see things in simple enough terms to lead to direct political action'. Helen says that 'this position is seen as not committed enough (by the hard-line feminists) and in fact it is hard to explain what I mean without seeming counter revolutionary'.

In *Monkey Grip*, released two years after this interview, Garner's fictional surrogate Nora is working at the women's centre one day when she finds herself turning away from its politics in search of something more poetic. The book's narrator Nora describes how she is

> typing in the ugly bare room, copying an article about government attitudes towards the Halfway House, when music started in the dancing studio across the lane. It was Bette Midler singing *Do You Wanna Dance?*. The studio replays the song 'a dozen times or more, and as my fingers obediently typed my imagination went soaring off into those fantasies of violins and dim lights and perfumes and dresses and arms holding me, oh *yes!* I wanna dance!

Nora might be a feminist, but she's one who doesn't want the party line to stop her going to the party. In a later chapter, as Nora crawls on the floor letting down the hem on a housemate's pants, she tells him, in mock horror: 'If anyone from the women's centre saw me doing this ... my reputation would be shot to pieces'.

In her essay about *Monkey Grip*, a novel that emerged from the sexual and feminist revolutions of the 1970s, historian and gender studies academic Zora Simic writes that while Garner's book might have been the first nationally recognised novel of the Australian women's liberation movement, its place in the feminist canon is complicated. The novel's gritty realism – its portrait of drug-taking, improvised families and women's compromised sexual lives in a Melbourne community of musicians, painters and actors who inhabit inner-city music venues and theatres – was responsible for both the novel's success and its uneasy position as a women's liberation text. It was neither a polemic in the style of *The Female Eunuch*, nor an instruction manual for a women's liberationist lifestyle, like the movement journals *MeJane* and *Vashti's Voice* could be. *Monkey Grip* could be read as troublingly heterosexual, Simic writes, a novel that 'too easily let men off the hook'.

The women's movement might have shaped Helen – on the frontlines of abortion rights protests, at the consciousness-raising session and in the rehearsal room – but creative people aren't well suited to political organisations, she told Kerry: 'The best they can do is be revolutionary in their work, and not to service a revolutionary party or group. That is, they should think in a revolutionary way about the form of the art, as much as about the content.' Political action is driven by clarity, but as Garner already understood in 1975, art invariably relies on ambiguity, on reaching towards infinite possibility.

In *Monkey Grip* Garner created her revolutionary form: a story told from the point of view of a woman's consciousness, one that didn't conform to narrative conventions or political ideologies, and one that drew from life to make art. The novel follows a year in the life of single mother Nora, a woman who gives into, and intermittently tries to give up, her often debasing addiction to Javo, a junkie with 'eyes the colour of blue marbles' that burn in his face. (Javo's skin is always hot or sunburnt: there's a lot of heat in *Monkey Grip* – hot steps, hot bricks, hot concrete, hot mornings, rooms that are hot and full of dry air. Nora is constantly heading for the cool liquid of the pool, or towards the cold waves of the coast, as if seeking an antidote to the burns of her love addiction).

Garner fictionalised the countercultural world she and her friends inhabited in Carlton and inner-city Melbourne. Nora's lover Javo is based on a real-life actor who belonged to the Nightshift faction at the APG, a group that performed late-night shows in the Pram's back theatre. Inspired by radical politics and punk aesthetics, Nightshift members favoured heroin, and some occasionally dabbled in petty crime. As Helen did in real life, Nora takes a small part in an underground film about a group of heroin users. And Nora, like Helen, has a young daughter. Nora's Gracie dances and flits though the story, running with her brown, sand-encrusted limbs, in turn clingy and independent, tearful and light. In a politically progressive tribe that prides itself on being non-judgemental, Gracie gives her mother perhaps the most accepting and perceptive advice about how to handle her lover, whom she describes (with her perfect child's invention) as a 'drunkie'. 'Leave him alone,' Gracie tells Nora, noticing that her mother's efforts to talk to a pinned Javo just make him nervous.

The drama of *Monkey Grip* is straightforward,' writes the literary critic Merve Emre. 'Nora loves Javo, and Javo loves smack.' There's little in the way of plot or dramatic tension or resolution, days are baggy and events are lifelike. But behind 'a certain crookedness of form, a haziness of character, a bending back and forth of thought [is] a strangeness that startles us awake,' writes Emre, who compares Garner to Virginia Woolf. *Monkey Grip*'s great achievement, Emre perceptively notes, is the way it reports on a modern form of consciousness, of characters losing their self, becoming strangers to themselves again and again in drugs or in love, in intense consciousness and awareness of another. Sex can approximate an intermingling of consciousness – 'we fucked with a joy so intense and peaceful that our hearts were in our faces and we gave them to each other without a word', Nora narrates. Sometimes the sex is more prosaic, less about exchanging than taking: 'We came back into the house and lay on the bed, and fucked together, looking into each other's faces. And the next morning he stole the last five dollars from our food kitty.' Garner rarely sounds judgemental. She's too curious about how we crash through life without rationality, and how we have to 'cop it' when we fuck up.

Garner's suspension of judgement or equivocations about moral problems (like Nora's simple acceptance of Javo) is not unconnected to her rejection of aspects of feminist dogma, and to her insistence that an artist and intellectual has the right (even responsibility) to stand outside the movement. In one sense, then, there's a kind of irony that she is the one member of the *Betty Can Jump* collective who has her own entry in the encyclopedia of the Australian feminist movement (*Australian Feminism: A Companion*). Garner was not a voice of the women's liberation movement in the way that Anne Summers or Germaine Greer were. Her fame rests on her singular, often contrary, but always compelling literary voice.

While Garner was never beholden to feminist orthodoxies, she wrote for the feminist magazine *Vashti's Voice*, and an early anthology of women's poetry published by Kate Jennings, *Mother, I'm Rooted*. Meanwhile, the Whitlam government, thanks to lobbying from groups like WEL, introduced the Supporting Mother's Benefit, which gave her the time to write.

When she was sacked from her teaching job at Fitzroy High, after the Victorian Education Department traced back to her an anonymous article she had written in *The Digger* on answering a class of thirteen-year-olds' questions about sex, Helen tells me she considered other ways to support herself and her daughter: 'I thought maybe I could get a taxi licence and I could drive at night.' Alice would be safe at night with the other adults in her share house, she reasoned. She went to the training centre, with 'weird people sitting around trying to learn how to use the street directory and how to do change [for fares] and ... I only went about three times. It was kind of scary.' She was saved from night shifts when she met up with a friend who told her about the Supporting Mother's Benefit. The income enabled Garner to write during the daytime after dropping Alice off at school and peddling to the State Library. In the mid-1970s you would walk into the library, 'everything's quiet. Take your seat. And when you look up, it's 3 pm,' she tells me. (Now she doesn't think she could work there: 'It's fuckin' fun Central,' she tilts her head back and mocks being shocked. 'You know, everybody's planning their parties, they're laughing.')

In 1976, Hilary McPhee – the former head of the Marlowe Society who had programmed the festival of absurd theatre – was now the co-owner of a small independent publishing house with her friend Di Gribble. She recalls the day at their half-underground office in a laneway in East Melbourne when Helen 'arrived at the Jolimont Lane bunker to tell us rather diffidently that she thought she might have written a novel. Would we take a look?' The publishers read the manuscript overnight. McPhee writes that they found 'an original voice saying something that hadn't been said before under skies that were familiar from the opening lines: "In the old brown house on the corner, a mile from the middle of the city, we ate bacon for breakfast every morning of our lives."'

It is true that *Monkey Grip* was an original voice in fiction, but Garner was in a way writing on the page what the APG was performing on the stage. The APG's mission of telling Australian stories included stories drawn from their own community of young inner-city bohemians. In 1969, for example, the group staged a production of Romeril's *I Don't Know Who to Feel Sorry For*, a play Kerry performed in, playing opposite actor Peter Cummins as one half of an Australian counterculture couple living in a bedsit as their relationship falls apart. The audience was crammed into the small La Mama set and were seated as if they were visitors in the couple's home. As the actors moved, a direct look between the cast and audience members was 'inevitable', Graeme Blundell, the show's director, writes. 'On the nights it took off as a show, it was as if the audience members ... were inside the show as it unfolded.' I don't know if Helen saw the play (Alice was only a few weeks old when the play was performed), but she too was already writing about the life around her.

Claire remembers 'Helen was ... even at that time, all the time, she was always writing in her journal. She was always recording everything, watching and observing and reporting.' And her gift for crafting a compelling narrative was clear, as Kerry recalls in a memory of a community meeting she attended:

> There was some issue and people all stood up and spoke. After about twenty minutes, Helen stood up and she encapsulated everything that everybody had said so succinctly and then topped it with something which actually had a huge impact. She's got an amazing ability to do that, to gather all the threads together and put it into some sort of narrative.

But it was their Carlton consciousness-raising group, and Maggie Helmer's visit, that seemed to give Helen permission to say out loud things she had been thinking about her own life. 'It blew my mind to find that it was possible to set out things that had been on my mind for a long time, things about myself ... to find and act out single images of myself as a woman,' she told Kerry. And when she turned those thoughts into monologues and then performed them, noted Bernadette Brennan in her literary biography of Garner, the reactions of both women and men during performances of the show 'confirmed for Garner that women's interior experiences were valid and needed to be articulated'.

While Helen wrote some of *Betty Can Jump*'s most affecting scenes, as a show created by the collective through workshops, improvisation and research, no one individual was credited as a writer. I wondered, though, if Helen's later fame led to some of the collective to retrospectively cast her in their mind as the show's playwright – 'Helen wrote the script didn't she?' Evelyn asks me. She didn't write the script, but she took on a role that was akin to a dramaturge, according to Claire, someone who was 'able to take big ideas and reduce them to a human personal scale':

> We used to all go around saying all the time 'Of course, the personal is political' ... But if I were to tell a story about how I got up and did the dishes, it would be a recounting of an exceptionally dull moment, but she would invest it with the history of 'Why do women always do the dishes?' ... She had the ability to make it both profound and personal and meaningful.

Working with the women in the *Betty* collective and performing in the show was also a lesson for Helen in trusting herself and her abilities: 'Doing the play validated things,' she told Kerry in 1975. 'It was important to be able to work with other women, and to feel competent.' And she discovered just how much pleasure could be wrung from the process of writing something and seeing the reactions of other people to her words: 'I felt terribly pleased when people in the cast had liked the "women" speech, because it was the first time I had shown any non-discursive stuff to anyone.'

Kerry tell me that she believes the play, Garner's first experience writing for the public, was a formative experience for her: 'She got a lot of confidence out of it ... I think definitely it had a big impact on her life.' But Helen tells me she doesn't recall the time as one 'of fruitfulness'. She says she feels 'miscast' now 'in that role of being a voice that arose from a group. I don't feel comfortable about that.'

While *Monkey Grip* is not a play, I think you can trace connections between the novel and *Betty*. In *Monkey Grip* Garner shocked readers with her frankness about women's sexuality and bodies in scenes such as this description of a lover's bed: 'I was bleeding. I bled and bled, dark red flowers on his coarse sheets.' But these kinds of explicit descriptions can also be seen in *Betty Can Jump*, particularly the play's knowledge scene, where the cast talked about sex and packets of Supertampex and fucking, shocking audiences with its frank discussions of women's bodies. And the reaction of *Monkey Grip* readers mirrored that of *Betty Can Jump* audience members, argues Bernadette Brennan: audiences and readers, particularly women, were gripped by the same 'shock of recognition'.

When I asked Helen if I could interview her for this book, she told me she has avoided revisiting this period in her life, a time when her relationship with her parents was ruptured, her marriage was ending, she was struggling with single parenthood, and her teaching career was cut short. 'I don't look back very happily on that moment of my life and have resisted talking about it,' she wrote to me when I first made contact. But to her credit, she not only agreed to meet, but she responded to my many questions with patience and humour, and a candour regularly punctuated with profanities. At times she crossed her arms and legs as if to shield herself from more difficult memories; I felt guilty for asking her to think about a time she described as full of 'incredible smashing and breaking things'.

Helen tells me her memories of the play now are sketchy, but I wonder if it's possible that making *Betty*, spending nights and weekends talking with other women in the cast about their own lives in ways they hadn't talked about them before, finding connection with women throughout history and escaping into those roles on the stage, was a kind of saving grace for her. Her 1975 interview with Kerry suggests that time may not have been as relentlessly bleak as she remembers now. 'I look back on *BCJ* as an exciting time for lots of reasons,' Helen tells Kerry, 'one of them being that I fell hopelessly in love with one of the other women in the cast.' But while the collective experience might have been a kind of salve, being a member of a group was never going to be her natural home. The Pram Factory was an exciting place to visit, Carlton's open-all-hours carnival, but 'my character was not the personality type that was going to flourish well in that kind of milieu', she tells me.

She describes to Kerry going to a special meeting of the MWTG, and says she 'was horrified by the passivity of the women in the group': 'There was no attempt to push ideas, and there appeared to be no one who had done any preparation for the meeting in terms of strategy or tactics.' The desire women have 'to be part of a group or movement' seemed to hold women back from saying what they thought. They were 'embarrassed to articulate [their thoughts] for fear of offending,' she told Kerry. 'But there's not much point in doing a show merely to feel good; if you do a public thing – you must accept criticism.' Women are raised to seek approval and find it difficult to accept criticism, she adds, but 'there is no point in trying to be tactful either, because tact often destroys the point of what you want to say'.

Reading this interview, I thought about how, when you use your personal life to make plays or art or literature, it becomes, like any art or literature, something that opens itself up to the sphere of criticism. While the art may arise from the personal experience, criticism of the art – at least good criticism – isn't personal. But criticising young feminist writers and artists (as I did when I wrote that opinion piece) or in Helen's case criticising the art of the women's theatre group, can be taken (it's worth remembering) as a great personal harm.

What I find so interesting about this interview, conducted decades ago, was seeing the way Helen was already expressing the kind of critical approach to the women's movement – her desire to *talk* about things, to hash things out – that would, twenty years later, propel the narrative of *The First Stone*. 'It's not good enough any more to praise things just because they're done by women,' she tells Kerry. When I ask her about *The First Stone*, Helen is quick to acknowledge the huge blunder she made when she first read about the cases and wrote a sympathetic letter to the Ormond College master ('I'm writing to say how upset I am and how terribly sorry about what has happened to you ... if there was an incident, as alleged, this has been the most appallingly destructive, priggish and pitiless way of dealing with it'). 'I shot myself in the foot with that [letter],' she tells me. But she says, when she first started writing the book, she 'was just really curious. And I thought, "Oh, is this what's happening to feminism? ... I wonder what's going on, I'll see if I can find out."' But she hit a 'wall of hostility', particularly from a woman she knew at the college, an acquaintance who had supported the women to have their complaints dealt with within the college:

> everybody quickly withdrew and got behind the crenelations of their position. And there was nowhere to go for me after that. But in a way that was good, because it meant I had to interview hundreds of other people who had more tangential approaches to the whole thing. And I learnt a lot from writing that book. And I'm not sorry I wrote it. But I can see that it really enraged certain people. It's okay, nothing wrong with that.

The difficulty Helen ran into is that while the personal may be political, the women she was writing about understandably maintained the right to keep a space in their lives that was personal.

One morning, a few months after *The First Stone* had been released and the storm over the book was at its fiercest, I was at home in my share house in Sydney when the phone rang. The call was and remains one of the most unexpected of my life. It was Helen Garner, asking if I would meet her for a cup of tea. Over a table in a café at the Queen Victoria Building she asked me the question she asked so many others: why did the girls go to the police? I tried to explain, as best I could, but by then our positions were drawn and we were just colouring them in. Yet I couldn't help admiring Helen's commitment to the questions, to not ending the conversation even if she had finished her book. What if the *university* had listened to the girls? How would their lives have been different, I wonder? What if Garner's former friend at Ormond had said, 'Listen, let's talk,' rather than deciding she was beyond the pale? What if Helen had talked to us, the 'puritanical' editors? What if Anne Summers had listened to our voices before writing off a whole generation she seemed unwilling to see?

My instinct is for open discussion. But I also think we have to respect people who want to stay silent. At the end of the 1990s, I was in London and at an outdoor concert when I thought I glimpsed one of the Ormond girls in the crowd. Somewhere along the line I had heard she had left the country. I wanted to go up to her and ask her about her story, but some part of me, a part that respected her right not to talk about what she'd been through, stopped me. Women's voices are now easier to hear than ever, thanks to the generations before us, but we don't *have* to speak. I don't know if Jude Kuring has received messages I've tried to pass on, but she doesn't need to speak to me. Other women, whose stories fascinate, or fill us with horror, don't *have* to talk either.

When an audience member at Broadside asks Helen about her views on feminism, she responds: 'I couldn't say what my views of feminism are or were ... but if anyone said to me "Are you a feminist?" ... Well, what do you think? I'm an intelligent woman who has lived seventy-seven years in this world, of course I'm a feminist!' While she says she rejoiced, at the start of the #MeToo movement, at all the 'chickens coming home to roost', she can swing from being 'plunged back into that kind of rage you feel as a woman when you hear about what happens in this world ... and what people, some men do' to days when she feels at odds with the movement.

What attracts me about this position is not its certainty but its radical self-doubt and constant reassessment. There's no settling of scores. The $5 stolen by a lover is not the leading thought, it's the curious afterthought. There's an attempt to see things in perspective, to engage with another consciousness, with both sides. When *The First Stone* came out, academics Shane Rowlands and Margaret Henderson described Garner's role as both a feminist ethnographer and an ethnographer of feminism. They didn't necessarily mean it as a compliment but now I interpret it as meaning that she's a writer and feminist willing not only to examine herself, but to question feminist orthodoxies. Like Laura Kipnis, Katie Roiphe, Zadie Smith and Joan Didion. What these writers do, even as they risk the label of being 'bad feminists', is not weigh down women, or feminism for that matter, with the heavy load of being right and good all the time.

One of the things about writing diaries, the daily discipline of recording the small details that accrue each day, Helen tells her Broadside interviewer, author Sarah Krasnostein, is that when you go back to read them, it becomes impossible to believe in the stories you've told yourself, about how you were good and right and someone else wronged you. The way we rearrange the past in our heads to make ourselves 'less of a beast'. Reading her diaries, she realised with shock that there were times she had remembered being wronged when *she* had been the beastly one. When she writes, Helen is imagining herself – if not always perfectly – in other people's shoes.

In Garner's latest diary, as her third marriage disintegrates, she laments that there is some lack in her that makes her a failure at marriage. But I prefer to read it as a vindication of the 1970s ideal of the Pram communalism and the sisterhood's ideal of women's liberation. When she documents the disintegration of heterosexual marriages and failure of monogamy in her diaries, they don't read to me as proof of her own personal flaws, but rather as proof of a systemic flaw in the heterosexual nuclear set-up.

In her latest diary, Helen records how she pays close attention to X, a younger woman from an unnamed European country, with a manner that is feminine in a way she isn't. She watches with a fascinated awe as she opens gifts, and later tells her: 'I loved seeing you open the presents at your birthday party – it was almost like watching a little play.' Over course of the diary, we sense an almost an erotic charge between her and X, two women who could be friends. But X is, unbeknown to Helen, having an affair with Helen's husband, V. Her husband, almost as if he is terrified the two women might like each other *too much*, tells Helen X is not interested in her, and tells X that Helen dislikes her. It's as if he is in fear of the erotic potential leaking away from him, of women, together, and what they might say.

The desire to hash things out, a search for sisterhood despite our differences, is a characteristic of Garner's work. There can be a desire for connection and love, even when characters are rivals. Or completely different kinds of women. 'I dreamed about you and me becoming friends,' one character says to her lover's ex. Later, when we encounter these two women facing each other in another scene, one woman feels 'a throb of almost sexual tenderness' towards the other. 'With a force of will she kept the other woman's hand, studied with a peculiar flux of love her sun-wrinkled eyes, the marks of her shrewd expression. They could even smell each other.' By the end of this passage, the difference and distance between the women might still be there, but in that moment, it has dissolved.

Chapter 9
Betty today

In winter 2020, in between COVID lockdowns and what seems like hourly announcements of cancellations of live shows, a little window into the world outside my home in Sydney's inner west briefly opens up, and I set out for the three-minute walk to my local bowling club to see a show. Comedian Mandy Nolan and Irish folk singer Áine Tyrrell have travelled from Mullumbimby in northern NSW in a station wagon crammed with various people, and props that include Áine's guitar and amp and matching leopard-print jumpsuits. Mandy and Áine greet us at the door, where they take our tickets and hand us each a 'Country Witches Association Dismembership' [sic] card (I am member number 445). Like the play *Dimboola*, where the audience becomes a rural wedding reception party, Nolan and Tyrrell invite their audiences to take part in a general meeting of the Country Witches Association – the unauthorised bad sisters of the Country Women's Association. On stage, Mandy jokes about how men get all the best sex words, comparing the musical Latin syllables of 'fellatio' with the hard, clipped syllables of 'cunnilingus': 'What is *that*? It sounds like a throat infection.' Some of her best jokes are improvised. On a wall of club badges and memorabilia is a photo of Elvis, the King of rock'n'roll. It is mounted above a faded photo of Elizabeth II, Queen of the Commonwealth: 'Look!' Mandy points to the two pictures. 'If that's not white male privilege, I don't know what is.' When the show ends, Mandy and Áine unzip their pink leopard-print suits, whip off their bras, and invite the audience to unhook our own bras and swing them like lassos over our heads.

In 2018, after years when my visits to live shows were at best sporadic (small children! the costs!), I began a stint reviewing theatre for an arts website by night, while researching the women who had made film and theatre in the 1970s by day. As invitations to new plays began to fill my inbox, I started noticing how many of Sydney's stages were being given over to stories about women's lives. For one early review, I visited the Sydney Theatre Company's reprisal of Caryl Churchill's 1982 play *Top Girls* at the Sydney Opera House. The play opens at a dinner party hosted by shoulder-padded alpha executive Marlene (Helen Thompson) to celebrate her latest work promotion. The scene is a kind of fantasy dream sequence, with a tableaux of historical characters as Marlene's guests – a female Pope; Lady Nijo, a concubine to a Japanese emperor; the Victorian-era explorer Isabella Bird; and Dull Gret, a folkloric figure who led a female army into the underworld. In a series of revelations and non-sequiturs, the women talk to and over each other about the horrors of their lives: being raped as a child, being forced to give up children, always putting their husband's or employer's needs first. Like *Betty Can Jump*, Churchill's play searches for connections and patterns in the lives of women living in different eras. The script, almost four decades old, includes Lady Nijo's story about becoming pregnant to the emperor and being banished to the countryside. As I watched the performance, Deputy Prime Minister Barnaby Joyce's pregnant former staffer was fleeing the city and headlines that were threatening to derail the government. And at a time when the #MeToo movement was at its height, Gret's story about leading an avenging female army through hell to pay back the bastards who'd done them over felt like an allegory for our time.

A few months earlier, I had watched Emily Barclay, on another STC stage, perform Anna Barnes' one-woman show *Lethal Indifference*, a monologue based on Barnes' experiences working at a domestic violence centre. Directed by Jessica Arthur, the claustrophobic, menacing story takes place in a bedroom. The heavily pregnant and barefoot Barclay paced the room and fanned herself as she recounted the story of another woman, a recent immigrant to the country, who was imprisoned by her husband and hunted down when she tried to escape. And I saw writer, actor and director Nakkiah Lui's *Blackie*

Blackie Brown, a story starring Gamilaroi actor Megan Wilding as Dr Jacqueline Black (aka vigilante Blackie Blackie Brown). A cross between a Marvel comic hero and Hamlet, Blackie Blackie Brown held her great-great-grandmother's skull aloft as her disembodied ancestor's voice urged her to take vengeance on the 400 descendants of the four men who massacred her family. In April that year, I also saw Heather Mitchell play Catherine McGregor in *Still Point Turning*, Priscilla Jackman's dramatisation of McGregor's transition from a hypermasculine military officer and driven political adviser named Malcolm to transwoman Catherine, a sharp, witty writer and commentator on her two great loves: politics and cricket.

One of my favourite shows in 2018 was the Sydney Festival production *Wild Bore*, an anarchic show by comics Zoë Coombs Marr, Ursula Martinez and Adrienne Truscott that took aim at male critics who had patronised and misunderstood their work in reviews. *Wild Bore* used humour, surrealism and mockery – including a scene where Coombs Marr wore a giant plastic prosthetic nose. When another cast member dressed as Al Pacino stood on Coombs Marr's shoulders and draped her costume over Coombs Marr's face, the prop turned into a Pacino penis peeking out of his pants.

Even the overseas acts I saw performing in the 2018 festival featured stories about women and feminist themes. The Wooster Group from New York presented *The Town Hall Affair*, a re-enactment of the 1971 confrontation in New York's Town Hall between Norman Mailer and a panel of feminists, including Germaine Greer; Jacqueline Ceballos, New York president of the National Organization for Women; and Jill Johnston, a writer and dance critic with the *Village Voice*.

In 2021 theatres started to reopen after nearly two years of cancelled and interrupted performances. I sat in a small theatre at the Seymour Centre and watched Sheridan Harbridge's gripping performance as Tessa, a strutting criminal lawyer who becomes an anxious, self-doubting court witness to her own sexual assault in *Prima Facie*, playwright Suzie Miller's one-woman show staged by Griffin Theatre, a small company dedicated to staging new Australian shows.

Harbridge adopts multiple characters and moves through numerous timelines in the show, her ease-filled performance sitting in uneasy tension with her shift from a top barrister who saves men from gaol on a weekly basis, to a woman who grimly holds onto her sanity in a court system where her story is twisted and manipulated until it makes no sense.

I watched Elaine Crombie in the one-woman play *The Seven Stages of Grieving*, an update by Deborah Mailman and Wesley Enoch of their 1995 classic. The hour-long monologue delivered by Crombie is a personal and political rumination on seven phases of Indigenous history, from Dreaming through genocide to self-determination and reconciliation – something that won't be achieved until the names of those who die in custody, displayed on a two-storey-high screen behind her, stop multiplying.

And I finally had the chance to see Anita Hegh perform in Carissa Licciardello and Tom Wright's stage adaptation of Virginia Woolf's *A Room of One's Own*. The show reminded me how dazzlingly brilliant Woolf's mind and words were, although I wondered about the point of hearing them delivered, verbatim (albeit edited), on stage in a spare production. Hegh performed dressed in all black and mostly seated on a simple black chair on a black stage. Ella Prince intermittently appeared spotlit and mute in a glass box behind Hegh, wearing a changing series of costumes.

Months later, I read Woolf's book again, lying on a bed in a tiny cabin in a national park on the New South Wales south coast. Finally, the reason for the show seemed clear: to sit and listen to an uninterrupted woman for seventy-five minutes is still a revolutionary act. And there is no better argument – in both its form and its content – for the uninterrupted woman than Woolf's book. I followed her meanderings through Oxbridge lawns and libraries, along rivers where she imagines herself letting a fishing line down into the stream, and watching it:

> hither and thither among the reflections and the weeds, letting the water lift it and sink it, until – you know the little tug – the sudden

conglomeration of an idea at the end of one's line: and then the cautious hauling of it in, and the careful laying of it out? Alas, laid on the grass, how small, how insignificant this thought of mine looked.

By the river, free from the intrusions and obstacles men have placed in her path in the previous pages – chasing her off the lawns and barring her from libraries reserved for men – her thoughts are free, and she has one of the many small and larger epiphanies that fill her compact book. 'A good fisherman,' Woolf writes, puts such a fish 'back into the water so that it may grow fatter and be one day worth cooking and eating.' I read this passage inside a little room with fake-wood-veneered walls, between washing clothes, my daughter wandering in to ask the time, and checking my phone for a signal and messages from a friend I was driving to meet so we could rotate two children between us halfway through our holiday.

As I write now, I'm waiting to sit in darkened rooms to listen to more women tell stories uninterrupted. I'll soon see Glace Chase in the STC production *Triple X*, a play she wrote about a transwoman's love affair with an engaged Wall Street banker. I have a ticket to see Anchuli Felicia King's show *White Pearl* (again directed by Priscilla Jackman), a play that features six Asian Australian women in a story about Singapore-based Clearday Cosmetics and an ad for skin whitener that goes viral. And I'm excited that I will finally see Eryn Jean Norvill in the STC production of *The Picture of Dorian Gray*. I've been anticipating this production for two years – since my Twitter feed and arts pages first filled with praise of Norvill's performance as twenty-six characters from Oscar Wilde's story.

To see all the theatre being made by women in Australia right now would entail a commitment of time and energy few could sustain. But anyone who had seen *Betty Can Jump* in 1972 and somehow missed the intervening forty-five years of Australian performance culture could be forgiven for imagining the story of women in theatre since was one long final act of triumphant success. But the history of feminism has never been a simple story of steady progress.

The year 2009 represented a nadir of sorts for women in theatre. When director Neil Armfield with much fanfare announced his final season at Sydney's Belvoir St Theatre, he chose a series of shows almost entirely written and directed by men. The playwright Joanna Erskine wrote a blog about the alienation and disbelief she felt when she attended the season's launch and saw thirteen men lined up on stage, with just one woman, director Lee Lewis, at the end of the row. Ten years later, in 2019, arts writer Jane Howard traced the way the incident had led to an almost universal mea culpa from the industry over the following decade. It began in 2012 with a report commissioned by the Australia Council, Women in Theatre. The report's authors revealed that in each year since 2001 at the eight best-funded Australian theatre companies, women comprised as little as sixteen per cent of playwrights and fourteen per cent of directors. In 2009, women made up twenty-four per cent of playwrights and of directors. By 2019, Howard writes, things had turned around dramatically. Women made up forty-seven per cent of playwrights and fifty-eight per cent of directors. Not quite the domination of women on stage that my own admittedly selective theatregoing suggested, but you could at least call it parity.

Howard writes that the change was driven by interventions such as the Melbourne Theatre Company's Women in Theatre Program, which offered women not just professional development, but assistance with the costs of childcare. Where a decade earlier the most produced playwright in Australia was Shakespeare, Howard writes that in 2019 it was Nakkiah Lui. That year, Lui's plays *Black Is the New White* and *Blackie Blackie Brown* were being performed at the Malthouse, while the premiere of her latest play, *How to Rule the World*, was being staged around the country. But Howard also quotes *White Pearl* playwright Anchuli Felicia King, who moved to New York in 2014. As a student, King says she felt 'despair' watching so much of Australia's stage culture, including new plays, being imported from the US and from London rather than written by fellow Australian playwrights. Her vision is not so different from that of the Pram Factory actors, writers and directors, who imagined their task as creating a theatre culture that, while influenced by overseas trends, grew from Australian stories and Australian life.

Why does it matter whether actors tell women's stories on stage? Because, as trite as it sounds, seeing other worlds, imagining ourselves inside the costumes and under the skin of a character on the stage or on the screen, is one way we can imagine ourselves into a new world. Growing up in the postwar era, the daughter of a Methodist clergy family, my mother was taught the rules of life: 'no sex before marriage, no make-up, no dancing, no alcohol and always putting others first'. When she was six or seven years old and television was yet to arrive in Australia, she lived in a small country town east of Melbourne. She and her two brothers would run up to the main street behind their parents' backs. 'We would look through the cracks in the walls of the local theatre and see the films that were playing,' she remembers. Seeing characters on screen dancing and wearing make-up and kissing was a revelation to her. When she left home to train as a nurse, she walked from her nurses' dormitory in Prahran to the city to see Melbourne Theatre Company plays, and films at the city cinemas. 'I had very little money to pay for it so I would usually walk into the city and then back,' she tells me.

> I loved the staging. I loved the community spirit, the conversations and the buzz. And that was just so different to the life that I lived, you know, going to church and being prim and proper, and then you get the liveness of theatre, that was just so refreshing and exhilarating.

I grew up in a somnolent seaside town at the tip of the Mornington Peninsula, but when my mother's night shift schedule allowed, she would take my brother and me to live shows. When we moved to Melbourne, she took me to see a Melbourne Theatre Company production of *Top Girls*. That year, Madonna was on the television singing 'Like a Virgin', a Catholic girl in a white wedding dress writhing in palaces and on gondolas lusting after a man-lion in Venice, and I had a small role in a school production of *The Crucible*, a play about girls, victims of a sexually repressive, hypocritical society, who are imprisoned and sentenced to hang. As I sat in the audience watching *Top Girls*, witnessing a group of confident and strong women, led by a towering Pamela Rabe in a Pope's flowing red and white vestments,

I remember thinking of it as celebration of the girl power that was gathering strength and peaking in the 1990s. But *Top Girls*, I know now, is Caryl Churchill's trenchant critique of Thatcherism: individualism, the privatisation of state utilities and cuts to welfare benefits. Marlene's version of a top girl is really just Thatcherism and neoliberalism in feminism's name. She can't acknowledge that her success comes at the cost of other women, at the expense of a child she gives to her sister to raise.

Years later, when I saw the production of *Top Girls* in Sydney, the popularisation of Tarana Burke's grassroots #MeToo movement, driven by testimonies about Harvey Weinstein from women in the world of film, was having its own moment in Australia. The movement here similarly began to crack open first in the entertainment industries. Stories about celebrity television hosts groping and harassing women were followed by stories of inappropriate behaviour by actors from film and the stage. 'Who will be next?' we wondered, silently hoping it would not be *our* favourite star and then preparing for the worst.

I read and watched these women's stories as I was researching my PhD about the *Betty* women and the women who were making dozens of women's liberation films in Sydney during the same period. I was struck by the way that women in film and theatre were important parts of the resurgence of feminist movements both in the 1970s and then again nearly fifty years later. But while *Betty Can Jump* talked about sexual abuse by men throughout the history of white Australia, women at the Pram Factory didn't suffer from widespread sexual harassment themselves, at least according to Kerry. Sexual harassment 'was never an issue at the Pram Factory', she tells me. 'I often think about that, and I think "Was that because we were so terrifying?"' That's not to say women were not exploited in Australian theatre in the 1970s. Actress and filmmaker Jeni Thornley had been involved in the Monash University drama scene in the late 1960s before moving to Sydney and joining the Australian Arts Lab, an experimental theatre group in Paddington. She recalls feeling confused when she played a character called Miss Pink, and finding it 'odd being the only person in the cast who had to strip. Every rehearsal I had to strip to the waist.'

Kendall Feaver's new play *Wherever She Wanders*, staged by the Griffin Theatre Company in 2021, is set in a residential college at an elite Australian university, and is in many ways a theatrical update of *The First Stone*. The play opens during orientation week, where third-year student Nikki Faletau (Emily Havea) is campaigning to stop the festival of boozing and brutal induction ceremonies that take place to a soundtrack of college songs glorifying lecherous blokes. When Paige, a first-year student newly arrived from the country, wakes up one morning after a sexual encounter she barely remembers, Nikki seizes on her story to make Paige a poster girl for her campaign about consent. But what for Nikki is a clear-cut case of rape is, for Paige, a much murkier story involving two inebriated people. Was it rape or simply really bad sex? Feaver's script doesn't cast Nikki as an unimpeachable feminist heroine, and suggests Nikki might be projecting her own traumatising, unspeakable experiences onto Paige. When Nikki writes a viral article for *The Guardian* and turns Paige's story into the centrepiece of her social media campaign without Paige's consent, Feaver makes the provocative suggestion that Nikki may be harming Paige just as much – if not more – than the college boy with whose name Paige's will forever be linked whenever someone searches one of their names online.

I saw *Wherever She Wanders* while I was reading Diana Reid's 2021 book *Love and Virtue*, which features a similar plotline (except that the crusading student journalist who steals her friend's story makes it both her own story and unrecognisable to her erstwhile friend). Both stories pose challenging questions about feminism, women's agency and desire. But one of the things that dispirited me about Feaver's otherwise excellent play is the way it seemed to want to resurrect tired tropes about feminist generations in perpetual battle, one that requires the younger generation to commit symbolic matricide. Feaver's third main female character, Jo Mulligan (Fiona Press), the college's first ever female head, is grudgingly sympathetic to Nikki's petitions, but ultimately exasperated by Nikki's complaints about every little microaggression, and by her apparent passivity in looking for an all-protective saviour mother figure. A former activist who led Reclaim the Night Marches when she was younger, Jo has ascended to head of the college, but she only manages to stay there by adopting a 'boys will be boys' nonchalance. When Nikki *does* take matters into her own hands and writes an exposé of college life, Jo becomes as much her target as the culpable boys.

Feaver's play suggests depressingly that an older woman rising to the top of the pile has to come at the expense of her having any real feeling for young women with less power. Meanwhile, a young feminist firebrand can only make her name if the woman who paved the road for her is disgraced and loses *her* job. Feaver's otherwise complex play, in other words, implies that feminist history is a generational battle that can only have one winner.

We can't simply close our eyes and ears to generational differences, but talking across and over each other – like the women who assemble for Marlene's dinner party – doesn't take us very far either. The *Betty Can Jump* women used stories and conversations from real life to jolt audiences into action with a shock of recognition, to make them laugh and cry. Women making theatre today have picked up the sock and buskin masks to make shows with some of the same rebellious spirit that informed *Betty Can Jump*. Their stories can make us cry. And then a performer like Mandy Nolan, reflecting on the horrific tally of women dying at the hands of partners and ex partners, uses absurd humour and makes us laugh. All we need is a random lottery that selects one man a day for a knock on his door from a committee authorised to take their dick away in a bucket, and the problem will be solved, she suggests. 'I reckon it'll take two weeks, tops.'

Afterword

'What do you make of us? Do we seem like we were all a bit mad?'

As we leave her office and walk down the stairs at the end of our interview, Helen Garner wants to know what I think of the crowd of artists, activists, writers and performers she was knocking around with in the 1970s.

'I have to fight against romanticising those years,' I say as we pause outside the sprawling Victorian-era market building where she works to take a photo I'd promised a friend in my book group.

It's easy to project myself, like one of those historical episodes of *Doctor Who*, into that world. I can imagine I am friends with Yvonne and rolling a joint under a tree at the Carlton Gardens while watching a rehearsal for a moratorium march sketch. Being fascinated – and a little awed – by Helen's direct conversation and noticing gaze. Having flings with one of the show-off performers, like the bookseller and political idealist Jon Hawkes.

'Oh no, don't romanticise it,' says Helen. She looks horrified.

'A part of me really wishes I had been there. We lived at the tail end of the world you all created. We could still rent a room in a share house next to the university for $50 a week, live on Austudy and have enough left over to buy a beer when we went to see a friend's band.'

'Before everything changed,' Helen nods. 'Are there still share houses?'

'Not in the same way, I don't think. You now need three part-time jobs to get by.'

As I walk away, a young woman with wavy shoulder-length brown hair, wearing a floral dress and black stockings, sails by on a red bike. She could be a latter-day Nora, crisscrossing the wide streets of the inner city between the North Melbourne market, her Brunswick home and the Fitzroy Swimming Pool. In *Monkey Grip*, Helen describes Nora's tyres pumped up so hard they 'whirred on the glossy bitumen'. In these moments, flying on her bike, Nora seems *free*.

It's not good history to romanticise any era. But I keep finding myself thinking there *is* something indelibly romantic about the world Helen and her tribe inhabited in Melbourne in the early 1970s. I know this is, in part, because of the way the novels and histories and documentaries about this period have helped foster a mythology about the time and place. A world where you could go from watching a strange surrealist show of tumbling acrobats, singing and slapstick at the Pram Factory, to a game of pool at Johnny's Green Room with friends, before seducing a new lover at the Albion and having breakfast with an old lover at Tamani's. More than once Kerry uses the word 'vortex' to describe the world where they lived, worked and played, bounded by Rathdowne, Lygon, Elgin and Faraday streets.

'The thing about the Factory was it had a big energy,' Helen says. 'You would come home just sore from laughing ... Everyone wanted to be a part of it.' I am rapt with attention when she tells me how, whenever she felt like a chat, she could visit someone in the Tower while Alice played with other children on the outdoor terrace. Then I listen to the Skyhooks song 'Carlton (Lygon Street Limbo)', and I'm reminded of the darker side of their world, and how the life force and the death force are entangled in all of us. Shirley Strachan sings about a night, after 'the sun sets over Carlton', when 'stars begin to shine'. The stars he sees are in the sky, but they are also the 'grey-haired writers and drunken fighters' and the 'night-time junkies and long-haired monkeys'. The Pram Factory lasted for eleven years. The factions became more fractious, the audience dwindled – or it spread too thin over too many shows – and the wheels stopped turning. In 1980 the building's owners put the place up for sale, and when the group entered voluntary liquidation and administrators sold off assets to pay creditors, someone (perhaps desperate for a final fix) nicked the lighting system. John Romeril, who a decade earlier had conjured up a character called Life emerging from a coffin, dressed as Death at the auction and stood in another coffin while the suits auctioned the building. He remembers: 'The light on the hill hadn't just gone out – it had been pinched.'

Cultural studies people talk about 'conjunctions', the way certain things can happen at particular times and places. *Marvellous Melbourne*, the Pram Factory's first play, was about a city transforming in the 1880s. The population was booming, the first telephone exchange opened, and the Melbourne International Exhibition saw arts and crafts and new inventions from industry and agriculture sent from around the world and displayed at the newly opened Royal Exhibition Building. The city was a goldrush-sprinkled cocktail of culture, technology and politics. Almost a century later, a generation of writers, playwrights, performers, filmmakers and artists who came out of the rapidly expanding universities of the 1960s helped forge another transformative age. Thanks to a new and flush-with-cash Australia Council, cheap inner-city rents, and the political and cultural experiments flowing in from overseas, by the end of the 1970s, a different kind of Australian culture had emerged.

Leaving Helen's office, I keep walking, past the grounds of University High School, where my mother spent a year before her country parents, the Methodist minister and his wife, decided they couldn't afford the board for her to live in the city. I think she still regrets not having that opportunity, but during that year she spent in the city she received another kind of education, when she witnessed a backyard abortion. She went on to train at Alfred Hospital, topping her year in midwifery. She was assisting in surgeries where doctors gave women unsanctioned abortions at the same time Helen was offering women who came off the plane from New Zealand a cup of tea and someone to lean on. I text my mother to say that Helen was delighted at the gift of champagne and homemade chutney my mother and her partner had insisted I take for her.

I drop my bags at my room above Naughtons on Royal Parade. It's now a slick hotel and restaurant, but at the end of the 1980s it was a student haunt, and one of the first pubs I drank in when I was seventeen and ordered too many drinks there during Orientation Week. In the early evening, I walk through the University of Melbourne's main campus to meet friends for dinner. The grounds seems greener and lusher and even more beautiful than I remember. I pass three students sitting in a garden of ferns, cycads, conifers and cactuses that looks like a scene from a university in a future utopia. I supress the instinct to stop and ask where they've been, what they're doing and where they are going (and the thing I really want to say – I went here *too*).

I want to walk through Union House, a building a friend has told me would soon be knocked down to make way for new student housing. It will be replaced by a new student union building on Swanston Street, in the middle of a campus that has grown and taken over whole city blocks. Although I haven't set foot on campus for more than twenty-five years, I work my way through the maze of more than a century's worth of construction and find the building easily. Inside it hasn't changed nearly as much as I had expected. The ground-floor dining area – where I worked for two years picking up dirty plates and stacking a giant dishwasher (and dodged heckles led by an oafish private school boy I knew from my daily high school bus trip) is smaller, but still recognisable. A function room where I served beers while bands played is locked, but hanging on one wall I can see a giant handmade sign that reads 'Consent is Sexy!' Like one of those oversized office cards that people circulate when someone leaves, it is filled with autographs – the promises to keep in touch have been replaced (I imagine, the writing was too small) with pledges from signees promising to touch only when given permission.

The food co-op on the first floor, with its clear glass jars of rice, lentils and dates, hasn't moved. Neither has the union's theatre department offices. It is late on a Friday and the building is mostly empty. Outside the theatre office, three or four students wearing black are talking in voices that project across the large landing: 'I'll see you there in an hour!', 'See ya!' As they walk off, I notice they've left behind a rack of oddly matched clothes, a sequined frock and a few flimsy items hanging like the rejects from the last low-budget play. Next door, a set of arts and culture department offices has evicted the old *Farrago* office, where I spent almost as many hours as I did at lectures, laying out pages while looking out large plate-glass windows to see who was coming into the building from the union lawn.

Like the *Betty* women, who learnt how to put a show together by locking men out, I learnt how to edit a magazine when the *Judy's Punch* collective shut men out of the *Farrago* office for a month during the mid-year break to put together the annual women's magazine. Collective action is how we make change, but it also changes us. Working with other women in the *Betty* collective, Helen told Kerry, validated her and helped her 'feel competent' in the male world of the Pram Factory. But in the end, as much as the collective experience opened up a world for her, she found working with others had its limits. 'I don't function well in groups,' Helen tells me.

In 1975, Helen was already thinking about the tension between the individual and others and creative work. I think my own fascination with collectives perhaps stems from the fact that I am also not very good at them. I still blush when I think of the argument I had with one of my co-editors at *Farrago* that was so loud the drama department next door could hear every word (they later told me). I was mortified that she had signed off an article she wrote defending a protest that stopped a visiting politician from speaking by using the by-line 'Editors'. Freedom of speech, having a voice, I was learning, was a messy, difficult idea.

Upstairs, I look for the Women's Room and find it is now named the Queer Space. Through the window I can see someone has set up the couch with a pillow and sheets. I walk past other new rooms and spaces. There's one for students with disabilities, signs for Islamic prayer rooms for men and for women, a department for Indigenous students, and leaflets scattered about the building promoting trans awareness. On the top floor, I walk past the rooms where the various religious groups had their offices when I was at university: the Islamic Students Society and the ecumenical chaplain. The latter office was occupied by a man I knew as a solid, short and gentle presence, the sort of man who could easily play a lesser cabinet minister in a Keating government. When the Dalai Lama came to visit Australia, I visited the chaplain to ask him to contribute to a special issue of the student paper on religion and revolution, philosophy and politics. When I sat down in his office, he must have seen I was in search of counsel as much as copy. 'Are you here as an editor, or are you here for yourself,' he asked kindly. I couldn't believe in dogma or the Christian faith I had been brought up with – the revolution of the 1970s had made sure of that – but I was floundering in some ways to find solid ground. (He ended up writing a piece in defence of the radical agnostic, someone who has opened doors and windows to allow 'stale air to be drawn off' and replaced with something fresh, but never settling on certainty.)

As I leave the union building, I try the doors to the Union Theatre where, in 1989, students performed a twentieth-anniversary production of the musical *Hair*. The director recruited me to design the cast's costumes; I turned over op shops for 1960s clothes and I tie-dyed flared jumpsuits, sewed fringes on jeans, and made velvet and silk vests. At the start of rehearsals many of the cast wore polo necks and neat jeans and summer frocks, but their method-acting approach meant their own clothes became looser and hippier as the weeks went on, until rehearsals began with group hugs. The fact that we were performing *Hair* in 1989 (and still listening to Jim Morrison and Joni Mitchell, as well as the Pixies and the Pet Shop Boys), is a sign of just how in thrall some of us were to the generation before us. I remember other student theatre too: an experimental show in the university's underground carpark adapted from Dostoyevsky; and an all-woman production of *Hamlet* in 1989 upstairs in the Union Building's rehearsal room, with a cast that included a young actor called Cate Blanchett.

It was all interesting and exciting, but I'm sure it didn't have the same culture-shifting impact of the writers and performers who emerged from the universities in the 1960s to form the Australian Performing Group. By the early 1990s, some of the most interesting live theatre was coming from the Ilbijerri Theatre Company, performed in small spaces off campus (which, in my first freelance job, the *Melbourne Times* sent me to report on).

The next morning, I meet an old friend for breakfast. When I was eighteen and he was a few years older, I moved into the Swanston Street terrace he and his friends were moving out of to start my own share house, one that became home to a changing mix of actors, artists and a heroin-addicted law student. Though my friend and I never lived in the same house, we followed each other between rentals in Carlton and Collingwood and Fitzroy, wheeling fridges handed down from parents between households, leaving the seagrass matting on the floor and the Blu Tack stains we couldn't always scrub from the walls. Now, I think, we are part of the reason why inner-city housing is increasingly scarce and unaffordable – so many of us who lived in share houses while we were students over the last five decades decided we liked it so much we never left. A week later, Helen replies to my email asking if I've correctly remembered our conversation outside her office. 'All this is reminding me of a dream I found in the old diary I've just finished editing,' she replies. She dreamt she was at a 'retro 70s event' in Carlton. 'I ran into a woman I used to share a house with back then, when we were single mothers. We shrugged at the retro show. "Not like the real thing, is it?" she said, and walked away. A younger woman sat down beside me and said with an intense, challenging curiosity, "What's not the same? What's different?" I sighed, weary at the thought of having to talk about it, and said, "The households. The households are gone."'

My friend, a writer, prefers to eat at places that are older than he is, and we order coffee and eggs at the Lygon Street café that Helen used as a setting for many of Nora and Javo's breakfast meetings and chance encounters. My friend wants to know how my interview with Helen went. The conversation is still swirling around in my head. We'd talked about what seemed like an eternally unsolvable problem between men and women. The Coalition government has been staggering through weeks of almost daily allegations of sexual abuse and scandals at Parliament House. Some of the men now in the headlines were our political opponents when we were university students. Women are furious.

My own fury has been all too personal. 'Got the rags on, have you?' a character taunted in *Betty*'s knowledge scene. Half a century later, at my ten-year-old's primary school, a group of boys have been harassing girls with 'jokes' about rape, comments about their bodies, taunts about being 'on their periods' and going to 'the LGBTBBQ'. A deputy principal is sympathetic and concerned and makes all the right noises, but keeps emphasising that 'we had no idea this was going on', and seems to imply the fault is with the girls: 'They need to speak up and tell us every time something like this happens.'

I'd driven from Sydney to Canberra with two friends for the March4Justice, a nationwide protest of women mobilised by anger at a new wave of sexual assault stories that began when Brittany Higgins, a former staffer in the Coalition government, alleged she had been raped in a minister's office. To get to the rally, we walked past the lawns of Old Parliament House, where the activist and actor Gary Foley had helped set up the Aboriginal Tent Embassy in 1972, later calling it a kind of 'theatrical performance' (Foley would also later work on shows with Pram Factory members).

In 1975, 800 women took over (Old) Parliament House for a Women and Politics conference that turned into another piece of political theatre. Told by the invitation from government to wear 'formal dress', many participants turned up in men's suits and bow ties, women wrote 'Lesbians are lovely' on the Parliament House toilet mirrors, and draped underwear over statues.

Nearly half a century later, the mood at March4Justice is sombre – most protestors are following the organisers' black-clothes dress code. As we stop to take selfies, a woman walking past us up the hill is dressed as a suffragette and is holding a sign: 'I can't believe I'm still protesting this shit.' Higgins fronts the crowd with a brave speech. Scott Morrison and Marise Payne, the Minister for Women, refuse to leave the building. Later that day Morrison tells parliament that we protestors are fortunate to live in a country where police won't shoot us for demonstrating, as if, in a country settled at gunpoint, he could measure his response by the lowest of bars.

The second-wave feminist Biff Ward and Whitlam's women's adviser Elizabeth Reid are in the crowd. Julia Zemiro, the television host and actor who was a regular performer at La Mama in the 1990s, is MC, introducing speakers including Wakka Wakka/Wulli Wulli woman Dr Tjanara Goreng Goreng and ANU student president Madhumitha Janagaraja.

Helen had told me her first instinct on hearing the stories coming out of Canberra was: 'Those guys should be strung up by the heels like Mussolini or something ... I mean, just some frightful punishment should be visited upon them.' She added:

> I also think that we're in a fallen world. It doesn't matter what we think people *should* do, they're never going to do it. Some things might change, but there's stuff about men and sex and women that are just not amenable to social control, and never will be.

'That's what I believe,' my friend says when I summarise the gist of this conversation. 'I know,' I sigh. I want to resist their notion that, as fallen beings, the problems between men and women of sex and power are intractable. But lately I've been feeling more despair than hope. Commentators keep calling this latest moment an unprecedented 'reckoning', but I had been wondering if there was anything truly different about it. Women have been speaking out about these things for a long time. In the 1970s, women started Reclaim the Night marches, they opened rape crisis centres, and they campaigned to overturn laws that allowed husbands to rape wives with impunity. *Betty Can Jump* had told stories about women's abuse and rape. Its opening scene depicted Australia as a colonised country where violence against women was government-sanctioned from the day officers raped convict women the moment they tumbled onto the shore.

My friend and I discuss the most recent scandal – leaked pictures showing a liberal staffer masturbating over a female MP's desk. In the confused and confusing first reporting, it seemed that he might have been motivated by revenge against MPs who didn't support the marriage equality vote. 'In the 1970s he would have been seen as a hero,' I joke to my friend.

More details about the office pleasure seeker, I learnt later, muddied the story, with suggestions of revenge porn and misogyny and a strange cast of characters. But it did make me think about one of the great schisms between second-wave feminism and contemporary feminism: while both generations have loudly railed against rape and male violence, many second-wave feminists also had great faith in the liberating powers of sex. Throwing off sexual repression, along with the idea that sex had to be contained within heterosexual marriage, was a key tenet of the counterculture and the New Left in the 1960s. The movement was strongly influenced by thinkers such as the German Jewish philosopher Herbert Marcuse. Inspired by both Freud and Marx, Marcuse had argued that an authoritarian capitalist society depended on the repression of our instincts for erotic pleasure and sex, while our energies and desires are redirected into overwork and overconsumption. The anti-war movement embraced this idea with the slogan 'Make love, not war'. The group gropes at La Mama, the Pram plays where cast members did cartwheels in the nude, and the sexual permissiveness at the Tower and the share houses of Carlton, were inseparable from the idea that sex, politics and art were interlinked.

Australians were at the forefront of this movement. Germaine Greer, influenced by libertarian ideas she'd encountered when she moved to Sydney and joined a group known as the Sydney Push, championed a revolution led by women's orgasms. Dennis Altman argued for a polymorphous sexuality that would queer and break down heterosexual and monogamous institutions (a radical position that, in part, accounts for his long ambivalence about, and his belated endorsement of, the marriage equality movement). Their arguments about the transformative potential of sexual freedom were seductive, but they were also fatally flawed. When Greer posed nude for the underground magazine *Suck*, legs above her shoulders to allow the best view of her pubic hair and vulva, she was betrayed by her male colleagues on the editorial board, who failed to live up to an agreement to pose nude themselves.

The idea that sex might dismantle the entire capitalist–military system was, before long, replaced by a more sobering realisation that capitalism – from Playboy clubs to almost every ad campaign ever made – was an expert system for coopting and commodifying sex. And the New Left notion that libidinous sexual drives might undermine the deadening, alienating workplace was soon discredited by the evidence that powerful men, again and again, would use their positions at work to harass or force women into unconsenting sex. (When Hugh Hefner died and eulogies credited him with single-handedly kickstarting the sexual revolution against a puritanical feminism and a repressed 1950s culture, it was staggering how the role of feminists in liberating women sexually was not just written out but reversed. Meanwhile, Hefner's crushingly long list of rules for Playboy bunnies – from the height of their heels to the size of their waist measurements – were glossed over in the rush to call him the great liberator. Yet he hired detectives to follow bunnies after work, enforced rules about who they could and could not have relationships with, and charged them for costume repairs. His vision of sexual liberation was for men only).

Helen was part of this movement, formed first by libertarian ideas, then by the sexual revolution and women's liberation. But she also believes that relations between men and women might forever be shot through with a shadow side that is ancient and intractable and eternally bleak. 'You can't go through any sort of psychoanalysis without accepting that people have got these drives inside them that are so deep and dark. It's a wonder the landscape is not strewn with corpses, because everyone's filled with rage and grief,' she tells me. 'But it's not a very popular view,' she adds. 'It comes in handy to have had some kind of religious background – you understand the idea of a fallen world.'

It's her religious background that has left a chasm between the way she sees things and the way her daughter does, Helen adds. 'There are certain concepts that I've got that she either doesn't have or resists.' Helen tells me of a conversation she'd had with her daughter that morning, when she told her about a discussion she had just had in the tearoom at the Castlemaine Writers Festival with four other women. 'They were all women of mature years, and we got talking about all the scandals that are happening in Canberra and elsewhere and ... they were sort of rather more nervously saying ... that drinking makes people very vulnerable.' She told the tearoom group, '"Women shouldn't drink until they are helpless, they just shouldn't," and everyone agreed, "No! They shouldn't. They really shouldn't. It's crazy."' The discussion had left them 'feeling quite ... pleased with ourselves for having agreed on something', Helen says.

When Helen told her daughter this story, she retorted: 'Men are the ones that have got to change ... why are women not allowed to get drunk?'

'But we live in a fallen world,' Helen replied.

This difference of experience, of generational perspectives, is a chasm of understanding, one that might become smaller, or at least different, over time, but one that is not likely to ever close entirely. It's not the kind of rupture Helen experienced with *her* parents, but it's a gap that takes good faith and good intentions to bridge.

When I began writing this book, I told an academic, a woman from my generation whom I admire immensely, that I envisaged it as a kind of bridge-building between feminist generations. 'That's a really admirable intent, but I'll never forgive her for *The First Stone*,' she told me.

I understand her position, but in this case I'm no good at maintaining rage. The notion that we are all fallen has its flip side in another religious idea, the notion of forgiveness. I don't find it easy to live with anger, and I think I forgave Helen a long time ago. But, more importantly, I hope – if she ever remembers – she forgives me for leafleting a talk she gave when she published *The First Stone*, asking her audience to listen to us, not her. Perhaps that is one reason why I recoiled so strongly when I read that a fight had recently broken out about who is allowed to speak. In the middle is a bookshop that opened in Carlton the year the APG was moving from La Mama to the Pram Factory. One side seems not to want to listen to a (mostly younger generation's) experiences about gender, sex and identity, and ideas that my children take for granted about their friends' rights for their bodies to be transformed, in reality or symbolically, so they can be the person they are. Another side seems to want to silence the voices of an older generation – a generation who fought against the oppression embedded in pregnancy, unsafe abortion and being female-bodied. The demands that the bookshop apologise for having hosted an older feminist writer two years earlier, and then the threats of boycotts from other women when the bookshop made the apology, make me despair. As does the idea that there can only be only good people, and good intentions, on one or the other side.

My breakfast date likes to talk about how the 1960s and 1970s were an unprecedented moment when our culture shifted from a 'closed' to an 'open' one. Michelle Arrow in *The Seventies*, describes the extraordinary speed at which, over just a few short years, social attitudes about issues such as women working outside the home, sex outside marriage, and homosexuality, radically shifted. It was a social revolution that was long overdue, but it was not embraced by everyone. And it came with costs. After we talk, Helen emails to say that revisiting this time had left her 'saddened and churned up … I can hardly think about those years without a sort of angst. I had a heavy heart for days.' (Walking towards the difficult thing is what she does, I thought when I read her email.)

There was excitement and joy in creating something new. But there was also the murderous toll of the Vietnam War, women's lives lost in an illegal abortion industry, and families fractured, sometimes irreversibly, by cultural shifts. At the Pram, behind the ideals of tolerance and experimentation, behind the jokes about someone drilling holes in all the teaspoons to thwart the heroin users, was a darker tale of talents that were wasted.

What I feel a kind of nostalgia for is a past when there was so much hope for a much better future. One where a war could be ended by masses marching, where gender did not stop anyone from being the person they could be, where children could be brought up by all the adults in a community, and where work, play and politics were indistinguishable.

After breakfast I walk with my friend out into the bright blue autumn light. We take a detour to see La Mama, now behind a temporary fence while it is rebuilt after a fire burned down the building in 2018. The fireplace Betty Burstall stoked while she nurtured performers will be rebuilt too. Shakahari, the restaurant that opened in 1972, and where Vic Marsh worked part-time as a waiter and started a journey into Eastern mysticism and coming out as a gay man, is now next door. Other places are no more. The original Johnny's Green Room, where the APG name was dreamt up over a pool game, is gone, as is the Albion – now transformed beyond recognition into a women's clothing store.

The site where the Pram Factory once stood is unrecognisable too. It now has a ghost life in the memories of those who were there, in their production diaries, the articles they wrote and the interviews and stories they have saved in the archives. And it has had afterlives in Laurel's work with Circus Oz, in Micky's photos, in Evelyn's work with the Kadimah Theatre, in Helen's books, and in the countless women's shows that followed in the years after Kerry first had the idea for a women's play.

I thought about the legacy of other women: the doctor couple who helped promote my mother's family planning talks had a daughter who became a GP specialising in women's health. In one of life's strange coincidences, she has moved to Sydney and was on duty the day I visited my local practice while writing this book. I spoke to her about a problem that, like the *Betty* knowledge scene that was played out in the dark, women still don't talk enough about. I thought about my own family, and how it had been upended by the women's and sexual and cultural revolutions that were beginning when I was born, splintering and reforming into its own barely recognisable shapes by the time I reached adulthood. The ground shifted, and we learnt how exhilarating, but also how tiring, it could be to live in a world that changes and then changes again at ever faster speeds.

When I researched her papers at the Mitchell Library in Sydney, Kerry told me she'd put them away hoping that 'someone like you would come along'. Making *Betty Can Jump* 'just sort of sits there in my mind as this kind of light bulb', she tells me. 'It's like a flash of light shining on everything that happened afterwards. And it was like a culmination of years of frustration and inarticulacy, and then suddenly being able to express things that were not expressible before.' When I think of Kerry I imagine her still-straight back, her dancer's and yoga devotee's posture. But I also think of circles. The consciousness-raising circle, and the three nested circles in Micky's poster design for *Betty*. A small circle pulsating out towards two bigger ones that suggests to me the way that ideas and political movements were spreading at in the 1970s. Like soundwaves radiating out. And a circle has no beginning or end: you can travel in any direction, there's no obvious forwards or backward. That seems to me to a good representation of both the non-hierarchical ideals (if not always the practice) of women's liberation, and the notion that feminist history can go in circles, each generation facing the same issues, albeit in different ways.

When we think of 'revolution' in history we usually think of a sudden and ground-shifting event. But a 'revolution' is also a movement around a circle, something we have to keep repeating. Kathie Sarachild, the woman credited as coming up with the term 'consciousness raising', was also credited with coining the phrase 'Sisterhood is powerful', one that was a popular slogan on banners and badges, on T-shirts and in the headlines of women's newspapers. There are good reasons why this phrase has dropped out of use: the notion of sisterhood can be a homogenising term that can make the many differences between women invisible. There were Indigenous women in the second-wave feminist movement, women like Pat Eatock, who ran for an ACT seat in federal parliament for the Black Liberation Front, to name just one example. But their voices weren't heard nearly as much as they should have been. In *Talkin' Up to the White Woman*, Aileen Moreton-Robinson makes the point that feminist struggles such as the fight for abortion rights – one of the signature campaigns of second-wave feminism – were often in opposition to the struggles of Indigenous women, who were fighting racist policies such as forced sterilisations.

Throughout the 1980s and 1990s, the notion of sisterhood faded while that other second-wave slogan – 'The personal is political' – persisted, its emphasis on the *personal* being more adaptable to a neoliberal era when the notion of the 'collective' and the sisterhood has become less fashionable. But I think the notion of sisterhood is worth rethinking. It is a more useful metaphor for feminists than the mother–daughter one, with its connotations of batons being handed down, of rivalries and hierarchies. The women behind *Betty Can Jump* weren't perfect, and they weren't representative of *all* women. But their ideas about collective creation, about sharing income and childcare and the spotlight, and rejecting the heterosexual nuclear family, had revolutionary potential.

I remember Helen describing how she felt like she had stuck her head out of the water to take a breath for the first time when she discovered women's liberation. Back home in Sydney, I listen to our interview and she uses another water metaphor:

I don't know if you could call what's happening now a revolution. It's more like, just this enormous scream of rage and pain ... What worries me is that it will just die down, and the waters will close over again. And we'll trudge on, and nothing will have changed.

Sometimes it feels like nothing ever changes. As I was writing my doctoral thesis, an acquaintance from long ago contacted me and offered me his 'quiet opinion' about my ideas, and his help 'smoothing out the prose'; I was struck by how his offer read like a contemporary version of the man in Chapter 5 who attended an early meeting to discuss *Betty Can Jump*, only to constantly interrupt to tell the assembled women that they would never get anywhere if they didn't 'accept help from men'. When Kerry emailed me to apologise for her messy archives (they were, in fact, a goldmine of material that left me constantly amazed at her prescience in keeping them), I thought about how it can take more than a lifetime for us as women to shake off our proclivity for apology. And I realised, when I recently began meeting on Sundays with a group of women from my neighbourhood – a visual artist, a filmmaker and children's author, two musicians, a teacher, and a public communications expert – that we were holding our own version of consciousness-raising meetings, trying to understand how being a woman in this world can still sometimes feel like being trapped underwater, gasping for air.

As I walk away from the new La Mama, down Faraday Street towards Lygon Street, I can picture a troupe of actors skipping home from a moratorium march, dressed in black costumes, their faces blazing, their wild hair held down by slashes of red bandanas. On the corner, the make-up emporium becomes the old Albion Hotel again. Kerry, her hair hennaed, pushes the frosted-glass saloon doors open and walks out onto the street from the bar, leading Micky and Helen and half a dozen other women in an animated conversation. Across the road at Tiamo, Yvonne is smoking a rollie cigarette. Two mothers walking by stop to talk outside an empty café. Their two children, four or five years old, chase each other around three upturned milk crates. They clamber up on one of the crates at the end, jump across the next two and leap off.

Photographs

Notes

Introduction

p. 13-16 The reconstruction of the play's preview night is an imagined scene based on oral interviews conducted with surviving cast and crew, recollections of Pram Factory members published on Sue Ingleton's The Pram Factory website, interviews Kerry Dwyer conducted with cast and crew members (c. 1975), and Helen Garner's account of the night in *Dissent* (Garner 1972a).

p. 15 'Helen notices the men ...' Garner 1972a, p. 47.

p. 15 'To Claire, the men look ...' Claire Dobbin c. 1975 interview with Kerry Dwyer.

p. 18 'Second-wave activists ...' Curthoys 1994, p. 427; Magarey 2004.

p. 18 'Australian feminist scholar Margaret Henderson ...' Henderson 2012, p. 10.

p. 19 'they graffitied slogans ...' Arrow 2019, p. 127.

p. 19 'Women at the University of Adelaide ...' Magarey 2018, p. 34.

p. 19 'Elizabeth Reid knew ...' See Reid 2018, pp. 20–25; Arrow 2019, pp. 134–36.

p. 20 'saw girls outnumber boys ...' Parr 2015.

p. 22 'a headline about Katie Way ...' For an account of the spat between Way and Banfield, see Gabriella Paiella's 2018 story in *The Cut*, 'What's Going on Between the Writer Who Broke the Aziz Ansari Story and This TV Host?', 17 January, <www.thecut.com/2018/01/babe-net-aziz-ansari-story-writer-emails-ashleigh-banfield.html>.

p. 23 'There is an irony ...' Henderson 2006, pp. 158–59.

p. 23 'Another feminist scholar, Avtar Brah ...' Brah 2019.

p. 23 'We've come to think of Germaine Greer ...' Greer and Summers have come to be seen by feminists and non-feminists alike as the 'personification of Australian women's feminism' the feminist scholar Margaret Henderson has observed (Henderson 2006, pp. 72, 149).

p. 24 'Perhaps more surprising ...' *Betty* is mentioned in brief in Tim Robertson's gloriously freewheeling, gonzo-like tale of the Pram Factory (2001), written as an insider. Gabrielle Wolf's unsurpassed scholarly history of the Pram (2008) also pays attention to the play in a chapter that discusses the impact of feminism on the APG.

Chapter 1: A leap of faith

p. 27   'In 1961, eighteen-year-old Kerry Dwyer ...' This paragraph draws on the author's interviews with Kerry Dwyer, 2 May 2018, 10 March 2020 and 18 August 2021.

p. 27   'female students are outnumbered ...' There were approximately three men to every woman in Australian higher education in 1961 (see Parr 2015).

p. 28   'Menzies stood outside ...' See 'Opening of the Baillieu Library (21 March 1959)', The Robert Menzies Collection, University of Melbourne, <www.menziescollection.esrc.unimelb.edu.au/biogs/ E003859b.htm>.

p. 28   'Publisher and writer Hilary ...' McPhee 2001, p. 36.

p. 28   'The Literature Censorship Board ...' Mullins 2020, pp. 36–37.

p. 28   'J. Metcalfe favours restricting ...' Metcalfe 1961, 'More of Lady Chatterley', Farrago, Friday 24 March, p. 5.

p. 29   'For the first time, women can buy ...' See 'The pill', National Museum Australia, <www.nma.gov.au/online_features/defining_moments/ featured/the_pill>. See also Arrow 2019, p. 17.

p. 29   'One writer, Peter Mayne ...' Mayne 1961, 'Sexual freedom aids the student', Farrago, Friday 24 March, vol. 37, no. 3, p. 5.

p. 29   'An opinion piece by Wendy Neilson ...' Neilson 1961, 'Wendy Nielson replies on abortion article', Farrago, Friday 17 March, p. 4.

p. 29   'greatly disturbs one correspondent ...' Leithhead 1961, 'Sexy Farrago a symbol of Sodom', Farrago, Friday 28 April, p. 4.

p. 29   'In an address ...' Anonymous 1961, 'Women wasted at university', Farrago, Friday 17 March, p. 1.

p. 29   'the Farrago editors write ...' Editors 1961, 'So girls look better without gowns?', Farrago, Friday 17 March, pp. 1, 3.

p. 30   'On the day of the contest ...' Editors 1961, 'Uproar as Miss University reaches climax in Wilson Hall', Farrago, Friday 19 May, p. 1.

p. 30   'Kerry notices all of this ...' This paragraph draws on the author's interviews with Kerry Dwyer, and Sue Ingleton's descriptions of the Architecture faculty's theatre world in the early 1960s in an interview published in the Melbourne University Student Theatre Archive (see <must.unimelb.edu.au/2008/01/01/interview-with-suzanne-ingleton>).

p. 30   'Kerry also gravitates ...' Kerry Dwyer interviews with author.

p. 31   'Graeme remembers her ...' Graeme Blundell interview with author.

p. 31   'Micky Allan, one of Kerry's ... ' Micky Allan interview with author.

p. 31   'sit an exam in homecraft ...' See Brennan 2017, p. 13.

p. 31   'My boyfriend at the time ...' Helen Garner interview with author.

p. 31   'A student theatre crowd ...' See Blundell 2008, pp. 52–53.

p. 31   'To Graeme ...' See Blundell 2008, p. 53.

p. 32   'Kerry finds the student ...' Kerry Dwyer interviews with author.

p. 32   'In 1964, on a Wednesday afternoon ...' Kerry Dwyer and John Helmer interviews with author.

p. 32   'The barman loudly ...' The event is reported in Anonymous 1964, 'Girl thrown out: pub scandal', *Farrago*, Monday 20 July, p. 1.

p. 32   'A couple of days later ...' Anonymous 1964, 'Girl thrown out: pub scandal', *Farrago*, Monday 20 July, p. 1.

p. 33   'There were more than a dozen theatre groups ...' See the Melbourne University Student Theatre Archive <must.unimelb.edu.au>.

p. 33   'Commonwealth Scholarship student Hilary McPhee ...' See Wolf 2008, p. 6.

p. 33   'In a review of the season ...' Faust 1963, 'The Season of the Absurd in review', *Farrago*, Monday 17 June.

p. 33   'As part of the program ...' See the program at 'Theatre of the Absurd (1963)', Melbourne University Student Theatre Archive, <must.unimelb. edu.au/2017/08/01/theatre-of-the-absurd>.

p. 33   'the drama on university campuses ...' Max Gillies interview with author.

p. 34   'Hibberd told interviewer ...' Berry 1967, 'White With Wire Wheels', *Farrago*, Friday 14 July.

p. 34   'David Kendall later recalled ...' See 'White with Wire Wheels: Then and Now', Melbourne University Student Theatre Archive, <must.unimelb. edu.au/article/jack-hibberds-white-with-wire-wheels-then-and-now>.

p. 34   'The play's ocker stereotypes ...' See Wolf 2008, pp. 37–38.

p. 34   'Kerry misses out ...' This description of Kerry Dwyer's time in France draws from, and directly quotes from, her account of the time in her article 'From Grotowski to *Betty Can Jump*', published in *Australasian Drama Studies* in 2017, as well as her memories of the time published on Sue Ingleton's The Pram Factory website (see <wayback.archive-it. org/10989/20180903014625/https://www.pramfactory.com/ memoirsfolder/Dwyer-Kerry.html>.

p. 35   'Kerry had also met ...' Kerry Dwyer interviews with author.

p. 37   'growing political discontent ...' See Stein 1967, 'The Australians: they could be brought home now', *Farrago*, Friday 14 April, p. 5; King 1967, 'Big protest on Vietnam', *Farrago*, Friday 7 July, p. 1; Brown 1967, 'Rights not promises', *Farrago*, Friday 8 September, p. 3.

p. 37   'that Menzies had overseen ...' See Reid 2012, p. 4.

p. 37   'Historian Michelle Arrow ...' See Arrow 2019, p. 6.

p. 38   'even the beauty queens ...' See photospread 1967 'Bachelor girls', *Farrago*, Friday 12 May, pp. 6–7.

p. 38   'Helen's biographer Bernadette Brennan ...' See Brennan 2017, p. 22.

p. 39   'Helen was born ...' The following passages draw on Brennan 2017, pp. 12–15, Helen Garner c. 1975 interview with Kerry Dwyer; Garner' interview with author, and Garner's interview with Clare Wright and

Yves Rees 2020 on their podcast Archive Fever <www.archivefeverpod. com/s2ep02>.

Chapter 2: From La Mama to the Pram

p. 43   'They built a mud-brick house ...' See Hilary McPhee's 2012 *Memoirs of a Young Bastard: The Diaries of Tim Burstall*, published by Melbourne University Press, for an account of this community.

p. 43   'In 1967, Betty and Tim ...' See Cass 2017, p. 223; Wolf 2008, p. 10.

p. 43   'Betty settles on ...' See Jones 2017, p. 42; Wolf 2008, p. 10.

p. 44   'They subscribe to ...' See Bill Garner interviewed in Cass 2017, p. 27.

p. 44   'Brian Davies brings ...' See Blundell 2008, p. 99.

p. 44   'now pulls beers for SP bookies ...' See Meg Clancy's c. 2005 Pram Factory memories, <wayback.archive-it.org/10989/20180903014601/ https://www.pramfactory.com/memoirsfolder/Clancy-Meg.html>.

p. 44   'One day they take turns ...' The description of the workshop draws from Bill Garner in Cass 2017, p. 28; Bill Garner interview with author; Kerry Dwyer's c. 2005 Pram Factory memories; and Blundell 2008, p. 99.

p. 45   'The word went around ...' Blundell 2008, p. 99.

p. 45   'John Romeril describes ...' See John Romeril's c. 2005 Pram Factory memories, <wayback.archive-it.org/10989/20180903014900/https:// www.pramfactory.com/memoirsfolder/Romeril-John.html>.

p. 45   'under the umbrella title ...' Gabrielle Wolf writes that the Hibberd season 'loudly signalled that the New Wave had begun' (2008, pp. 7–8). The series of Brainrot plays saw Hibberd's emergence as an important new force in theatre; influenced by absurdism and Pinter's portrayal of characters with exaggerated traits, Hibberd was unafraid to highlight and exaggerate vulgar Australian characters, Wolf notes (2008, p. 8).

p. 45   'Writing to Graeme Blundell ...' See Blundell 2008, p. 99.

p. 46   'that aren't white and male ...' Graeme Blundell (2008, p. 127) writes: 'We lived in a town that was fast becoming the multicultural capital of Australia and this fact passed us by.'

p. 46   'Kerry would later recall ...' See Dwyer 1993.

p. 46   'pommy accents to get ...' See Kerry Dwyer's c. 2005 Pram Factory memories. Victor Marsh writes in his 2004 book *The Boy in the Yellow Dress*, 'A new emerging generation is no longer satisfied with the cultural cringe that would have them tugging a forelock in the direction of Britain. It is still a rarity to hear an Australian accent on the stage.'

p. 46   'the APG were aware of ...' See Wolf 2008, p. 73–74.

p. 46   'John Romeril has described ...' John Romeril's c. 2005 Pram Factory memories.

p. 46   'a visit from the vice squad ...' For an account of *Norm and Ahmed* and *Whatever Happened to Realism* and the vice squad incident, see Blundell 2008, pp. 127–38; Dwyer 1993; and Wolf 2008, pp. 51–57.

p. 47　'audiences at La Mama shows ...' Blundell 2008, p. 100.

p. 47　' Writing in *Carlton News* ...' Hibberd 1970.

p. 47　'The audience crams ...' See Blundell 2008, p. 136.

p. 48　'they sit down at tables ...' See Glickfeld 1970.

p. 48　'Actor Peter Cummins recalls ...' See the 1994 documentary *Pram Factory* (directors Anna Grieve and James Manché).

p. 48　'protesting Australia's involvement ...' Denise Varney (2011, pp. 58–59) sees the turn by artists and activists to left-wing politics as a reaction to 'a long period of conservative rule that brought prosperity but also an unwanted involvement in military actions [in the Korean and then Vietnam wars] ... The stage was set for dissenters to form an anti-war and anti-conscription movement that acted as an extra-parliamentary opposition to the Menzies Government.'

p. 48　'linked the group's growing ...' Timlin 1974.

p. 49　'Bill Garner similarly described ...' Garner B 1971.

p. 49　'new members influenced ...' Dwyer 1993.

p. 49　'The strike began ...' See Richard Vinen's 2018 book *The Long '68: Radical Protest and Its Enemies* (Penguin, London).

p. 49　'Australian theatre scholar Denise Varney ...' Varney 2011, pp. 45–48.

p. 49　'British playwright and critic ...' Wandor 1984, p. 77. Grant Tyler Peterson similarly describes the events of 1968 as challenging the 'boundaries between public life and artistic practice' (2018, p. 74). Denise Varney (2011, p. 51) notes a similar development of 'cultural radicalism' in theatre groups forming in New York and San Francisco, notably the 1969 New York production by the Performance Group of the play *Dionysus* in a factory, which involved improvisation and audience interaction. *Dionysus*, writes Varney, 'marked the diversification of the radical movement into a range of oppositional cultural practices, of which theatre and performance, along with music and dance, would be a dynamic site of activity for youth culture'.

p. 50　'spurred by a Marxist belief ...' Wolf (2008, p. 19) is paraphrasing Kerry Dwyer's description of the APG philosophy here. Writing in *The Bulletin*, Glickfeld (1970) also makes it clear that the APG's political motives were balanced by the group's creative and pragmatic efforts to raise funds, including a 'Ring-A-Play service': 'Telephone Blundell, offer the Group co-operative $40 or $50, and it will descend on your home, church or social centre to perform in the space you provide in the clothes they arrive in. The play will be lewd and abrasive and pick its nose at the sexual hypocrisy and political ineptness of the older generation, but it is Australia as many of the young know and suffer it today.'

p. 50　'using acrobatics and commedia dell'arte ...' Kerry Dwyer's c. 2005 Pram Factory memories. See also Wolf 2008, p. 17.

p. 50   'Some of the La Mama actors ...' Blundell 2008, p. 119.

p. 50   'Bill Garner remembers ...' Bill Garner's c. 2005 Pram Factory memories, <wayback.archive-it.org/10989/20180903014641/https://www.pramfactory.com/memoirsfolder/Garner-Bill.html>.

p. 50   'Leonard Glickfeld described ...' Glickfeld 1970.

p. 50   'Kerry has written about the day ...' Kerry Dwyer's c. 2005 Pram Factory memories.

p. 52   'seen on YouTube today ...' See 'Melbourne moratorium against Vietnam War (This Day Tonight, ABC, 1970)', ABC Education, <www.youtube.com/watch?v=3R5zKW3Y1U4>.

p. 52   'Bill Garner later writes ...' Bill Garner's c. 2005 Pram Factory memories.

p. 52   'Kerry describes the point ...' Dwyer 1993.

p. 52   'in a 1968 interview ...' See Brown et al. 1968, p. 66.

p. 53   'The Carlton group likewise ...' Dwyer 1978–79, p. 150.

p. 53   'Kerry repeats his theory ...' Kerry Dwyer interviews with author. Author note: Just as Brecht's epic theatre rejected naturalism in favour of encouraging audiences to question the world on stage (and, by extrapolation, the world beyond the stage), this newer, more explicitly political theatre, wanted to encourage audiences to become self-consciously creative actors in the world.

p. 53   'Bill Garner would describe ...' See Garner B 1971. Garner acknowledges ongoing divisions between those APG members whose interests were more theatrical and those who were more politically orientated, but he insists that the APG's political plays and actions had radicalised even the most 'wishy-washy left-liberals' in the company.

p. 53   'the Sunday workshop at La Mama was ...' Kerry Dwyer's c. 2005 Pram Factory memories.

p. 53   'Months of searching ...' Blundell 2008, pp, 167–68.

p. 54   'The sprawling building dated from ...' See Blundell 2008, p. 168; 'Freeman's Livery Stables' entry on the Carlton Community History Group website, <www.cchg.asn.au/travel.html>. See also APG member recollections in the 1994 documentary *Pram Factory* (directors Anna Grieve and James Manché).

p. 54   'John Timlin recalls ...' *Pram Factory* 1994 (film).

p. 54   'Timlin says the name ...' Timlin 1974.

p. 54   'Suggestions such as Lindsay Smith's ...' Blundell 2008, p. 145.

p. 55   'A group of lecturers ...' Max Gillies and Claire Dobbin interviews with author, see also Wolf 2008, pp. 9–11.

p. 55   'introducing students to Brecht's ...' Epic theatre, Wolf (2008, p. 7) writes, encourages audiences to 'critically evaluate and consider ways to improve their society'. Varney (2011, p. 29) similarly writes: 'Epic theatre generates in the spectator a metatheatrical appreciation of the way in which the story is told rather than immersion in the story itself.' As Varney (2011, pp. 29–31) writes, Brecht's techniques would later be incorporated into APG shows: collage, montage, stories being interrupted by songs that allowed audiences to reflect on characters' decisions, and an open rather than closed story structure.

p. 55   'also attracts Evelyn Krape ...' Evelyn's memories are drawn from her interview with the author.

p. 56   'Max Gillies tells me ...' Max Gillies interview with author.

p. 57   'the 1970s government of Victoria ...' The show was a political satire about power and corruption in the city during the economic boom of the 1880s that was 'acerbically directed at the present', Graeme Blundell (2008, p. 173) writes.

p. 57   'connection between the young men ...' Max Gillies interview with author.

p. 57   'Covering their faces with handkerchiefs ...' Meg Clancy's c. 2005 Pram Factory memories.

p. 57   'days as a printery ...' Kerry Dwyer's c. 2005 Pram Factory memories.

p. 57   'Tony Taylor remembers ...' Tony Taylor's c. 2005 Pram Factory memories, <wayback.archive-it.org/10989/20180903014936/https://www.pramfactory.com/memoirsfolder/Taylor-Tony.html>.

p. 57   'DIY approach to renovating ...' Meg Clancy's c. 2005 Pram Factory memories.

p. 58   'We used to go down and get ...' Evelyn Krape interview with author.

p. 58   'enjoying the communal meals ...' Robin Laurie's c. 2005 Pram Factory memories, <wayback.archive-it.org/10989/20180903014742/https://www.pramfactory.com/memoirsfolder/Laurie-Robin.html>.

p. 58   'Tim Robertson writes ...' Robertson 2001, p. 38.

p. 58   'took advantage of increasingly affordable ...' Founding member of Ubu experimental film collective John Clark purchased an offset printer in 1968 to produce the anti-war and anti-censorship film magazine *Ubunews* (see Mudie 1997, pp. 10–11).

p. 58   'these groups acted as ...' Hughes 2015; see also Varney 2011, p. 59.

p. 59   'American programs had dominated ...' The introduction of television in the mid-1950s, Michelle Arrow (2017) notes, had 'raised the stakes in the debate about a national culture [and] concerns about the dominance of American television programs'.

p. 59   'always been Australian plays ...' See Arrow 2002.

p. 59   'argued that Australia's performing arts ...' See Arrow 2017, which quotes Gorton saying that the government's intention was to 'show the rest of the world that there are other things than avant-garde kangaroos and Ned Kellys in this great country of ours'. See also Tomsic 2017, p. 195.

p. 60   'APG to formalise its structure ...' Timlin 1974; Wolf 2008, pp. 106–107.

p. 60   'There was a sense …' Max Gillies interviewed in the 1994 documentary *Pram Factory* (directors Anna Grieve and James Manché).

p. 60   'a scheme where members pooled …' Claire Dobbin and Max Gillies interviews with author.

p. 60   'Robin Laurie remembers a kind of …' Robin Laurie interviewed in the 1994 documentary *Pram Factory* (directors Anna Grieve and James Manché).

p. 60   'John Smythe recalls …' See John Smythe's c. 2005 Pram Factory memories, <wayback.archive-it.org/10989/20180903014913/https://www.pramfactory.com/memoirsfolder/Smythe-John.html>.

p. 61   'Laurel Frank remembers …' Laurel Frank interview with author.

p. 61   'Hibberd wrote the most amazing …' Vic Marsh interview with author.

p. 61   'where the group's energy …' Laurel Frank interview with author.

p. 61   'Max recalls one meeting …' Max Gillies interview with author.

p. 62   'From the group's earliest years …' Varney (2011, p. 65) notes that between 1970 and 1981 Hibberd and Romeril 'wrote 31 per cent of the APG's locally written plays and performance texts'.

p. 62   'La Mama's July 1969 …' See La Mama 1969.

p. 62   'seem to be women …' It is difficult to be precise due to the ambiguous gender of some of the actors' names.

p. 62   'described by theatre scholar …' See Varney 2011, p. 64. Varney later adds (pp. 71–72) that the gender divisions that saw men write the plays and women act 'reproduced [women's] social subordination by taking their place in the more subordinate spheres of theatre, including acting'.

p. 62   'the production was dominated …' Kerry Dwyer's c. 2005 Pram Factory memories.

p. 63   'with actors on stage …' Max Gillies interview with author.

p. 63   'the radical nature of the play …' Dwyer 1993.

p. 63   'Kerry described the show …' Kerry Dwyer interviews with author.

p. 63   'no one else felt as strongly …' Kerry Dwyer's c. 2005 Pram Factory memories.

p. 63   'Yvonne Marini writes that …' Yvonne Marini's c. 2005 Pram Factory memories, <wayback.archive-it.org/10989/20180903020853/http://www.pramfactory.com/memoirsfolder/Marini-Yvonne.html>.

p. 64   'Claire Dobbin would later recall …' Claire Dobbin c. 1975 interview with Kerry Dwyer.

p. 64   'In a 1984 interview …' Quoted in Glow 1984, p. 129.

p. 64   'When I talked to her in 2020 …' Claire Dobbin interview with author.

p. 64   'The absence of a language …' Kerry Dwyer's c. 2005 Pram Factory memories. Wolf (2008, pp. 91–92) cites Dwyer's unhappiness during this period, and adds that critics agreed Williamson didn't write adequately for women.

p. 64   'Helen described the feelings …' Garner 1972b.

p. 65   'attendance at football matches ...' Vic Marsh interview with author.

p. 65   'Kerry believes there was a disconnection ...' Kerry Dwyer interviews with author. Wolf (2008, p. 9) argues that the group's use of Australian accents and language was both a way of defining their project and making explicit their embrace of the working class, even while the group's working-class credentials were complicated by the largely middle-class, university-educated background of many members. Wolf (2008, p. 19) suggests that 'Beyond their work in the streets, they never entertained a broad, general, cross-class audience.'

p. 65   'Kerry had hoped *Marvellous Melbourne* ...' Dwyer 2017, p. 187.

p. 65   'glimpse of a spiritual dimension ...' Kerry Dwyer's c. 2005 Pram Factory memories.

p. 65   'the beginning of many bitter ...' Dwyer 1993.

p. 65   'one night at the APG ...' Yvonne Marini's c. 2005 Pram Factory memories.

p. 66   'it was their active involvement ...' Dwyer 2017, p. 188.

Chapter 3: As a woman ...

p. 67   'as Kerry Dwyer wraps ...' This reimagined scene is based on Kerry Dwyer's writings about the period, her interviews with the author, Graeme Blundell's description of the period (2008, p. 143) and archival records (e.g. Australian Performing Group 1972a).

p. 68   'Carlton Women's Liberation Group's early ...' Although memories of where the meeting with Helmer/Dyllan occurred varied in my interviews with Dwyer, Frank and Allan, in her c. 1975 interview with Kerry Dwyer, Helen Garner recalled Dyllan coming to a meeting 'when 40 women were crowded into a house in Rathdowne Street'.

p. 68   'Kerry and Helen's friend, Micky ...' Micky Allan interview with author.

p. 68   'when Kerry and Graeme had offered ...' Micky Allan c. 1975 interview with Kerry Dwyer.

p. 68   'Maggie had taught drama ...' John Helmer interview with author.

p. 69   'an actor who had performed alongside ...' Peter Kovner interview with author.

p. 69   'The Caravan Theatre was ...' Greeley 2015, p. 206.

p. 69   'In 1967 Bobbi ...' Bobbi Ausubel interview with author.

p. 69   'The first women's liberation play ...' Greeley 2015, p. 179. Although the company created the play on the cusp of the organised women's movement and consciousness-raising groups emerging in the United States, it explored the experiences of being a woman in a way that was analogous with consciousness-raising groups. The play became a mainstay of the company's performances for the next half a dozen years.

p. 70   'a folk music club in Harvard Square ...' Peter Kovner interview with author.

p. 70   'lead men and women in the audience ...' Bobbi Ausubel interview with author.

p. 70   'Helen feels so uncomfortable ...' Helen Garner c. 1975 interview with Kerry Dwyer.

p. 70   'Kerry tells the workshop ...' Kerry Dwyer's memory of the workshop in her interview with author.

p. 70   'Helen acts out bringing ...' Helen Garner c. 1975 interview with Kerry Dwyer.

p. 71   'I was estranged ...' Helen Garner interview with author.

p. 71   'feels like a theatre widow ...' Brennan 2017, p. 24.

p. 71   'When I speak to Helen now ...' Helen Garner interview with author.

p. 71   'one of Melbourne's first consciousness-raising ...' In her history of the women's liberation movement, Jean Taylor writes that small groups of women would come together to 'explore our conditioning', often discussing weekly themes such as sexuality, friendships and love, but nearly always with the intention of analysing their situation and taking political action (2009, pp. 101–103). Taylor describes groups picking topics such as 'virginity', or 'family relationships' to discuss each week, and notes how women who attended the first consciousness-raising groups in Melbourne described the experience as all-consuming (see also Reid 2018, p. 16).

p. 72   'Yvonne Marini was born ...' The passage about Yvonne Marini draws on her c. 2005 Pram Factory memories and the author's interview with Evelyn Krape.

p. 73   'Student Laurel Frank ...' This passage draws on the author's interview with Laurel Frank.

p. 73   'Kerry's visits to markets ...' Blundell 2008, p. 145.

p. 74   'In her memoir, second-wave feminist ...' Brownmiller 1999, pp. 20–21.

p. 74   'Another early women's liberationist ...' Quoted in Press 2017.

p. 75   'Marilyn Lake, a historian ...' Lake 1999, p. 233.

p. 75   'while the Canberra Women's ...' Reid 2018, p. 11.

p. 75   'by 1973 there were ...' Taylor 2009, p. 102.

p. 75   'Libby Lloyd, a qualified osteopath ...' Libby Lloyd interview with author.

p. 75   'Feminist author Sara Dowse ...' Interviewed in the 2020 documentary *Brazen Hussies* (director Catherine Dwyer).

p. 76   'When I visit Julie Gibson ...' Julie Gibson interview with author.

p. 76   'Libby Lloyd's daughter ...' Justine Lloyd interview with author.

p. 76   'Kerry says now that ...' Kerry Dwyer interviews with author.

p. 76   'Jealousy and possessiveness was frowned ...' Ponch Hawkes' c. 2005 Pram Factory memories, <wayback.archive-it.

org/10989/20180903014715/https://www.pramfactory.com/
memoirsfolder/Hawkes-Ponch.html>.

p. 77   'One night in 1971 ...' Dennis Altman correspondence with author 2021.

p. 77   'Pram actor Tony Taylor ...' Tony Taylor's c. 2005 Pram Factory
         memories.

p. 77   'Vic Marsh, who joined ...' Vic Marsh interview with author.

p. 77   'Pram member Bob Thorneycroft ...' Bob Thorneycroft's c. 2005 Pram
         Factory memories, <wayback.archive-it.org/10989/20180903014943/
         https://www.pramfactory.com/memoirsfolder/Thorneycroft-Bob.html>.

p. 77   'Bill Garner recalls ...' Bill Garner's interview with Michael Cathcart for
         'How The Pram Factory shaped Australian theatre', first broadcast on
         the ABC on Monday 17 July 2017.

p. 77   'Bill Garner tells me ...' Bill Garner interview with author.

p. 78   'When Vic Marsh arrived ...' Vic Marsh interview with author.

p. 78   'Evelyn recalls a friend ...' Evelyn Krape c. 1975 interview with Kerry
         Dwyer.

p. 78   'complaints about their personal ...' Brennan 2017, p. 25.

p. 79   'Carol Hanisch described ...' Hanisch 1970, p. 76.

p. 80   'They needed to be matched ...' Lake 1999, p. 235.

p. 80   'Kerry, Micky and Helen were ...' Kerry Dwyer interviews with author.

p. 80   'Helen recalls being drawn ...' Helen Garner c. 1975 interview with
         Kerry Dwyer.

Chapter 4: Rehearsals for revolution

p. 81   'Micky Allan remembers ...' Micky Allan 2018 interview with author.

p. 81   'Meetings could devolve ...' Robin Laurie's Pram Factory memories
         c. 2005.

p. 81   'Quite a lot of knitting ...' Max Gillies interview with author.

p. 81   'Graeme Blundell writes ...' Blundell 2008, p. 172.

p. 82   'Meg Clancy supported ...' Meg Clancy's c. 2005 Pram Factory
         memories.

p. 82   'According to Kerry ...' Kerry Dwyer's c. 2005 Pram Factory memories.

p. 82   'unacknowledged power of romantic ...' Kerry Dwyer interviews with
         author.

p. 82   'Timlin, in "Pramocracy" ...' Timlin 1974.

p. 83   'In September 1971 ...' The descriptions of the rehearsal period in this
         chapter draw on the author's interviews with Kerry Dwyer, as well as
         Kerry Dwyer's *Betty Can Jump* production diaries (see Dwyer 1971,
         Dwyer 1971–72); an article she later wrote for *Lip* magazine (Dwyer
         1978–79); her Pram Factory memories c. 2005; and her article for
         Australasian Drama Studies (Dwyer 2017).

p. 84   'Claire recalls the mood ...' Claire Dobbin interview with author.

p. 86   'The closest Helen ...' Helen Garner interview with author.

p. 86   'She would later tell Kerry ...' Helen Garner c. 1975 interview with Kerry Dwyer.

p. 86   'But when she hears ...' Laurel Frank c. 1975 interview with Kerry Dwyer; Laurel Frank interview with author.

p. 86   'Micky now recalls ...' Micky Allan interview with author.

p. 86   'The collective received ...' Australian Performing Group, 1972f.

p. 86   'Micky's design evokes ...' My thanks to Dr Laura Prieto for her observation of the significance of this stylistic motif.

p. 87   'Jude had a reputation ...' Evelyn Krape interview with author.

p. 87   'Jude was also famous ...' Soosie Adshead's c. 2005 Pram Factory memories of Jude Kuring, <wayback.archive-it.org/10989/20180903020845/http://www.pramfactory.com/memoirsfolder/Kuring-Jude.html>.

p. 87   'She was a droll ...' Claire Dobbin interview with author.

p. 87   'Claire remembers Yvonne ...' Claire Dobbin interview with author.

p. 87   'Evelyn recalls that she ...' Evelyn Krape interview with author.

p. 87   'Claire remembers Evelyn ...' Claire Dobbin interview with author.

p. 88   'remembers her as ...' Vic Marsh interview with author.

p. 88   'Kerry longed for a ...' Kerry Dwyer's c. 2005 Pram Factory memories.

p. 89   'Helen, who has begun learning yoga ...' Helen Garner interview with author.

p. 89   'Yvonne would recall how these exercises ...' Yvonne Marini c. 1975 interview with Kerry Dwyer.

p. 89   'unheard of at the Pram Factory ...' See Dwyer 2017, p. 190.

p. 90   'Evelyn recalls many late-night ... ' Evelyn Krape interview with author.

p. 90   'Kerry's aim was to create ...' Dwyer 1978–79, p. 150.

p. 90   'Evelyn Krape felt like a ...' Kerry Dwyer's c. 2005 Pram Factory memories.

p. 90   'I remember lying on the ground ... ' Evelyn Krape interview with author.

p. 91   'Claire, however, sees more ...' Claire Dobbin interview with author.

p. 91   'While Claire describes creating ...' Claire Dobbin interview with author.

p. 91   'Through consciousness-raising, the rigour ...' Dwyer 2017, p. 193.

p. 91   'Some of the stories they found ...' Laurel Frank interview with author.

p. 92   'An APG News item ...' Australian Performing Group 1972a.

p. 92   'Writing in the radical journal *Dissent* ...' Garner 1972a, p. 49.

p. 92   'the material Laurel and Kay ...' Kerry Dwyer's c. 2005 Pram Factory memories.

p. 92   'Evelyn recalls the "nights ..."' Evelyn's recollections of this night are from Evelyn Krape c. 1975 interview with Kerry Dwyer.

p. 93   'The historical stories Laurel and Kay ...' Laurel Frank interview with author.

p. 93 'Evelyn describes it as process ...' Evelyn Krape c. 1975 interview with Kerry Dwyer.

p. 94 'You seemed impenetrable ...' Evelyn Krape c. 1975 interview with Kerry Dwyer.

p. 94 'Evelyn now recalls Claire ...' Evelyn Krape interview with author.

p. 94 'Helen, too, remembers ...' Helen Garner interview with author.

p. 94 'He had gone overseas ...' Kerry Dwyer's c. 2005 Pram Factory memories.

p. 95 'Micky Allan was planning costumes ...' Micky Allan interview with author. The slides are now in the State Library of New South Wales with Kerry Dwyer's archives.

p. 95 'Sometimes the slides bonded ...' Laurel Frank interview with author.

p. 95 'Kerry had been trying to ...' Kerry Dwyer's c. 2005 Pram Factory memories.

p. 95 'Vic was an actor ...' Vic Marsh interview with author.

p. 96 'Vic was in Sydney facing charges ...' Vic Marsh recounts the story in his 2014 memoir, *The Boy in the Yellow Dress*.

p. 96 'Her activism introduced her to Vic ...' Carmen Lawrence interview with author.

p. 96 'Hewett has said ...' See Novakovic 2009.

p. 97 'marked by poetic and musical ...' See Moore 2016.

p. 97 'We had closed rehearsals ...' Helen Garner c. 1975 interview with Kerry Dwyer.

p. 97 'When Graeme Blundell attended ...' Vic Marsh interview with author.

p. 98 'Vic made me laugh ...' Helen Garner c. 1975 interview with Kerry Dwyer.

p. 98 'Kerry recalls Vic as ...' Kerry Dwyer's c. 2005 Pram Factory memories.

p. 98 'In the opening convict ship scene ...' Vic Marsh interview with author.

p. 98 'Vic had to "wear the sins ..."' Claire Dobbin interview with author.

p. 98 'Without income from me ...' Carmen Lawrence interview with author.

p. 98 'Kerry remembers Carmen also contributing ...' Kerry Dwyer's c. 2005 Pram Factory memories.

p. 99 'Claire recollects Carmen would ...' Claire Dobbin interview with author.

p. 99 'Fifty years on, Carmen ...' Carmen Lawrence interview with author.

p. 99 'Iola Mathews, one of ...' See Mathews 2019, p. 26.

p. 99 'the women's liberation principle ...' See Reid 2018 (p. 16) for a description of this practice.

p. 99 'Yvonne Marini later commented ...' Yvonne Marini c. 1975 interview with Kerry Dwyer.

p. 100 '*Betty*'s production philosophy ...' See Dwyer 1978–79, p. 150.

p. 100 'an APG News editorial noted ...' Australian Performing Group 1972a.

p. 100 'as Kerry remarks now, "I was about ..."' Kerry Dwyer interviews with author.

p. 100 'to coincide with Germaine Greer's ...' Kerry writes that they timed the opening night 'to coincide with Germaine Greer's visit (The Female Eunuch was newly published – a great source of inspiration to us)' (Kerry Dwyer's c. 2005 Pram Factory memories).

p. 100 'We had to work every day ...' Kerry Dwyer interviews with author.

p. 100 'Evelyn's memory differs ...' Evelyn Krape interview with author.

p. 100 'the unilateral decisions made ...' Dwyer 1978–79, p. 151.

p. 101 'Helen reflected on the difficult ...' Garner 1972a, pp. 47–50.

p. 101 'personal tensions can be more urgent ...' In her production diary, Kerry similarly notes that 'personal problems and interpersonal problems assumed greater significance than theatrical ones'.

p. 101 'Kerry's diary contains a note ...' Dwyer explains: 'That's Kristin Green who married David Williamson but I don't recall her being involved at all and I don't know why her name is there ... She might have come to a couple of the sessions, but it didn't work out for her to be involved in it' (Kerry Dwyer interviews with author). This concern for supporting women who had caring responsibilities extended to women outside the group: Dwyer's production diary also records a discussion about giving proceeds from coffee sales during the performances to either 'Carlton women's lib or a daycare organisation', although she cannot now recall if this happened.

p. 101 'the demanding rehearsal schedule ...' Dwyer 1978–79, p. 150.

p. 101 'Claire doesn't remember it being ...' Claire Dobbin interview with author.

Chapter 5: *Betty's run*

p. 103 'As the theatre fills ...' See Gary Foley, 'A reflection on the first thirty days of the embassy', archived at the Koori History Website Project, <www.kooriweb.org/foley/essays/pdf_essays/embassy.pdf>.

p. 104 'He rounds the women up ...' An annotation in Kerry Dwyer's production diary describes a direction for actors in this scene: 'feel like a raw, aching cunt, a huge hole, expanding but still have sense of power, ability to withstand pain, endure'. The notes describe the 'Aim of the scene' is showing women's 'sexual degradation, their association with animals, and therefore their subhuman nature, as well as their ability to endure'.

p. 104 'It was a "total coincidence" ...' Kerry Dwyer interviews with author.

p. 104 'Helen wrote that the night ...' Garner 1972a, pp. 49–50.

p. 105 'photos in this book ...' Micky Allan email to author, 15 October 2021.

p. 105 'In an APG News story ...' Garner 1972b.

p. 105 'Kerry describes the show ...' Kerry Dwyer interviews with author.

p. 105 'We were afraid ...' Garner 1972a, p. 50.

p. 105 'a near-complete script ...' *Betty Can Jump* collective 1972a.

p. 108   'Kerry recalls the impact ...' Kerry Dwyer's c. 2005 Pram Factory memories.

p. 108   'Unlike other scenes that were ...' Garner 1972a, pp. 47–49.

p. 108   'The collective wanted ...' Note in Kerry Dwyer's production diary.

p. 109   'a column Lawson wrote ...' Lawson's words were published in *The Bulletin*, vol. 17, no. 871, 24 Oct 1896.

p. 110   'Evelyn leapt up onto ...' Evelyn Krape and Vic Marsh interviews with author.

p. 110   'In this scene Vic is ...' In a review of the play in *The Australian*, Tim Dare (1972) describes Marsh wearing a placard that reads 'penis power'. Dwyer's production diary also include references to Vic wearing football bladders to represent giant balls and Yvonne wearing a giant wedding ring around her neck (Dwyer 1971).

p. 111   'the group commissioning ...' Kerry Dwyer interviews with author.

p. 111   'Micky remarks on how ...' Micky Allan c. 1975 interview with Kerry Dwyer.

p. 111   'Vic remembers how each ...' Vic Marsh interview with author.

p. 111   'feminist street theatre in the UK ...' Wandor 1984, p. 82.

p. 112   'Aili Paal Singer, the actor ...' Aili Paal Singer interview with author.

p. 112   'the *Betty* cast's basic costume ...' Vic Marsh interview with author.

p. 112   'the APG eschewed ...' Timlin 1974.

p. 112   'Audiences in the round ...' Wolf (2008, p. 62) quotes Blundell, who says: 'It was always important that the audience should be able to see itself reacting [because] when it really took off it was as though the audience were participating with the performers.'

p. 113   'Sometimes we heard ...' Garner 1972a, p. 50.

p. 113   'Some of them were weeping ...' Garner 1972a, p. 47.

p. 113   'Women would "fall about ..."' Laurel Frank c. 1975 interview with Kerry Dwyer.

p. 113   'Evelyn described the production ...' Evelyn Krape c. 1975 interview with Kerry Dwyer.

p. 113   'the response was unprecedented ...' Dobbin quoted in Glow 1984, p. 133.

p. 113   'Jane Clifton had not yet joined ...' Jane Clifton interview with author.

p. 114   'keen to receive positive reviews ...' The APG kept clippings of reviews (now held in State Library Victoria's Australian Performing Group Records collection, see Folio 33).

p. 114   'sent letters to prominent ...' Australian Performing Group 1972b.

p. 114   'Carmen Lawrence agrees ...' Carmen Lawrence interview with author.

p. 115   'Laurel singles out ...' Laurel Frank interview with author.

p. 115   'was little rivalry ...' Garner 1972a, p. 47.

p. 115   'criticised for not being *of* ...' For a discussion of Greer's relationship to the movement see Sheehan 2016 and Lilburn et al 2000.

p. 115 'make any extravagant claims ...' Garner 1972a, p. 47.

p. 116 'humourless women's liberationists ...' See A Taylor (2014) for a discussion of how feminists (in particular Germaine Greer) have used humour to undermine the humourless feminist stereotype and insert feminist speech into public discourse.

p. 117 'lone female reviewer ...' Beatrice Faust was the only woman to have a by-line in the *Betty Can Jump* review clips kept by APG, although there could have been other female reviewers.

p. 117 'Evelyn recalls deliberately injecting ...' Evelyn Krape interview with author.

p. 118 'The *Melbourne Times*' reviewer wanted ...' Mayhead likewise writes that 'it covers too much too lightly'.

p. 118 'the feminist journal *Lip* ...' Dwyer 1978–79, p. 151.

p. 118 'Claire reflected on the reasons ...' Claire Dobbin c. 1975 interview with Kerry Dwyer.

p. 118 'Evelyn described the historical scenes ...' Evelyn Krape c. 1975 interview with Kerry Dwyer.

p. 118 'Micky told Kerry in 1975 ...' Micky Allan c. 1975 interview with Kerry Dwyer.

p. 119 'Helen summed up ...' Helen Garner c. 1975 interview with Kerry Dwyer.

p. 119 'created an immediate rapport ...' Garner 1972a, p. 49.

p. 119 'Kerry uses similar reasoning ...' Kerry Dwyer interviews with author.

p. 120 'When Claire spoke to Hilary Glow ...' Glow 1984, pp. 130–31.

p. 120 'Vic now describes ...' Vic Marsh and Kerry Dwyer interviews with author.

p. 120 'She qualifies this point ...' Evelyn Krape said a similar thing to Kerry in 1975: 'What we needed was an overall structure to unify those segments, and that is the problem with any group-developed show.'

p. 120 'Garner wrote that in one sense ...' Garner 1972a, p. 50.

p. 120 'It was "amateurish", Helen ...' Helen Garner interview with author.

p. 120 '*Betty* was also "thoroughly in ..."' Australian Performing Group 1972a.

p. 121 'In a position paper ...' Blundell & Hutchinson 1972.

p. 121 'Members of "the *Betty Can Jump* ..."' Australian Performing Group 1972d.

p. 122 'Kerry led a workshop ...' See Kerry Dwyer's production diary 1971–72.

p. 122 'Evelyn and twelve women ...' See *The Age*, 30 September 1972, p. 1.

p. 122 'Claire later acknowledged ...' Quoted in Glow 1984, p. 132.

p. 123 'The performance scholar and playwright ...' Tait 1993, p. 73. In Tait's next book about later Australian women's theatre, *Converging Realities*, she explicitly makes the link between Butler's work and way theatre can reveal gender as a performance (1994, p. 43).

p. 123 'echoes Butler's now famous ...' Butler 1990/2007, p. 34.

p. 123   'A preview of the show ...' Anonymous, '...A woman enters', *The Sun* (Melbourne), 20 January 1972.

p. 123   'removed his exaggerated costume ...' Dwyer 1971–72.

p. 123   'a point about women's social conditioning ...' Buckley 1973.

p. 124   '*Betty Can Jump* was not a perfect ...' Laurel Frank interview with author.

p. 124   'When the show's four-week ...' Claire Dobbin told Hilary Glow: 'It so obviously tapped a response in the community and we were packed out for six weeks' (Glow 1984, p. 133).

p. 124   'Measured by box office ...' See Australian Performing Group 1973. The next highest grossing plays were *Compulsory Century* ($5685), the *APG Revue* ($5612) and *Brumby Innes* ($5016).

p. 124   'APG News singled out ...' See Australian Performing Group 1972c.

p. 124   'When I tell Helen ...' Helen Garner interview with author.

Chapter 6: *Betty* rocks the Pram

p. 125   The opening Christmas party scene is reconstructed from Claire Dobbin c. 1975 interview with Kerry Dwyer; and Claire Dobbin interview with author.

p. 125   'Fifty years later, Claire ...' Claire Dobbin interview with author.

p. 126   'Micky explains to me ...' Micky Allan interview with author.

p. 126   'Kerry recollects that the men ...' Kerry Dwyer's c. 2005 Pram Factory memories.

p. 126   'Helen describes the scene ...' Garner 1972, p. 47.

p. 126   'Claire has similar memories ...' Claire Dobbin c. 1975 interview with Kerry Dwyer.

p. 126   'When Kerry interviews her in 1975 ...' Helen Garner c. 1975 interview with Kerry Dwyer.

p. 126   'her delayed reaction in *Dissent* ...' Garner 1972, p. 47.

p. 127   'The "APG men were grim ..."' Dwyer 2017, p. 192.

p. 127   'Micky describes to me ...' Micky Allan interview with author.

p. 127   'reactions to the knowledge scene ...' Garner 1972a, p. 50.

p. 127   'Claire now thinks the Pram men ...' Claire Dobbin interview with author.

p. 127   'The Pram men I speak to ...' Author interviews with Bill Garner, Graeme Blundell, Max Gillies and John Timlin.

p. 128   'Claire tells me that ...' Claire Dobbin interview with author.

p. 128   'Women "were quite at liberty" ...' Claire Dobbin quoted in Glow 1984, p. 130.

p. 128   'John Romeril remembers ...' John Romeril's c. 2005 Pram Factory memories.

p. 128   'Carmen Lawrence recalls ...' Carmen Lawrence interview with author.

p. 129   'Max, for his part ...' Max Gillies interview with author.

p. 129   'the way APG meetings were run ...' Robin Laurie's c. 2005 Pram Factory memories.

p. 129   'activist and writer Jo Freeman ...' See 'The Tyranny of Structurelessness', <www.jofreeman.com/joreen/tyranny.htm>.

p. 129   'Helen didn't attend APG ...' Helen Garner interview with author.

p. 129   'In 1975, Micky reflected ...' Micky Allan c. 1975 interview with Kerry Dwyer.

p. 130   'A Stretch of the Imagination ...' See 'Chronology of Shows' on Sue Ingleton's The Pram Factory website, <wayback.archive-it. org/10989/20180903020257/http://www.pramfactory.com/chrono. html>.

p. 130   'The APG's next show ...' See the Pram 'Chronology of Shows'.

p. 130   'Gabrielle Wolf writes that ...' Wolf 2008, p. 118.

p. 130   'Laurel later remarked that ...' Laurel Frank c. 1975 interview with Kerry Dwyer.

p. 130   'Laurel told me that ...' Laurel Frank interview with author.

p. 130   'APG member Geoffrey Milne ...' Quoted in Wolf 2008, p. 105.

p. 130   'John Romeril describes the changes ...' John Romeril's c. 2005 Pram Factory memories.

p. 131   'In 1973, Helen profiled ...' Garner 1973.

p. 131   'did not stop Evelyn lamenting ...' Quoted in Buckley 1973. 'Shit work' was a common women's liberation phrase. Hanisch used it in her reference to women in left groups being left with menial tasks (1970, p. 77), and Mainardi uses it in 'The politics of housework' (1970, p. 29) in reference to the domestic chores borne predominantly by women.

p. 131   'begin to be renegotiated ...' Denise Varney (2011, p. 74) writes that debates over issues such as childcare were common at the Pram Factory, including whether it was the collective's responsibility to provide childcare for members.

p. 132   'the day of the show's final ...' Minutes of Executive Meeting, 6 March 1972, found in Dwyer 1971–72.

p. 132   'An internal bulletin in March ...' Australian Performing Group 1972d.

p. 132   'While the APG had cleaning ...' Kerry Dwyer interviews with author.

p. 132   'Rose Chong recalls that ...' See Rose Chong's c. 2005 Pram Factory memories, <wayback.archive-it.org/10989/20180903020742/http:// www.pramfactory.com/memoirsfolder/Chong-Rose.html>.

p. 132   'the men were "severely ..."' Helen Garner c. 1975 interview with Kerry Dwyer.

p. 132   'Laurel tells me she ...' Laurel Frank interview with author.

p. 133   'responsibilities to share childcare ...' Kerry Dwyer interviews with author.

p. 133   'Evelyn recalls she and Claire ...' Evelyn Krape interview with author.

p. 133   'Not all mothers ...' Jenny Walsh's c. 2005 Pram Factory memories, <wayback.archive-it.org/10989/20180903020957/http://www.pramfactory.com/memoirsfolder/Spence-Bruce.html>.

p. 133   'In a report of a 1975 ...' Australian Performing Group 1975.

p. 134   'Genuine efforts were made ...' Kerry Dwyer interviews with author.

p. 134   'Written by the New Zealand–born feminist ...' Varney 2011, pp. 150–56.

p. 134   'Helen Garner describes the play ...' Garner 1972b.

p. 135   'In her 1975 interview with Kerry ...' Brennan (2017, p. 25) also writes that 'the production caused ructions within the male-dominated APG and added to the escalating tensions within the group'.

p. 135   'Kerry remembers: "There were men ..."' Kerry Dwyer interviews with author.

p. 135   'In May 1972, simmering tensions ...' See Australian Performing Group 1972e.

p. 137   'John Timlin writes in ...' Timlin 1974.

p. 137   'Claire Dobbin tells me ...' Claire Dobbin interview with author.

p. 138   'John Romeril "would lope ..."' See Meg Clancy's c. 2005 Pram Factory memories.

p. 138   'Carol Porter wrote ...' See Carol Porter's c. 2005 Pram Factory memories, <wayback.archive-it.org/10989/20180903020925/http://www.pramfactory.com/memoirsfolder/Porter-Carol.html>.

p. 138   'Working without writers ...' Dwyer 1978–79, p. 150.

p. 138   'In 1975, *Betty* collective members ...' Collective member c. 1975 interviews with Kerry Dwyer.

p. 138   'Max agrees that he ...' Max Gillies interview with author.

p. 139   'In her feature on ...' Garner 1973.

p. 140   'Claire conceded the APG ...' Claire Dobbin c. 1975 interview with Kerry Dwyer.

p. 140   'an interview with Suzanne Spunner ...' Spunner 1979, p. 369.

p. 140   'Claire tells me now ...' Claire Dobbin interview with author.

p. 140   'Kerry has said ...' Kerry Dwyer quoted in Garner 1973.

p. 140   'Laurel recalled that ...' Laurel Frank c. 1975 interview with Kerry Dwyer.

p. 140   'In her *Meanjin* article ...' Spunner 1979, pp. 368–69.

p. 141   'The "Back Theatre" provided ...' Micky Allan c. 1975 interview with Kerry Dwyer.

p. 141   'grew out of local women's ...' The theatre scholar Peta Tait writes that some of the cast in the earliest MWTG shows were members of a 'North Fitzroy consciousness-raising group' (1993, p. 55). Sylvie Leber tells me that the founders were members of an activist group of feminists rather than a consciousness-raising group.

p. 141   'Sylvie's story was ...' Leber 2019.

p. 141 'Sylvie was born ...' Sylvie Leber interview with author.

p. 142 'Women from the APG also joined ...' See Wolf 2008, p. 147.

p. 142 'women within the APG were tired ...' Evelyn Krape c. 1975 interview with Kerry Dwyer.

p. 142 'The MWTG, like the *Betty* ...' See Tait 1993, p. 46.

p. 142 'Writing in 'Pramocracy' ...' Timlin (1974) also notes that by 1974 APG income was subsidised by the Australian Council for the Arts and the Victorian Ministry for the Arts to the tune of $75,000, about 42 per cent of total income: 'It is possible that this relative prosperity ... has also had an effect on our identity ... we are no longer the struggling players, firmly lodged within the counter culture.'

p. 143 'The short play highlighted ...' Spunner 1977, p. 10.

p. 143 'The mother–daughter scene ...' Sylvie Leber interview with author.

p. 143 'Of the eight women ...' See Leber 1977. See also Tait 1993, p. 48.

p. 143 'funding that Elizabeth Reid ...' See Reid 2018, pp. 20–25. See also Arrow 2019, pp. 134–36.

p. 143 'In a January 1975 meeting ...' Melbourne Women's Theatre Group 1975a.

p. 143 'The following month ...' Melbourne Women's Theatre Group 1975b.

p. 144 'Directed by Evelyn Krape and ...' Tait 1993, p. 87.

p. 144 'A press release issued ...' Melbourne Women's Theatre Group 1975c.

p. 144 'Ponch Hawkes recalls ...' Ponch Hawkes' c. 2005 Pram Factory memories.

p. 144 'Robin Laurie, who performed ...' Robin Laurie's c. 2005 Pram Factory memories.

p. 145 'In her history of the group ...' Tait 1993, p. 8.

p. 145 'Conflicts developed, and many ...' Dobbin quoted in Glow 1984, pp. 131–35.

p. 145 'It gave women confidence ...' Tait 1993, p. 42.

p. 145 'Pram member John Smythe ...' See John Smythe's c. 2005 Pram Factory memories.

p. 146 'Robin Laurie recalls APG actor ...' Robin Laurie's c. 2005 Pram Factory memories.

p. 146 'When I ask him about it ...' Robert Meldrum interview with author.

p. 146 'Evelyn, for one ...' Evelyn Krape interview with author.

p. 146 'Sylvie did not join ...' Sylvie Leber interview with author.

p. 146 'Robin Laurie recalls that towards ...' Robin Laurie's c. 2005 Pram Factory memories.

p. 146 'The lines between the ...' Bill Garner interview with author.

p. 146 'The MWTG lasted until ...' See Tait 1993, p. 45.

p. 147 'By 1978 in Melbourne ...' Spunner 1980.

p. 147 'Kerry recalls now ...' Kerry Dwyer interviews with author.

Chapter 7: *Betty's legacy*

p. 149   'When I visit Kerry ...' Kerry Dwyer interviews with author.

p. 149   'Yvonne would later write ...' Yvonne Marini's c. 2005 Pram Factory memories.

p. 149   'definitely all about us ...' Claire Dobbin interview with author.

p. 150   'When Kerry interviewed the *Betty* ...' Collective member c. 1975 interviews with Kerry Dwyer.

p. 151   'Evelyn had grown up in ...' Evelyn Krape interview with author.

p. 152   'Sue Ingleton recalls Jack ...' Sue Ingleton's c. 2005 Pram Factory memories, <wayback.archive-it.org/10989/20180903020839/http://www.pramfactory.com/memoirsfolder/Ingleton-Sue.html>.

p. 152   'Max Gillies described Evelyn ...' Max Gillies interview with author.

p. 152   'Bob Thorneycroft recalls ...' Bob Thorneycroft's c. 2005 Pram Factory memories.

p. 153   'When Claire reflected in 1975 ...' Claire Dobbin c. 1975 interview with Kerry Dwyer.

p. 153   'In 1974 she toured ...' See Wolf p. 151.

p. 153   'Robertson recalls Claire's energies ...' See Robertson 2001, p. 103.

p. 153   'another form of higher consciousness ...' Albert Rotstein interview with author.

p. 154   'Timlin remembers Yvonne ...' John Timlin correspondence with author.

p. 155   'Yvonne reflected years later ...' Yvonne Marini's c. 2005 Pram Factory memories.

p. 155   'Yvonne's parents had been ...' Albert Rotstein interview with author.

p. 155   'she describes as "cosmic ..."' Yvonne Marini's c. 2005 Pram Factory memories.

p. 156   'Vic was struggling with his ...' Vic Marsh interview with author.

p. 156   'Max Gillies remembers ...' Max Gillies interview with author.

p. 156   'For Kerry, the birth ...' Kerry Dwyer's c. 2005 Pram Factory memories.

p. 156   'Graeme describes how ...' Blundell 2008, p. 87.

p. 157   'the Classification Board's recently ...' Blundell 2008, p. 196.

p. 157   'The film was a huge success ...' It was 'one of the most commercially successful 1970s Australian films ever made', writes the media studies scholar Catherine Lumby (2008, p. 24).

p. 157   'But as Graeme has written ...' Blundell 2008, p. 195.

p. 158   'Graeme tells me he "only saw ..."' Graeme Blundell interview with author.

p. 158   'scenes and dialogue were improvised ...' See Lumby 2008, pp. 21–22.

p. 158   'some early "misgivings" ...' Graeme Blundell interview with author.

p. 158   'a source of tension ...' See Kerry Dwyer's c. 2005 Pram Factory memories.

p. 158   'While audiences queued ...' Magarey 2014, pp. 23–24.

p. 159   'Kerry, meanwhile, recalls ...' Kerry Dwyer's c. 2005 Pram Factory memories.

p. 159   'She compares the experience ...' Kerry Dwyer's c. 2005 Pram Factory memories.

p. 159   'made by the Sydney Women's Film ...' The films included Jeni Thornley's *Maidens*, a four-generational portrait of her maternal family. Like *Betty*, it looked at history through 'women's eyes'.

p. 159   'When she was accepted ...' Kerry Dwyer interviews with author.

p. 160   'After *Betty*, Micky continued ...' Micky Allan interview with author.

p. 161   'curator Yvette Dal Pozzo ...' Dal Pozzo 2020.

p. 161   '*Betty* was her first experience ...' Laurel Frank c. 1975 interview with Kerry Dwyer.

p. 162   'When Kerry offered Laurel ...' Laurel Frank interview with author.

p. 162   'there was excess of ...' Laurel Frank's c. 2005 Pram Factory memories, <wayback.archive-it.org/10989/20180903020808/http://www.pramfactory.com/memoirsfolder/Frank-Laurel.html>.

p. 162   'Bob Thorneycroft declares ...' Bob Thorneycroft's c. 2005 Pram Factory memories.

p. 162   'Yvonne Marini described ...' Yvonne Marini's c. 2005 Pram Factory memories.

p. 162   'It attracted APG members ...' Laurel Frank's c. 2005 Pram Factory memories.

p. 163   'Laurel's own performing career ended ...' Laurel Frank's c. 2005 Pram Factory memories.

p. 163   'There was a productive tension ...' Laurel Frank's c. 2005 Pram Factory memories.

p. 164   'They used the same 24-hour ...' Meg Clancy's c. 2005 Pram Factory memories.

p. 164   'Peta Tait argues that ...' Tait 1998, p. 504.

p. 165   'Max describes Jude ...' Max Gillies interview with author.

p. 165   'Helen remembers at one point ...' Helen Garner interview with author.

p. 165   'At some time in the mid-1970s ...' Kerry Dwyer c. 1975, 'Letter to Jude'.

p. 165   'The play was a huge success ...' Bobbi Ausubel interview with author.

p. 166   'When Jehane died ...' See C Levy, '"Silkwood" actor Jehane Dyllan Reuther dies', *Washington Post*, 16 August 1991, <www.washingtonpost.com/archive/local/1991/08/16/silkwood-actor-jehane-dyllan-reuther-dies/a822d9eb-5710-420d-a2e4-17fa8fef0519>.

p. 167   'She now says it is "very hard ..."' Carmen Lawrence interview with author.

p. 168   'The filmmaker Martha Ansara ...' Martha Ansara interview with author; and Summers 1973.

Chapter 8: *Betty* and Helen

p. 170 'In another novel ...' *The Children's Bach* (Garner 1984/2018, pp. 58, 17).

p. 171 'she writes of a day she sees ...' Garner 2015.

p. 171 'In one climactic scene ...' Garner 2021, p. 164.

p. 173 'Nora grabs a bowie knife ...' Garner 1977/2018, p. 19.

p. 173 'In Helen's most recent diary ...' Garner 2021, p. 24.

p. 173 'she records in her *Yellow Notebook* ...' Garner 2019, p. 76.

p. 173 'Literary critic James Wood ...' Wood 2016.

p. 173 'When her third husband ...' Garner 2021, pp. 7, 33.

p. 177 'she described my co-editors ...' Garner 1995.

p. 177 'a phantom version of the book ...' See Garner 2021, p. 6.

p. 178 'In 1975 Helen was ...' Helen Garner c. 1975 interview with Kerry Dwyer.

p. 178 'The centre was a large office ...' See Taylor 2013, p. 91–92.

p. 179 'Nora describes how she is ...' Garner 1977/2018, pp. 128, 209.

p. 179 'historian and gender studies academic ...' Simic 2019, pp. 139–52.

p. 180 'Creative people aren't well suited ...' Helen Garner c. 1975 interview with Kerry Dwyer.

p. 181 'The drama of *Monkey Grip* ...' Emre 2019.

p. 181 'we fucked with a joy ...' Garner 1977/2018, p. 98.

p. 181 'stole the last five dollars ...' Garner 1977/2018, p. 202.

p. 181 'entry in the encyclopedia ...' Grahame 1998b, p. 425.

p. 181 'Garner wrote for the feminist ...' Simic 2019, pp. 145–50.

p. 182 'Helen tells me she considered ...' Helen Garner interview with author.

p. 182 'the day at their half-underground ...' McPhee 2001, p. 142.

p. 183 'Graeme Blundell, the show's ...' Blundell 2008, p. 136.

p. 183 'Claire remembers 'Helen was ...' Claire Dobbin interview with author.

p. 183 'And her gift for crafting ...' Kerry Dwyer interviews with author.

p. 183 'It blew my mind to find ...' Helen Garner c. 1975 interview with Kerry Dwyer.

p. 183 'And when she turned those ...' The *Betty* performances also taught her an important writing lesson, Brennan adds: 'brevity and structure were powerful tools of communication' (2017, pp. 25–26).

p. 184 'that was akin to a dramaturge ...' Claire Dobbin interview with author.

p. 184 'Doing the play validated things ...' Helen Garner c. 1975 interview with Kerry Dwyer.

p. 184 'Kerry tell me that ...' Kerry Dwyer interviews with author.

p. 184 'But Helen tells me ...' Helen Garner interview with author.

p. 185 'this description of a lover's ...' Garner 1977/2018, p. 59.

p. 185 'the reaction of *Monkey Grip* readers ...' Brennan 2017, p. 35.

p. 188 'academics Shane Rowlands ...' Rowlands and Henderson 1996.

p. 189 'pays close attention to X ...' Garner 2021, p. 12.

Chapter 9: *Betty* today

p. 196 'arts writer Jane Howard traced ...' Howard, 'How Australian theatre rebalanced its gender disparity', ABC Arts, 13 April 2019, <www.abc.net.au/news/2019-04-13/australian-theatre-fixed-its-gender-imbalance-in-a-decade/10942452?nw=0&r=HtmlFragment>.

p. 198 'Actress and filmmaker Jeni Thornley ...' See Kenny 2018a.

Afterword

p. 203 'He remembers: "The light ..."' John Romeril's c. 2005 Pram Factory memories.

p. 208 'a kind of "theatrical ..."' See E Howell, 'Performing political history: an interview with Gary Foley', 5 October 2017, archived at The Commons, <commonslibrary.org/performing-political-history-an-interview-with-actor-academic-and-activist-gary-foley>.

p. 208 '800 women took over ...' See Arrow 2019, pp. 126–27.

p. 210 'cartwheels in the nude ...' Robertson 2001, p. 93.

p. 216 'There were Indigenous women ...' Arrow 2019, p. 79.

p. 216 'Aileen Moreton-Robinson makes the point ...' Moreton-Robinson 2020, p. 171.

Sources

Interviews

Oral interviews by the author, 2017–22

Micky Allan, 22 October 2018, Daylesford

Martha Ansara, 30 August 2017, Port Kembla

Bobbi Ausubel, 29 April 2019, San Francisco

Graeme Blundell, 12 February 2022, Sydney

Claire Dobbin, 15 October 2020, Sydney and Melbourne

Kerry Dwyer, 2 May 2018, 10 March 2021, 18 August 2021, 3 April 2022, Sydney

Laurel Frank, 21 October 2018, Melbourne

Bill Garner, 28 March 2022, Sydney and Melbourne

Helen Garner, 26 March 2021, Melbourne

Julie Gibson, 31 August 2019, Capertee Valley

Max Gillies, 26 November 2021, Sydney and Melbourne

John Helmer, 10 February 2021, Sydney and Melbourne

Peter Kovner, 25 April 2019, Cambridge, Massachusetts

Evelyn Krape, 20 October 2020, Sydney and Melbourne

Carmen Lawrence, 23 September 2020, Sydney and Perth

Sylvie Leber, 20 October 2021, Sydney and Melbourne

Libby Lloyd and Justine Lloyd, 19 February 2021, Sydney

Vic Marsh, 22 October 2020, Sydney and Perth

Robert Meldrum, 26 October 2021, Sydney and Melbourne

Albert Rotstein, 28 October 2021, Sydney and Melbourne

Aili Paal Singer, 25 April 2019, Cambridge, Massachusetts

Jeni Thornley, 8 March 2018, Sydney

Morgaine Williams (author's mother), various dates, Sydney and Gisborne

Other interviews by the author, 2017–22

Dennis Altman, 15 February 2021, online correspondence

Jane Clifton, 24 March 2022, email

Oral interviews by Kerry Dwyer, c. 1975

Archived in the Australian Performing Group records, c. 1979–92 (unprocessed collection), 1344469, Box 2, State Library of New South Wales, Sydney:

Micky Allan

Claire Dobbin

Laurel Frank

Helen Garner

Evelyn Krape

Yvonne Marini

Website

Sue Ingleton's Pram Factory site includes a show chronology and memories of APG members: <wayback.archive-it.org/10989/20180903013433/https://www.pramfactory.com>

Select bibliography

Arrow, M 2002, *Upstaged: Australian Women Dramatists in the Limelight at Last*, Pluto Press, Sydney

Arrow, M 2017, 'The popular is political', Annual NSW History Council Lecture, The Mint, Sydney, 5 September, broadcast as 'The ocker and social change in 70s Australia', *Big Ideas*, Radio National, 17 January 2018, <www.abc.net.au/radionational/programs/bigideas/the-ocker-and-social-change-in-70s-australia/8944466>

Arrow, M 2019, *The Seventies: The Personal, the Political, and the Making of Modern Australia*, NewSouth, Sydney

Australian Performing Group 1972a, 'Women's Play – Betty can jump, APG News January 1972', Australian Performing Group Records, 1968–1981, MS 11436, Box 7, State Library Victoria, Melbourne

Australian Performing Group 1972b, 'Letters to reviewers', Australian Performing Group Records, 1968–1981, MS 11436, Box 45, State Library Victoria, Melbourne

Australian Performing Group 1972c, 'APG News March 1972, APG's Current Financial Situation', Australian Performing Group Records, 1968–1981, MS 11436, Box 7, State Library Victoria, Melbourne

Australian Performing Group 1972d, 'Internal Bulletin No. 5, 6–7 March 1972', Australian Performing Group Records, 1968–1981, MS 11436, Box 7, State Library Victoria, Melbourne

Australian Performing Group 1972e, 'Internal Bulletin 7, 2 May 1972', Australian Performing Group records, c. 1979–1992 (unprocessed collection), 1344469, Box 2, State Library of New South Wales, Sydney

Australian Performing Group 1972f, 'APG News November 1972, Activities', Australian Performing Group records, c. 1979–1992 (unprocessed collection), 1344469, Box 1, State Library of New South Wales, Sydney

Australian Performing Group 1973, 'Administrator's Report January '73', Australian Performing Group Records, 1968–1981, MS 11436, Box 1, State Library Victoria, Melbourne

Australian Performing Group 1975, 'Executive Report', Australian Performing Group Records, 1968–1981, MS 11436, Box 1, State Library Victoria, Melbourne

Betty Can Jump collective 1972a, 'Betty Can Jump script', unpublished script, Australian Performing Group Records, 1968–1981, MS 11436, Box 45, State Library Victoria, Melbourne

Betty Can Jump collective 1972b, 'Betty Can Jump slides', Australian Performing Group records, c. 1979–1992 (unprocessed collection), 1344469, Box 2, State Library of New South Wales, Sydney

Betty Can Jump collective 1972c, 'Sources used for Betty Can Jump', appendix of unpublished script, Australian Performing Group Records, 1968–1981, MS 11436, Box 45, State Library Victoria, Melbourne

Blundell, G 2008, *The Naked Truth*, Hachette Australia, Sydney

Blundell, G & G Hutchinson 1972, 'A proposal: the AGP Collective – relationship of the parts to the whole. Why are we here?', position paper, 21 February, Australian Performing Group Records, 1968–1981, MS 11436, Box 1, State Library Victoria, Melbourne

Brah, A 2019, 'Generations of feminism?', panel event with Avtar Brah, Clare Hemmings, Niharika Pandit, Priya Raghavan and Anne Phillips, London School of Economics and Political Science, London, 23 January

Brennan, B 2017, *A Writing Life: Helen Garner and Her Work*, Text Publishing, Melbourne

Brown, H, K Morris, R Schechner, P Schumann & J Seitz, J 1968, 'With the Bread & Puppet Theatre: an interview with Peter Schumann', *TDR*, vol. 12, no. 2, pp. 62–73

Brownmiller, S 1999, *In Our Time: Memoir of a Revolution*, Dial Press, New York

Buckley, J 1973, 'A tale of two women', *Living Daylights*, 23–29 October, pp. 6–7

Butler, J 1990/2007, *Gender Trouble*, Routledge, New York

Caravan Theatre 1969a, 'Press release: How to Make a Woman', Bobbi Ausubel Papers, 1965–1990, MC 958, Schlesinger Library, Radcliffe Institute, Harvard University, Cambridge, Massachusetts

Caravan Theatre 1969b, 'Caravan Theatre Newsletter', Bobbi Ausubel Papers, 1965–1990, MC 958, Schlesinger Library, Radcliffe Institute, Harvard University, Cambridge, Massachusetts

Caravan Theatre 1972, 'How to make a woman', Bobbi Ausubel Papers, 1965–1990, VHS, Vt-206_0001, Schlesinger Library, Radcliffe Institute, Harvard University, Cambridge, Massachusetts

Caravan Theatre n.d., 'Loeb', Bobbi Ausubel Papers, 1965–1990, VHS, Vt-206_0001, Schlesinger Library, Radcliffe Institute, Harvard University, Cambridge, Massachusetts

Cass, A (ed.) 2017, *La Mama*, Melbourne University Press, Melbourne

Curthoys, A 1994, 'Australian feminism since 1970', in N Grieve & A Burns (eds), *Australian Women: Contemporary Feminist Thought*, Oxford University Press, Melbourne, pp. 425–47

Dal Pozzo, Y 2020, 'Micky Allan: a live-in show', National Gallery of Australia <medium.com/national-gallery-of-australia/micky-allan-a-live-in-show-21961892625>

Dare, T 1972, 'At last, home-grown women's lib hits the stage', *The Australian*, 2 February

Dwyer, K 1971–72, 'Women Book 1 and Women Book 2 – Betty Can Jump', Australian Performing Group records, c. 1979–1992 (unprocessed collection), 1344469, Box 2, State Library of New South Wales, Sydney

Dwyer, K c. 1975, 'Letter to Jude', Australian Performing Group records, c. 1979–1992 (unprocessed collection), 1344469, Box 2, State Library of New South Wales, Sydney

Dwyer, K 1978–79, 'Betty Can Jump', *Lip 1978–79*, Lip Collective, Melbourne, pp. 150–55

Dwyer, K 1993, 'Lecture: International Theatre Conference, University of Western Sydney – 1993', Australian Performing Group records, c. 1979–1992 (unprocessed collection), 1344469, Box 5, State Library of New South Wales, Sydney

Dwyer, K 2017, 'From Grotowski to *Betty Can Jump*', *Australasian Drama Studies*, no. 71, pp. 178–93

Emre, M 2019, 'On the dizzy edge', *London Review of Books*, vol. 41, no. 6, 21 March

Faust, B 1972, 'Betty jumps with some verve', *Sunday Review*, 5 February

Freeman, J 1970, 'The tyranny of structurelessness', <www.jofreeman.com/joreen/tyranny.htm>, accessed 13 May 2019

Garner, B 1971, 'APG Newsletter April 1971, Politicization of the A.P.G. 1968–1971', Australian Performing Group records, c. 1979–1992 (unprocessed collection), 1344469, Box 7, State Library of New South Wales, Sydney

Garner, B 2007, 'Enter the new wave Melbourne', conference panel, Enter the New Wave Symposium, University of Melbourne, 26–28 September, www.doubledialogues.com/article/enter-the-new-wave-melbourne, accessed 1 July 2018

Garner, B 2017, 'The philosopher improver', in A Cass (ed.), *La Mama*, Melbourne University Press, Melbourne, pp. 27–30

Garner, H 1972a, 'Betty Can Jump', *Dissent: A Radical Quarterly*, Winter, no. 28, pp. 46–50

Garner, H 1972b, 'APG News August 1972', Australian Performing Group records, c. 1979–1992 (unprocessed collection), 1344469, Box 1, State Library of New South Wales, Sydney

Garner, H 1973, 'Where's woman in the worlds men create?', *The Digger*, 10–24 March, p. 9

Garner, H 1977/2018, *Monkey Grip*, Text Publishing, Melbourne

Garner, H 1984/2018, *The Children's Bach*, Text Publishing, Melbourne

Garner, H 1995, *The First Stone*, Picador, Sydney

Garner, H 2015, 'The insults of age', *The Monthly*, May

Garner, H 2019, *Yellow Notebook: Diaries 1978–1987*, Text Publishing, Melbourne

Garner, H 2020, *One Day I'll Remember This: Diaries 1987–1995*, Text Publishing, Melbourne

Garner, H 2021, *How to End a Story: Diaries 1995–1998*, Text Publishing, Melbourne

Glickfeld, L 1970, 'Whatever happened to La Mama?', *The Bulletin*, 29 August, pp. 43–44

Glickfeld, L 1972a, 'A play for women's lib', *Australian Jewish News*, 11 February

Glickfeld, L 1972b, 'Betty's the best', *The Bulletin*, 26 February

Glow, H 1984, 'Women's theatre and the APG', *Meanjin*, vol. 43, no. 1, pp. 129–38

Grahame, E 1998a, 'Melbourne women's liberation', in B Caine, M Gatens, E Grahame, J Larbalestier, S Watson & E Webby (eds), *Australian Feminism: A Companion*, Oxford University Press, Melbourne, pp. 456–57

Grahame, E 1998b, 'Garner, Helen', in B Caine, M Gatens, E Grahame, J Larbalestier, S Watson & E Webby (eds), *Australian Feminism: A Companion*, Oxford University Press, Melbourne, p. 425

Greeley, L 2015, *Fearless Femininity by Women in American Theatre, 1910s to 2010s*, Cambria Press, Amherst, New York

Greer, G 1970, *The Female Eunuch*, Granada, Sydney

Grossberg, L 2019, 'Cultural studies in search of a method, or looking for conjunctural analysis', *New Formations*, no. 96, pp. 38–68

Grotowski, J 1968, *Towards a Poor Theatre*, Simon & Schuster, New York

Hanisch, C 1970, 'The personal is political', in S Firestone & A Koedt (eds), *Notes from the Second Year: Women's Liberation, Major Writings of the Radical Feminists*, New York Radical Women, New York, pp. 76–78

Hanisch, C 2006, 'The personal is political: introduction', <www.carolhanisch.org/CHwritings/PIP.html>, accessed 30 March 2017

Hemmings, C 2019, 'Generations of feminism?', panel event with Avtar Brah, Clare Hemmings, Niharika Pandit, Priya Raghavan and Anne Phillips, London School of Economics and Political Science, London, 23 January

Henderson, M 2006, *Marking Feminist Times: Remembering the Longest Revolution in Australia*, Peter Lang, Bern

Henderson, M 2012, 'Wonders taken for signs: the cultural activism of the Australian women's movement as avant-garde reformation', *Lilith: A Feminist History Journal*, nos 17–18, pp. 107–20

Hibberd, J 1970, 'Untitled report Carlton News 16 December', Australian Performing Group Records, 1968–1981, MS 11436, Folio 33, State Library Victoria, Melbourne

Hibberd, J 1972, 'Letter to the APG – Internal Bulletin 7, 2 May 1972', Australian Performing Group records, c. 1979–1992 (unprocessed collection), 1344469, Box 2, State Library of New South Wales, Sydney

Hughes, J 2015, 'A work in progress: the rise and fall of Australian filmmakers co-operatives, 1966–86', *Senses of Cinema*, no. 77

Ingleton, S 2005, The Pram Factory, website now archived by the Theatre and Dance Platform project, University of Melbourne, <wayback.archive-it.org/10989/20180903013433/https://www.pramfactory.com>

Jennings, K (ed.) 1975, *Mother I'm Rooted: An Anthology of Australian Women Poets*, Outback Press. Melbourne

Jones, L 2017, 'A small history of 205 Faraday Street, Carlton', in A Cass (ed.), *La Mama*, Melbourne University Press, Melbourne, p. 42

Kenny, K 1996, 'Live from the mouths of babes', in K Bail (ed.), *DIY Feminism*, Allen & Unwin, Sydney, pp. 139–51

Kenny, K 2018a, 'Girls on film', *Saturday Paper*, no. 216, 4–10 August

Kenny, K 2018b, 'Circus Oz *Model Citizens* review', *Daily Review*, 14 January

Kenny, K 2019, '#MeToo and déjà vu: Australian sexual harassment activism from the 70s to today', in N Kon-yu, C Nieman, M Scott & M Sved (eds), *#MeToo: Stories from the Australian Movement*, Picador, Sydney, pp. 1–16

Lake, M 1999, *Getting Equal: The History of Australian Feminism*, Allen & Unwin, Sydney

La Mama 1969, 'La Mama Program July 1969', Australian Performing Group records, c. 1979–1992 (unprocessed collection), 1344469, Box 1, State Library of New South Wales, Sydney

Leber, S 1977, 'Notes on performance', *Lip*, nos 2–3, Lip Collective, Melbourne

Leber, S 2019, 'How come you're so sane? A personal account of rape and rape crisis work in Victoria', in N Kon-yu, C Nieman, M Scott & M Sved (eds), *#MeToo: Stories from the Australian Movement*, Picador, Sydney, pp. 29–42

Lilburn, S, S Magarey & S Sheridan 2000, 'Celebrity feminism as synthesis: Germaine Greer, *The Female Eunuch* and the Australian print media', *Continuum: Journal of Media & Cultural Studies*, vol. 14, no. 3, pp. 335–48

Lumby, C 2008, *Alvin Purple*, Currency Press, Sydney

McPhee, H 2001, *Other People's Words*, Picador, Sydney

Magarey, S 2004, 'Feminism as cultural renaissance', *Hecate: An Interdisciplinary Journal of Women's Liberation*, vol. 30, no. 1, pp. 231–46

Magarey, S 2013, 'Sisterhood and women's liberation in Australia', *Outskirts: Feminism Along the Edge*, vol. 28, <www.outskirts.arts.uwa.edu.au/volumes/volume-28/susan-magarey>

Magarey, S 2014, *Dangerous Ideas*, University of Adelaide Press, Adelaide

Magarey, S 2018, 'Beauty becomes political: beginnings of the women's liberation movement in Australia', *Australian Feminist Studies*, vol. 33, no. 95, pp. 31–34

Mainardi, P 1970, 'The politics of housework', in S Firestone & A Koedt (eds), *Notes from the Second Year: Women's Liberation, Major Writings of the Radical Feminists*, New York Radical Women, New York, pp. 28–31

Marsh, V 2004, *The Boy in the Yellow Dress*, Clouds of Magellan, Melbourne

Mathews, I 2019, *Winning for Women: A Personal Story*, Monash University Publishing, Melbourne

Mayhead, G 1972, 'How it feels to be a woman', *Herald* (Melbourne), 3 February

Melbourne Women's Theatre Group 1971, 'Miss Daisy Bovine robbed of title', *MeJane*, vol. 1, no. 3, p. 3

Melbourne Times 1972, 'Betty and a Jock Strap', review from *Melbourne Times*, Australian Performing Group records, c. 1979–1992 (unprocessed collection), 1344469, Box 2, State Library of New South Wales, Sydney

Melbourne Women's Theatre Group & K Ansara 1974, 'The Great Frying Pan – festival flyer', Australian Performing Group records, c. 1979–1992 (unprocessed collection), 1344469, Box 2, State Library of New South Wales, Sydney

Melbourne Women's Theatre Group 1975a, 'Minutes, 3 January 1975', Australian Performing Group Records, 1968–1981, MS 11436, Box 20, State Library Victoria, Melbourne

Melbourne Women's Theatre Group 1975b, 'General meeting – 5 February 1975', Australian Performing Group Records, 1968–1981, MS 11436, Box 20, State Library Victoria, Melbourne

Melbourne Women's Theatre Group 1975c, 'Press release', Australian Performing Group Records, 1968–1981, MS 11436, Box 20, State Library Victoria, Melbourne

Moore, N 2016, 'Performing 1971: Dorothy Hewett's The Chapel Perilous', Westerly, vol. 61, no. 2, pp. 126–43

Moreton-Robinson, A 2020, Talkin' Up to the White Woman: Indigenous Women and Feminism, University of Queensland Press, Brisbane

Morgan, R (ed.) 1970, Sisterhood Is Powerful, Random House, New York

Mudie, P 1997, Ubu Films: Sydney Underground Movies 1965–1970, UNSW Press, Sydney

Mullins, Patrick 2020, The Trials of Portnoy: How Penguin Brought Down Australia's Censorship System, Scribe, Melbourne

Novakovic, J 2009, 'The Chapel Perilous: the paradigm of fertility overshadowed by the quest', Double Dialogues (Enter the New Wave), Winter, no. 11

Parr, N 2015, 'Who goes to university? The changing profile of our students', The Conversation, 25 May, <theconversation.com/who-goes-to-university-the-changing-profile-of-our-students-40373>, accessed 10 February 2018

Press, J 2017, 'The life and death of a radical sisterhood', The Cut, 15 November, <www.thecut.com/2017/11/an-oral-history-of-feminist-group-new-york-radical-women.html>, viewed 17 February 2019

Radic, L 1972, 'Betty takes a step in the right direction', The Age, 4 February

Reid, E 2018, 'How the personal became political: the feminist movement of the 1970s', Australian Feminist Studies, vol. 33, no. 95, pp. 9–30

Reid, J 2012, 'Menzies, Whitlam, and social justice: a view from the academy', Sir Robert Menzies oration on higher education, University of Melbourne,

23 October, <www.uws.edu.au/__data/assets/pdf_file/0013/405202/ INC3553_VC_Menzies_Oration_Speech.pdf>, accessed 2 December 2018

Robertson, T 2001, *The Pram Factory: The Australian Performing Group Recollected*, Melbourne University Press, Melbourne

Rowlands, S & M Henderson 1996, 'Damned bores and slick sisters: the selling of blockbuster feminism in Australia', *Australian Feminist Studies*, vol. 11, no. 23, pp. 9–16

Sarachild, K 1970, 'A program for feminist "consciousness raising"', 'The Personal is Political', in S Firestone & A Koedt (eds), *Notes from the Second Year: Women's Liberation, Major Writings of the Radical Feminists*, New York Radical Women, New York, pp. 78–80

Sheehan, RJ 2016, 'If we had more like her we would no longer be the unheard majority: Germaine Greer's reception in the United States', *Australian Feminist Studies*, vol. 31, no. 87, pp. 62–77

Simic, Z 2013, '"Women's writing" and "feminism": a history of intimacy and estrangement', *Outskirts*, vol. 28, <www.outskirts.arts.uwa.edu.au/volumes/ volume-28/zora-simic>

Simic, Z 2019, '"Unmistakably a book by a feminist": Helen Garner's *Monkey Grip* and its feminist contexts', in M Arrow & A Woollacott (eds) 2019, *Everyday Revolutions: Remaking Gender, Sexuality and Culture in 1970s Australia*, ANU Press, Canberra, pp. 139–59

Spunner, S 1977, 'She'll be right mate: the Migrant Women Show', *Lip*, nos 2–3, Lip Collective, Melbourne

Spunner, S 1979, 'Since Betty jumped: theatre and feminism in Melbourne', *Meanjin*, vol. 38, no. 3, pp. 368–77

Spunner, S 1980, 'Feminism from then till now', *Theatre Australia*, February, pp. 28–30

Summers, A 1973, 'Where's the women's movement moving to?', *MeJane* vol. 1, no. 10. pp. 6–8

Summers, A 1975, *Damned Whores and God's Police*, Penguin, Melbourne

Tait, P 1993, *Original Women's Theatre: The Melbourne Women's Theatre Group 1974–77*, Artmoves, Melbourne

Tait, P 1994, *Converging Realities: Feminism in Australian Theatre*, Currency Press, Sydney

Tait, P 1998, 'Theatre', in B Caine, M Gatens, E Grahame, J Larbalestier, S Watson & E Webby E (eds), *Australian Feminism: A Companion*, Oxford University Press, Melbourne, pp. 503–504

Taylor, A 2014, 'Germaine Greer's adaptable celebrity: feminism, unruliness, and humour on the British small screen', *Feminist Media Studies*, vol. 14, no. 5, pp. 759–74

Taylor, J 2009, *Brazen Hussies*, Dyke Books Inc, Melbourne

Taylor, J 2013, 'Gestetner', in A Bartlett & M Henderson (eds) *Things That Liberate*, Cambridge Scholars Publishing, Newcastle-upon-Tyne, pp. 91–92

Timlin, J 1974, 'Pramocracy', Australian Performing Group Records, 1968–1981, MS 11436, Box 7, State Library Victoria, Melbourne

Tomsic, M 2017, *Beyond the Silver Screen: A History of Women, Filmmaking and Film Culture in Australia 1920–1990*, Melbourne University Press, Melbourne

Tyler Peterson, G 2018, '"A revolutionary proposal': Alexander Trocchi, dramaturgies of disruption and situationist genealogies', in K McLoughlin (ed.), *British Literature in Transition, 1960–1980: Flower Power*, Cambridge University Press, Cambridge

Varney, D 2011, *Radical Visions 1968–2008: The Impact of the Sixties on Australian Drama*, Rodopi, Amsterdam and New York

Wandor, M 1984, 'The impact of feminism on theatre', *Feminist Review*, vol. 18, no. 1, pp. 76–92

Wandor, M 2001, *Post-war British Drama: Looking Back in Gender*, Routledge, London

Wolf, G 2008, *Make it Australian: The Australian Performing Group, the Pram Factory and New Wave Theatre*, Currency Press, Sydney

Wood, J 2016, 'Helen Garner's savage self-scrutiny', *New Yorker*, 12 December

Films

Alvin Purple, 1973, Tim Burstall

Brazen Hussies, 2020, director Catherine Dwyer

Dimboola, 1979, director John Duigan

Helen Garner's Monkey Grip, 2014, director Fiona Tuomy

Maidens, 1978, director Jeni Thornley

Pram Factory, 1994, directors Anna Grieve and James Manché

Radio and podcasts

'How the Pram Factory shaped Australian theatre', presenter Michael Cathcart, first broadcast Monday 17 July 2017, ABC Radio National

'The Day's Residue', 2020, Clare Wright and Yves Rees with Helen Garner

Acknowledgements

If I could travel back in time to the 1970s, I would thank the *Betty* women – some of them in the 20s, others barely in their 30s – not just for giving me this story to tell you, but for changing the world for my generation. I am particularly in debt to Kerry Dwyer, for the records she made and then preserved for years. And I owe many thanks to the *Betty* cast and crew I interviewed: Micky Allan, Claire Dobbin, Laurel Frank, Helen Garner, Evelyn Krape and Victor Marsh. Without fail they all generously agreed to confront and examine the small pieces of story I held up to them, ghostly versions of their past selves, and they gave me more stories of consciousness raising and confrontations and collectives. I'm also immensely grateful for the memories and reflections of Dennis Altman, Bill Garner, Graeme Blundell, Jane Clifton, Max Gillies, John Helmer, Carmen Lawrence, Sylvie Leber, Robert Meldrum, Albert Rotstein and John Timlin. Thank you to Tenille Hands and Susan Thomas for their generous help with photographs at the Academy Library UNSW Canberra. Many thanks too to the special collections staff at the State Library of NSW and the State Library of Victoria for access to their archives.

I'm eternally thankful to Michelle Arrow, who first told me about *Betty* when I visited her Macquarie University office at the beginning of my research for a doctorate on film and theatre in the Australian women's liberation movement. "How about looking at a play called *Betty Can Jump*? No one's really researched that yet," she suggested, and this is the result. When I finished my PhD, Michelle, along with Bernadette Brennan, Phillipa McGuinness and Patti Miller, all gave me crucial support and encouragement that helped turn this project from a few sample chapters and outline to a commissioned project. And take a bow Martin Shaw, über agent and pappa of books, who backed this story from the beginning. The exclamation marks that decorated his emails as we pitched this story were weekly mainlines of hope and happiness. And I can't thank my publisher, the fiercely fabulous Terri-ann White, enough: she did not hesitate to publish this tale, even when her books for 2022 were, quite literally, full. Thank you as always to Emma Wise, my invaluable first reader. And many thanks to Nicola Young, who improved the manuscript on every page.

To complete this book, I was fortunate to receive support from the NSW Government through Create NSW and the small project grant scheme. I was also grateful to receive a 2021 Varuna Writers' Space Fellowship, and at the end of 2021 I was lucky to spend a week working in the new studio on the Varuna grounds completing final chapters. Thank you to the Varuna staff, particularly Rebecca Goosen, Carol Major and Veechi Stuart, and thank you to Helen Bodycomb, Chris Hammer and Donné Restom for writerly solidarity.

Much of the research for this book took place while I was writing my doctorate, and I owe many thanks to my supervisor, Margie Borschke, for pushing me to think about the questions I was asking, and for constantly saying 'good, but let's make it better'. Thanks too to my associate supervisor Willa McDonald for her support and for her keen editorial eye, and to Alana Hadfield for sharing her research expertise. Special thanks, too, must go to Kate Rossmanith, who opened a window to research, and to Wendy Bacon for the loveliest of letters.

Many thanks to my thesis examiners, Zora Simic, Alison Bartlett and Laura Prieto: their generous words and enthusiastic encouragement were the ballast I needed to embark on this book just weeks after finishing my PhD. And thanks to all those who provided a sense of community in the academy, particularly Isobelle Barrett Meyering, Rosa Campbell, Bridget Griffen-Foley and Justine Lloyd. And thanks to Kate Fullagar, Catharine Lumby and Stefan Solomon for advice. Thank you to Peter Doyle and Bridget Griffen-Foley (again) for keeping me employed and buoyed at key times. A special mention to Andrew Nette, who showed me a couple of things about rocking the boat when we were undergraduates, and was the best brains trust and friend to meet up with again years later as we tackled doctorates together.

Much of the early research for this book was supported by a three-year Australian Government research scholarship. I was also fortunate to receive a Macquarie University Postgraduate Research Fund grant that enabled me to travel to Cambridge (US), Boston and San Francisco for research and oral interviews. Thank you Bobbi Ausubel, Aili Paal Singer and Peter Kovner in the US for the stories. And special thanks to Tamar Brown at the Arthur and Elizabeth Schlesinger Library for access to the papers of the Bobbi Ausubel collection.

Thank you to my Sydney Writers' Room community for the shared solitude, particularly Eve Spence, Nadine Cameron and Ben Keating. Thanks to my book group sisters who create small and big revolutions every day: Maria Cirillo, Alex Grayson, Emma Maiden, Anastasia Polites, Vanessa Seagrove, Trudy Tweedie, Jeane Wells and Gabi Wynhausen, with a special thank you to Katherine McKernan and Lea Redfern for the unfailing cheering and wise words. Many people are part of my village of care and co-operation that makes everything else possible, other friends have encouraged and inspired me, accompanied me on field work and as plus ones to theatre and to talks, or patiently listened as I recited yet another anecdote I had found in the minutes of a Pram Factory meeting. I thank them all for their good natured company and good-humoured forbearance: special thanks to Mish Allen, Kim Bluett, David Bristow, George Catsi, Jackie Chowns, David Coady, Stephanie Cunio, Martin Graham, Geoff Holland, Anne Kwasner, Rozanna Lilley, Nici Lindsay, Patricia Lynch, Mishelle Predika, Melissa Putre, Owen Richardson, Guy Rundle, Andrew Scarborough, Beth Spencer, Kelly Stephens, Laurence White, Paul Williams and Jackie Woods. Particular thanks to Suzie Gasper and Helen Slonek for sharing the longest story with me. And thank you Noel Hester, for the employment and solidarity.

Thank you to my father Charles Kenny, for teaching me some of my first words but never dictating the script. Thank you to my mother, Morgaine Williams, who led a team of nurses onto the football field in 1965. When I came along she always made sure I had a book in my hands and knew how to take up my own space. And thanks too to my mother's partner (my second mother) Niq Morcos, for always raising the bar and raising my expectations every day.

Thanks to Laurel, Micky, Kerry and Lloyd Carrick, Ponch Hawkes, John Helmer and Margot Nash for the photographs. If any credits have been missed for photographs in this book, we would welcome correspondence to rectify the record for future editions.

Finally, thanks to my family, Andrew, Daniel and Alex, for their steady belief in me and in this work. You all kept things together in the present while I was often living in the 1970s. Thank you for everything.

The author's mother, kicking the ball (centre) at a football match she organised for nurses circa 1965.

Index

About Upswell

Upswell Publishing was established in
2021 by Terri-ann White as a not-for-profit
press. A perceived gap in the market for
distinctive literary works in fiction, poetry
and narrative non-fiction was the motivation.
In her years as a bookseller, writer and then
publisher, Terri-ann has maintained a watch
on literary books and the way they insinuate
themselves into a cultural space and are
then located within our literary and cultural
inheritance. She is interested in making books
to last: books with the potential to still be
noticed, and noted, after decades and thus
be ripe to influence new literary histories.

About this typeface

Book designer Becky Chilcott chose
Foundry Origin not only as a strong,
carefully considered, and dependable
typeface, but also to honour her late
friend and mentor, type designer Freda
Sack, who oversaw the project. Designed
by Freda's long-standing colleague,
Stuart de Rozario, much like Upswell
Publishing, Foundry Origin was created
out of the desire to say something new.